Publications on the Near East

Publications on the Near East

Poetry's Voice, Society's Song: Ottoman Lyric Poetry
Walter G. Andrews

The Remaking of Istanbul:
Portrait of an Ottoman City in the Nineteenth Century
Zeynep Çelik

The Tragedy of Sohráb and Rostám from the Persian National Epic,
the Shahname of Abol-Qasem Ferdowsi
Translated by Jerome W. Clinton

The Jews in Modern Egypt, 1914–1952
Gudrun Krämer

Izmir and the Levantine World, 1550–1650
Daniel Goffman

Medieval Agriculture and Islamic Science:
The Almanac of a Yemeni Sultan
Daniel Martin Varisco

Rethinking Modernity and National Identity in Turkey
Edited by Sibel Bozdoğan and Reşat Kasaba

Britons in the Ottoman Empire during
the English Civil Wars, 1642–1660
Daniel Goffman

Slavery and Abolition in the Ottoman Middle East
Ehud R. Toledano

Slavery and Abolition in the Ottoman Middle East

Ehud R. Toledano

University of Washington Press
Seattle & London

LIBRARY OF CONGRESS CATALOGING-IN-PUBLICATION DATA
Toledano, Ehud R.
Slavery and abolition in the Ottoman Middle East / Ehud R. Toledano.
p. cm. — (Publications on the Near East)
Includes bibliographical references (p.) and index.
ISBN 0-295-97642-X (alk. paper)
1. Slavery—Middle East—History. 2. Slave trade—Middle East—History. 3. Slavery and Islam—History. 4. Turkey—History—Ottoman Empire, 1288–1918. I. Title. II. Series.
HT1316.T65 1997
306.3'62'0956—dc21 97-9571
CIP

∞ The paper used in this publication meets the minimum requirements of American National Standard for Information Sciences—Permanence of Paper for Printed Library materials, ANSI Z39.48–1984.

For my children
Maya and *Iddo Toledano*
with unbounded love

CONTENTS

PREFACE

Slavery is one of those "mega-topics" in world history that continue to attract interest, both scholarly and nonscholarly. The lingering effects of slavery—in its strict sense now almost extinct—are being linked, often by groups with vested interests, to political and social issues that are still very much alive today, such as gaps in economic development between the countries that lost their people to slavery and those that exploited slave labor and benefited from it, race relations within formerly slave-owning societies, and persistent cultural attitudes and stereotyping. The intriguing complexity of the institution of slavery—never fully comprehensible—has spawned a wealth of studies covering a wide variety of societies around the globe. For a number of reasons, which I will discuss in various parts of this book, only a limited amount of work has appeared to date on slavery in Ottoman society, or for that matter in other Muslim societies. This deficiency has impeded the effective incorporation of slavery in those societies into the analytical framework of comparative slavery.

Thus, by bringing together in an easily accessible format my current thoughts on slavery in late Ottoman history, I hope at least partially to bridge the gap that exists between the study of Ottoman bondage and the study of slavery in other societies. If this book succeeds in attracting a broader audience than that of specialists in Ottoman, Arab, or Islamic studies—that is, the many who are interested in slavery as a social, cultural, and political phenomenon—it will have achieved its primary goal.

In looking at Ottoman slavery as a whole, it seems to me that one of its salient and most interesting features is the variety of modes of servility. It is precisely this variety that has constituted a major analytic impediment to the study of Ottoman slavery as a coherent social phenomenon. By electing to view the various manifestations of servile status in Ottoman society as emanating from and belonging to the notion of slavery, I am obviously taking a position in the debate, not only on Ottoman slavery, but also on slavery in Muslim and other societies. To demonstrate and sustain this view, I have put all the new, rewritten, and revised materials contained in this volume through a "grinder" that sorted them out, classified them, and wove them together according to the types of bondage that existed in the empire. Hence, the book's five chapters are all organized around the issue of unity and diversity, in an attempt to come up with a kind of loose model that, while accommodating all types, will still be able to further articulate our concept of the institution as a whole.

The Introduction ushers the reader into the world of Ottoman slaves and slave owners and provides the basic background for finding one's way in the labyrinth of Ottoman slavery. Chapters 1 and 2 cover the two components of *kul/harem*, or elite, slavery and discuss the paradox entailed in the dual notion of power and servility. Agricultural slavery as practiced by the Circassian refugees who entered the empire in the 1850s and 1860s is reviewed in chapter 3. Chapter 4 looks at how the Ottoman elite itself handled the varieties of slavery and the pressures of European abolitionism. Chapter 5 assesses the ways modern scholars and other writers have approached the same varieties and shows how they have developed a number of discourses on slavery. Finally, the Conclusion attempts to integrate the diversity and introduce some measure of unity into the analysis of nineteenth-century Ottoman bondage as a social institution.

In a way, the present volume is also an attempt to humanize the narrative and take it beyond the plane of numbers, tables, and charts—although I fully recognize the vital importance of these in the debate over the history of slavery anywhere. Stressing the social and cultural aspects of the history of Ottoman slavery, I shall examine the plight of the main "characters" in this nineteenth-century story: domestic slaves, female *harem* slaves, the sultan's *kul*s (officeholders of slave origins), court and elite eunuchs, Circassian agricultural slaves, slave dealers, and slave owners. They will all figure in the following pages and, whenever possible, be named and tell their own stories. When the records make that impossible, such persons will be presented as members of the various groups and categories they belonged to.

As I was preparing materials for this book, I realized the obvious—that the very language we use to depict slavery and social realities has meaningfully changed over the past decade. This reflects the gradual transformation of political culture, and the words we choose unmistakably position us upon the map charted by the discourse on slavery, or for that matter on any other sociocultural phenomenon. Thus, I found myself almost automatically changing "slave-girls" to "female slaves," "ladies" to "women," "he" to "he or she," "black" to "African," and "emigrants" to "refugees" (it did not take long to notice that the Russian expulsion of the Circassians from the Caucasus, which I had described as "emigration," would today be called "ethnic cleansing"). *Sic transit gloria mundi,* I guess.

This conveniently brings me to more mundane matters. For Turkish words I used modern Turkish transliteration conventions; for Arabic words I followed the rules of the *International Journal of Middle East Studies,* but since this book is aimed at a broader audience with no knowledge of Arabic, I have dropped all dots under letters (*d, h, t,* and *z*). In the notes, sources are cited in full only at first mention, then just by the author's last name and a shortened title.

The final version of this volume has greatly benefited from the penetrating reading and highly insightful comments of Professor Joseph C. Miller, to whom I am deeply grateful. For their kind hospitality and generosity, I wish to thank also the Department of History at the University of Pennsylvania, where I spent my 1993/94 sabbatical leave, researching and writing significant portions of this book. Final thanks go to Pamela J. Bruton, at the University of Washington Press, who did a superb copyediting job on the manuscript and helped clarify not a few statements and terms.

Parts of the following items have been used in various sections of this book. These were either thoroughly revised, updated with few changes, or just reassessed in light of recent research. In some cases, sections were taken out of articles and woven into the narrative in other chapters. I am grateful to the publishers of these works for permission to "mutilate" them and have them republished in the book:

The Ottoman Slave Trade and Its Suppression, 1840–1890. Princeton: Princeton University Press, 1982.

"Slave Dealers, Women, Pregnancy, and Abortion: The Story of a Circassian Slave-Girl in Mid–Nineteenth Century Cairo." *Slavery and Abolition* 2/1 (1981): 53–68. [Published by Frank Cass, London.]

"The Imperial Eunuchs of Istanbul: From Africa to the Heart of Islam." *Middle Eastern Studies* 20/3 (1984): 379–90. [Published by Frank Cass, London.]

"Ottoman Concepts of Slavery in the Period of Reform (1830s–1880s)." In *Breaking the Chains: Slavery, Bondage, and Emancipation in Modern Africa and Asia,* ed. Martin A. Klein, 37–63. Madison: University of Wisconsin Press, 1993. A slightly revised version appeared as "Late Ottoman Concepts of Slavery (1830s–1880s)" in *Poetics Today* 14/3 (1993): 477–506 [published by Duke University Press, Durham, N.C.].

"Shemsigul: A Circassian Slave in Mid-Nineteenth-Century Cairo." In *Struggle and Survival in the Modern Middle East,* ed. Edmund Burke III, 59–74. Berkeley and Los Angeles: University of California Press, 1993.

SLAVERY and ABOLITION

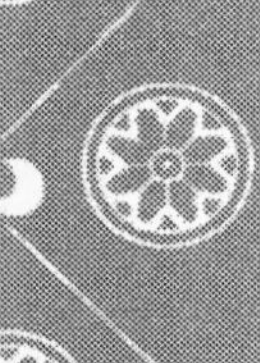

INTRODUCTION

Ottoman Slavery and the Slave Trade

SLAVERY HAS EXISTED IN many societies ever since antiquity. Where it was practiced, the legal owning of humans by other humans was accepted as a "natural" phenomenon, an integral part of the social fabric. This was so also in the vast lands that constituted the Ottoman Empire. Nonetheless, for millennia before the Ottomans set foot in those regions, men, women, and children had been reduced to slavery within their own societies or imported into them from both neighboring and faraway realms. In the Ottoman state, which conquered its vast territories in the fifteenth and sixteenth centuries, slavery was legal, and the slave trade flourished until the collapse of the empire during the First World War. But the traffic in slaves decreased dramatically toward the end of the nineteenth century, and the institution itself died out in the first decade of the twentieth. In some of the successor states in Arabia, however, the practice lingered on well beyond the Second World War, and actual bondage in various forms continues to exist covertly even today.

Ottoman slavery—like slavery in other societies—is neither completely understood by scholars nor easy to define. Some attempts to answer the question "who is a slave?" have resulted in definitions such as "one whose labor is controlled and whose freedom is withheld," a person "in a state of legal and actual servility or of slave origins," and even a "natally alienated and generally dishonored person" under "permanent, violent domination." Further below, I shall try to sort out some of this seeming tangle, but it is sufficient at this point to note that in Islamic legal terms, slavery grants one person ownership over another person, which means that the owner has rights to the slave's labor, property, and sexuality, and that the slave's freedoms are severely restricted.[1] But in sociocultural terms, slavery sometimes meant high social status or political power when applied to male slaves in the military and the bureaucracy (*mamlūk*s and *kul*s) and to female slaves in elite *harem*s. Even ordinary domestic slaves were often better fed, clothed, and protected than many free men and women. In any event, it is important to note that slavery was *both* an important, albeit involuntary, channel of recruitment and socialization into the elite and a major, though forced, means of linking individuals into patronage networks.

From the rise of the Ottoman state in the thirteenth century, slavery was familiar to and widely accepted by all walks of Ottoman society, and several types of slaves were known to the sultan's subjects. In fact, slavery gradually became a differentiated and broadly defined concept in many Islamic societies after the introduction of military slavery into the Abbasid Caliphate in the ninth century A.D. In the Ottoman Empire, military-administrative servitude, better known as the *kul* system, coexisted with other types of slavery: *harem* (quite different from male Western fantasy),[2] domestic, agricultural, and even military (on a limited scale at the periphery). While the latter types remained much the same until the period of reforms (1830s–1880s, what I prefer to call the "long Tanzimat"; see chapter 4), the *kul* system underwent profound changes.

From its inception, the *kul* system was nourished by periodic levies of the unmarried, able-bodied, male children of the sultan's Orthodox Christian subjects, mostly from the Balkans. This child levy

1. Although the broad definition provided here is mine, the best summary of the legal position of slavery in Islamic law is still R. Brunschvig's article "ʿAbd" in the *Encyclopædia of Islam*, 2d ed. (Leiden, 1960), vol. 1, pp. 24–40.

2. The best and most comprehensive account of the Ottoman imperial *harem* is Leslie P. Peirce, *The Imperial Harem: Women and Sovereignty in the Ottoman Empire* (New York and Oxford, 1993). Elite households emulated the style and structure of the sultan's household to the extent their finances allowed. For an analysis of the distorted male view of Ottoman *harem* life, see Billie Melman, *Women's Orients: English Women and the Middle East, 1718–1918* (Ann Arbor, 1992), especially pp. 59 ff.

was known as the *devşirme*. The children were reduced to slavery, converted to Islam, and rigorously socialized at the Palace School into various government roles with elite status. However, freeborn Muslims gradually entered government service, and the *kul* system evolved to accommodate this change, a process otherwise described in "old-school" Ottoman historiography as a manifestation of the empire's "decline." Ultimately, the child levy was abandoned during the seventeenth century, the Palace School lost its monopoly on the production of military-administrative slaves, and a new type of recruitment and socialization pattern, what I describe below as the *kul* type, came to prevail.[3]

As the *kul* system evolved, the classification of *kul*s as slaves gradually became irrelevant. Gibb and Bowen's somewhat dated work provides what is still a useful reference to the point:

> It is unfortunate that we should be obliged to use the word "slave" for persons of this status. For it is appropriate only in some ways. . . . everyone that belonged to it [the ruling elite] was held still to be a slave of the Sultan, though only a small minority were really eligible to be any such thing. The conventional slavery of the rest had a painful and real quality, however. It was actual enough to cost them what may be termed their civil rights.[4]

This meant that the sultan could confiscate the property of these "conventional" slaves or kill them, without legal process, whenever he so wished. However, over time, confiscations and executions became infrequent, being reserved for exemplary cases and meant to remind Ottoman officials "who was boss." Metin Kunt points out that confiscation of property took place only when an officeholder had been executed, which as early as the sixteenth century was not a common occurrence.[5]

3. The most thorough account of the impact of these developments on the scribal service and the emerging bureaucracy is Carter V. Findley's *Bureaucratic Reform in the Ottoman Empire* (Princeton, 1980). As will become evident later, however, I take a somewhat different view on the nature of official servility.

4. H. A. R. Gibb and H. Bowen, *The Islamic Society and the West* (Oxford, 1950), vol. 1, pt. 1, pp. 43–45.

5. Metin I. Kunt, *The Sultan's Servants: The Transformation of Ottoman Provincial Government, 1550–1650* (New York, 1983), p. 55. According to Kunt, the property

Since the female counterpart of *kul* servility was *harem* slavery, I shall now comment briefly on the actual nature of the imperial and elite *harems* in Ottoman society. The occidental image of the oriental *harem* is the locus of sexual romance and promiscuity, an extension of the legendary *Thousand and One Nights*. But as Billie Melman has shown, this image was very much the product of the male imagination and was not based on eyewitness accounts or on prolonged firsthand experiences. Occidental women travelers and ethnographers, on the other hand, "domesticated the exotic or . . . normalised and humanised the *harem*."[6] Their observations drew on a detailed and well-articulated body of ethnographic evidence, making their writings on Ottoman *harems* radically different from the literary tradition that propagated unrealistic images of oriental household customs and sexuality. The European women's *harem* was apparently a great deal closer to Ottoman realities, as current research convincingly demonstrates.

Throughout this book, but especially in chapter 1, I shall treat elite male *(kul)* and female *(harem)* slavery together under the construct of *kul/harem* slavery, since they were in fact two complementing elements of the same social institution. Hence, the term "*kul/harem* slaves" will be employed here to denote male military and civilian officeholders and female members of the elite who were slaves or had slave origins. When dealing with just one of the two components, I shall refer either to *kul* or to *harem* slavery separately.

The studies contained in the present book are all about late Ottoman history, that is, the last hundred years of the empire. As we examine Ottoman society at the beginning of the Tanzimat in the late 1830s, we find that the "real slave" population consisted of female and male, African and white, domestic and *kul/harem* slaves.[7] The overwhelming majority of Ottoman slaves were female, African, and domestic; males, white females, and *kul/harem* slaves were only a

---

of an heirless officeholder reverted to the sultan's private purse, whereas in the case of heirless *reaya*, it reverted to the Treasury.

6. Melman, *Women's Orients*, especially pp. 59 ff.; also consult Melman's exhaustive listings of women writers on the *harem* on pp. 59–76, 318–35.

7. This paragraph and the next draw on Ehud R. Toledano, *The Ottoman Slave Trade and Its Suppression, 1840–1890* (Princeton, 1982), pp. 14–90.

small minority. Although cruelty by slave traders and ill-usage by slave owners were repudiated, both the traffic and slaveholding were legal, socially acceptable, and a matter over which no serious moral question arose until late in the nineteenth century. The European powers had just passed the stage of abolition in the first quarter of the century and were turning their political, economic, and moral zeal to slavery in the Americas.

The continued existence of Ottoman slavery depended on the steady importation of slaves into the empire. Certain Islamic legal stipulations and ethical attitudes ensured that the slave population would constantly diminish, owing to early manumission, the free status accorded to the offspring of master-slave unions, and the mandatory liberation of such bonded mothers after the master's death (on concubinage, see further below). Thus, humanity at home inadvertently perpetuated the brutality from without. Slave breeding was not practiced in Ottoman society, and the only case that resembles it occurred among the Circassian slave class in the Caucasus, where parents would sell their children, mainly the girls, into the Ottoman *harem* market, often with the encouragement of the owner. Hence, the social and legal situation in the empire meant that the Ottoman slave population had to be replenished through conquest, forced recruitment, or trade. With conquest a thing of the past, and domestic enslavement of free persons both illegal and impracticable, the vast and complex slave-trading network became in the nineteenth century the only source of slaves for Ottoman elite households (sing., *kapı*).

African slaves were drawn from Central Africa (Waday, Bornu, Bagirmi) and the Sudan (the White and Blue Nile basins, Kordofan, and Darfur); Ethiopian slaves were imported from western Ethiopia, mainly from the Galla, Sidamo, and Gurage principalities; and Circassian and Georgian slaves reached the empire from the Caucasus. From Africa, slaves were run via Sahara Desert routes, the Ethiopian plateau, the Red Sea, the Nile Valley, the Persian Gulf, and the pilgrimage routes to and from Arabia. From the Caucasus, they were transported across the Black Sea and the Mediterranean. The number of slaves imported into the empire varied greatly from route to route and from period to period for the same route according to changing economic conditions in both the source region and the importing Ottoman province.[8]

To provide an order of magnitude (at which the purist expert would no doubt shudder) for the benefit of the uninitiated reader, I would say that the average number of slaves imported into the empire every year during much of the first seventy years of the nineteenth century (the apex of the traffic) ranged from 16,000 to 18,000.[9] The rise in the slave trade to the East coincided with the decline of the Atlantic traffic. That decline brought down slave prices as the market for them contracted. Consequently, slaves in large numbers became available for sale on the African market and for export to the East, in a development that was also related to the internal upheaval in central Sudan. This coincided with a rise in demand for slave labor in the Ottoman Middle East and North Africa, where economic growth occurred during the first half of the nineteenth century. Owing to all these developments, the slave trade was diverted from the West to the East.[10]

Prices of slaves in the empire varied according to the physical qualities and presumed skills of the individual slave but were also greatly affected by market conditions. These changed during the nineteenth century according to the changing circumstances in the

8. For the best available survey of economic conditions in the Ottoman Middle East, see Roger Owen, *The Middle East in the World Economy, 1800–1914* (London, 1981). For the Ottoman slave-trading network, see Toledano, *Ottoman Slave Trade,* pp. 14–54.

9. Thanks to the painstaking work of Ralph A. Austen for more than a decade, we now have a better idea of the numbers involved than we did when I first published my own estimates in 1982 (Toledano, *Ottoman Slave Trade,* pp. 81–90). Two of his recent articles are "The 19th Century Islamic Slave Trade from East Africa (Swahili and Red Sea Coasts): A Tentative Census," in *The Economics of the Indian Ocean Slave Trade in the Nineteenth Century,* ed. William Gervase Clarence-Smith, Special Issue of *Slavery and Abolition* 9/3 (1988), pp. 21–44; and "The Mediterranean Islamic Slave Trade out of Africa: A Tentative Census," *Slavery and Abolition* 13/1 (1992): 214–48. For the annual estimates provided here, I have added Austen's estimates for Egypt (second article, p. 218), which I had excluded in my book, and further revised some of my earlier figures, also incorporating Thomas M. Ricks's estimates for the Persian Gulf traffic (see his "Slaves and Slave Traders in the Persian Gulf, 18th and 19th Centuries: An Assessment," in Clarence-Smith, *Indian Ocean Slave Trade,* pp. 60–70). On the trans-Saharan slave trade, see also Michel Le Gall, "The End of the Trans-Saharan Slave Trade: A View from Tripoli, 1857–1902," *Princeton Papers on the Near East* 2 (1993): 25–56. On routes and the mechanism of the slave trade into the Ottoman Empire, see Toledano, *Ottoman Slave Trade,* pp. 14–54.

10. These changes in the slave trade are summarized in Patrick Manning, *Slavery and African Life* (Cambridge, 1990), pp. 136–40.

source regions, the political fluctuations that determined the safety of roads, the weather conditions that raised or lowered mortality during the passage, and the varying impact of state policies regarding prohibition. Upon entry into the empire, customs duties were regularly assessed by government officials, although dealers tried—when possible—to evade payment either through smuggling or by colluding with tax collectors in remote stations.[11]

To gain some sense of the size of the slave population uprooted from Africa to Ottoman territories, one should consider Ralph A. Austen's estimates that exports in the nineteenth century from East African Swahili coasts to Middle Eastern (Ottoman) and Indian (non-Ottoman) destinations were 313,000 and exports across the Red Sea and the Gulf of Aden (mostly Ottoman) were 492,000. Between 1820 and 1900, according to Austen, exports of African slaves to Ottoman Egypt reached 362,000, and exports to Ottoman North Africa (Algeria, Tunisia, and Libya) during the entire nineteenth century came to about 350,000.[12] For the sake of comparison, one can speak of three slave markets in Africa during the nineteenth century: the European export market, intended mainly for the Americas (including the Caribbean); the Muslim market, intended for the Ottoman (including Arab), Moroccan, Iranian, and Indian worlds; and the internal African market. The last was the largest and consisted mostly of women and children, whereas the European and the Muslim markets were roughly comparable in size, the Muslim being slightly smaller.[13]

11. For prices and taxes, see Toledano, *Ottoman Slave Trade,* pp. 62–72.

12. Figures for the East African exports are from Austen, "The 19th Century Islamic Slave Trade from East Africa," pp. 29 and 33; figures for the North African exports are from Austen, "The Mediterranean Islamic Slave Trade out of Africa," p. 226 (exports to non-Ottoman Morocco reached more than 300,000 during the same century). For the diminished size of the African diaspora in the Middle East and North Africa, see John O. Hunwick, "Black Africans in the Mediterranean World: Introduction to a Neglected Aspect of the African Diaspora," in *The Human Commodity: Perspectives on the Trans-Saharan Slave Trade,* ed. Elizabeth Savage (London, 1992), pp. 5–38; and Michael Brett's thesis on the issue in the introduction to the same volume. Against the evidence provided by the authors cited above, Albertine Jwaideh and J. W. Cox opine—a mere conjecture based on their study of the very limited area of the Gulf region and southern Iraq—that the small residuum of Africans in the Middle East belies the high estimates accepted by scholars for the slave trade ("The Black Slaves of Turkish Arabia during the 19th Century," in Clarence-Smith, *Indian Ocean Slave Trade,* p. 56).

13. See, e.g., Claire C. Robertson and Martin A. Klein, "Introduction: Women's Importance in African Slave Systems," in *Women and Slavery in Africa,* ed. Claire C. Robertson and Martin A. Klein (Madison, 1983), p. 4.

By the end of the long-Tanzimat period, the history of Ottoman slavery had taken a major turn. The suppression of the slave trade into the empire had become a common item in dealings between Britain and the Ottoman government. Slaveholding was still legal, but the slave trade had been prohibited by law. The traffic in Africans and Caucasians practically died out, although it would pick up from time to time on a small scale. Thomas Ricks tells us that the Persian Gulf traffic declined by 84–90 percent, with only fifty to a hundred slaves entering per annum, and Ralph Austen reckons that Egypt received then only about five hundred slaves a year, with just the North African branch (especially non-Ottoman Morocco) carrying on almost as earlier in the century.[14] Throughout the empire, slavery was gradually being transformed into free forms of service and patronage, such as raising freeborn, young girls in the household, socializing them into lower- or upper-class roles—as talent and need determined—and later marrying them off and setting them up in life *(çirak/çirağ* and *besleme).*[15] Ottoman elite culture was adopting a negative stance toward slavery and gradually disengaging from it on moral grounds (see chapter 4).

What happened during that half century? In the 1840s, British public opinion and the British government began to take an interest in the abolition of Ottoman slavery. An early success was scored with the reforming bey of Tunis, who in 1841 prohibited slavery and the slave trade in that semi-independent Ottoman province, following direct contacts with the British. Although the prohibition had a limited impact in Tunis, it was viewed with disfavor by Istanbul, and attempts to induce the Sublime Porte[16] to adopt similar measures soon proved futile.[17] Instead—and as an alternative method that would ultimately choke the institution through want of supply—

14. Ricks, "Slaves and Slave Traders in the Persian Gulf," p. 67; Austen, "The Mediterranean Islamic Slave Trade out of Africa," pp. 218 and 226.

15. This somewhat resembles the practice of keeping families of *muwallads* (persons legally no longer of slave status) in urban elite households in Iraq—especially in Baghdad—until recent times, which is described as being common among a small number of wealthy families (see Jwaideh and Cox, "The Black Slaves of Turkish Arabia," pp. 54–55).

16. The "Sublime Porte," often called just "the Porte," is a European term used to denote the Ottoman government.

17. On this, see Toledano, *Ottoman Slave Trade,* pp. 98–99.

a major effort was launched to suppress the slave trade into the empire. The goal of that long-term British drive was to extract from the Ottoman government edicts forbidding the trade in Africans and Caucasians on humanitarian grounds. The implementation of such edicts was then carefully monitored by British diplomatic and commercial representatives throughout the empire and reported back to London. In turn, London would press Istanbul to enforce the edicts, and so on.[18]

This policy yielded the prohibition of the slave trade in the Persian Gulf in 1847, the temporary prohibition of the traffic in Circassians and Georgians in 1854–55, the general prohibition of the African slave trade in 1857, and the Anglo-Egyptian and Anglo-Ottoman conventions for the suppression of the slave trade in 1877 and 1880, respectively. The campaign reached its climax with the participation of the Ottoman government in the negotiations leading to the conclusion of the Brussels Act against the slave trade, signed in 1890. It is immediately noticeable that from the mid-1850s onward, Caucasian slavery and slave trade were excluded from the realm of Anglo-Ottoman relations. In that area, the Porte initiated some major changes, acting alone and according to its own considerations (for details, see chapter 3).

In terms of attitudes, one should note that within the Ottoman Muslim elite, a general sense of moral and spiritual superiority toward Christian Europe prevailed. This feeling coexisted with the recognition of Ottoman military, technological, and economic inferiority. All this produced a clear disinclination in government circles to yield to British pressures regarding slavery and the slave trade. Thus, even when a number of edicts were promulgated by the Sublime Porte, their enforcement lagged behind and often required reiteration and reenactment, usually following British remonstrations. The situation was quite different when it concerned white (i.e., non-African) slavery and the traffic which kept it alive. Here, the Ottomans had to devise their own solution to the problem caused by the reintroduction of agricultural slavery into the empire.

18. The suppression of the Ottoman slave trade, only briefly delineated in this and the next few paragraphs, is described in detail in Toledano, *Ottoman Slave Trade*, from chap. 3 to the end. On this, see also Y. Hakan Erdem, *Slavery in the Ottoman Empire and Its Demise, 1800–1909* (London and New York, 1996).

One of the most important factors shaping the Porte's policy toward Caucasian slavery in the empire was the large number of Circassian refugees—estimates run from 500,000 to 1,000,000—who were forced by the Russians to leave their land and enter Ottoman territory from the mid-1850s to the mid-1860s. About 10 percent of the refugee population were unfree agricultural workers, which put the question of non-African slavery into a different perspective. Increased tensions between refugee slave owners and their slaves, at times causing violence and disturbance of public order, induced the Ottoman government in 1867 to design a special program for slaves who wished to obtain their freedom. Using an Islamic legal device for self-ransom, the Porte granted the slaves the tracts of land they were cultivating so that they could purchase their freedom from their masters.

In 1882, the authorities promoted this method to facilitate the conscription of Circassian and Georgian slaves. Such a step was necessary because only free men could be drafted into the army. Measures were also taken from the mid-1860s onward to restrict the traffic in Circassian and Georgian children, mostly young girls. Thus, by the last decade of the nineteenth century, the trade in Caucasian slaves had been reduced considerably. The remaining demand was then maintained only by the *harem*s of the imperial family and the households of well-to-do elites. The imperial *harem* at the time contained about four hundred women in a wide array of nonsexual household functions. Those *harem*s also continued to employ eunuchs, and as late as 1903, the Ottoman family alone owned 194 of them. In the nineteenth century, the eunuchs' political influence declined both as individuals and as a distinct corps in court politics (for details, see chapter 1). Whether officially abolished by the 1908 revolution, or only later by the new Turkish Republic, Ottoman slavery died piecemeal, not abruptly, with the end of empire.

Before moving on to review the profound changes that occurred in Ottoman slavery and the slave trade during the nineteenth century, it is necessary to briefly discuss two important points: the large female majority within the Ottoman slave population during the period under discussion and the debate over the mild nature of slavery in Ottoman society.

Muslim law, the Şeriat (Arabic Sharīʿa), does not recognize class distinctions among slaves but views them rather as one legal category.[19] Nevertheless, social conditions and cultural attitudes did not fail to produce a clear hierarchy among Ottoman slaves. This hierarchy was expressed in price and employment, as well as in social standing. At the top, we find the Circassian and Georgian slaves, and at the bottom, the Africans (with some internal differentiation favoring the Ethiopians). Accordingly, almost all African slaves served in menial jobs, along with a fair number of white slaves. However, many white female slaves, and a certain number of Ethiopian ones, became concubines, and often wives, to their masters.

If a concubine bore her master a child, that child was free, and the mother could not be resold and would automatically become free upon the death of her owner. In fact, a woman in that position, legally called *ümmüveled* (Arabic *umm walad*), could not be resold from the moment her pregnancy became known. Not infrequently, masters would free a woman in that position and marry her, especially if the baby was a boy. Thus, social mobility was at least a possibility for white slave women, even if not all of them did actually realize their aspirations (on the predicament of concubines, see further below). Although there was no legal obstacle to the upward mobility of nonwhite slaves, this avenue of socioeconomic betterment was not a realistic option for them.

Young women from the Caucasus were often sold by their own families—many already belonging to the slave class—in the hope that the women would rise to prominence in the imperial household or upper-class *harems*. Quite a few actually did, especially those who were beautiful and talented. Elite households often considered it their duty to marry off such young women, if they did not marry within the family. The rest served in household duties, never realizing the dreams and high aspirations of their youth.

The high female-to-male ratio among the slaves imported into the empire resembles the situation in the African domestic market but stands in sharp contrast to the 2–3:1 male-to-female ratio in the Atlantic slave trade. As in African societies at the time, so in the Ottoman Empire: female slaves were preferred to male slaves mainly for the hard work they performed in households and less for their

19. Brunschvig, "ʿAbd," pp. 26–31.

reproductive capacity.[20] Reproduction was more the incentive in the importation of female slaves from the Caucasus, though that too has been exaggerated, and many of these slaves worked in menial household jobs that did not necessarily lead to concubinage and childbearing.

Claire Robertson and Martin Klein argue with regard to slavery in African societies that to stress the biological functions of female slaves, and their concomitant easier assimilation into the slave-owning society, distorts the position and function of female slaves and underestimates their *productive* functions.[21] For Africa and the Americas, statistical evidence shows that fertility of female slaves was lower than that of free women, which shows that African female slaves were preferred to male slaves because of their productive, rather than reproductive, capacity. Although fertility studies regarding Ottoman female slaves have not been conducted, Robertson and Klein's other observations are also valid for Ottoman society. As in African Muslim societies, the requirements of gender segregation in the Ottoman Empire meant that the slaves used by well-to-do free women to perform their work for them had to be female. Thus, female slave labor often replaced female free labor to provide leisure for free, elite and sometimes non-elite women; the demand for female slave labor was created by the desire to reduce the burden on free women. Thus, free women might have paid a heavier price for abolition than did free men, as they were then pushed further down the social ladder to the less desirable, labor-intensive, low-status work.

This conveniently brings us to the discussion of the nature of Ottoman slavery, a question that is obviously part of a larger context, both Western and non-Western. The attempts by the British govern-

20. John Thornton, "Sexual Demography: The Impact of the Slave Trade on Family Structure," in Robertson and Klein, *Women and Slavery in Africa*, pp. 39–48. Thornton examines the impact of the slave trade to the Americas on the population that remained in Africa: the high male-to-female ratio in the Atlantic slave trade accounted for the inability of the slave population to reproduce itself and for the continued dependence of slaveholders on importation. In Africa, the productive age bracket (fifteen to sixty) showed 80 men to every 100 women, and in Angola, which was the hardest-hit region, 40–50 men to 100 women. This substantially increased the burden on women (pp. 39–41). The nineteenth-century East African traffic into the Ottoman Empire had a different impact on the remaining population since the overwhelming majority of the slaves imported were female.

21. Robertson and Klein, "Introduction," pp. 8–9, 10–11, and 16.

ment, beginning in the 1840s, to induce the Ottoman government to abolish slavery elicited a defensive reaction, which in later decades was articulated by Ottoman writers and developed into a small-scale polemic by the 1870s (for details, see chapter 4). The crux of the Ottoman argument was that slavery in the empire, as in other Muslim societies, was fundamentally different from slavery in the Americas. In the main, it was far milder because slaves were not employed on plantations, were well treated, were frequently manumitted, and could integrate into the slave-owning society. Islamic law, it was further maintained, encouraged owners to treat their slaves well, and manumission was considered a pious act, for which the believer could expect remuneration. It was virtually impossible for members of the Ottoman elite—many of whom were descendants of *kul/harem* slaves—to relate to slavery as did European abolitionists.

In the nineteenth century, Europeans and Americans had a rather undifferentiated view of slavery, tending to universalize the condition of plantation slaves in the United States South and leave no room for alternative, milder manifestations of slavery. In Western scholarship on slavery, a subtler view emerged in the 1940s and 1950s, when Frank Tannenbaum and Stanley Elkins argued that the Catholic-hierarchical cultures of Latin societies produced a mild form of slavery and "open" race relations, while the Protestant, capitalist individualism of North America conduced toward a harsher, "closed" type of slavery, which led to blatant discrimination against African Americans in the period following emancipation.[22] Later scholarship revised this thesis, stressing the impact of different economic conditions and levels of development rather than national or cultural factors.[23] It was accepted, however, that manumission was easier and

22. See Frank Tannenbaum, *Slave and Citizen: The Negro in the Americas* (New York, 1947); and Stanley Elkins, *Slavery* (Chicago, 1959). For a succinct summary of this point, see George M. Fredrickson, "Comparative History," in *The Past before Us: Contemporary Historical Writing in the United States,* ed. Michael Kammen (Ithaca and London, 1980), pp. 466–70.

23. See, e.g., David Brion Davis, *The Problem of Slavery in the Age of Revolution, 1770–1823* (Ithaca, 1975); David Brion Davis, *Slavery and Human Progress* (New York, 1984); Eugene D. Genovese, *The World the Slaveholders Made* (New York, 1969); Eugene D. Genovese, *Roll, Jordan, Roll* (New York, 1972); Carl N. Degler, *Perspectives and Irony in American Slavery* (Jackson, 1976); Franklin Knight and Peggy K. Liss, eds., *Atlantic Port Cities: Economy, Culture, and Society in the Atlantic World, 1650–1850* (Knoxville, 1991), introduction.

postemancipation race relations less constrained in Latin American societies. Degler argued that the earlier suppression of the slave trade to North America created the need for domestic reproduction of the slave population, resulting in better material conditions and less flagrant cruelty.

The examination of "open" and "closed" slave systems was later extended to non-American slavery, especially in Africa, the Far East, and—to a lesser extent—Muslim societies. Thus, for example, Peter Kolchin follows Pierre Dockés and Paul E. Lovejoy in distinguishing between a "society based on slavery" (i.e., in which slavery was a dominant productive institution) and a "society in which some slaves exist" (i.e., in which slavery was an economically marginal phenomenon); the latter category was described by Philip D. Curtin as a society where "the slave was not a labor unit," for example, in Muslim societies.[24] In general, scholars have tended to accept the views expounded by members of the studied societies themselves, namely that "their" slavery was milder, better integrated, more "open." This, in turn, would also explain—or explain away, as some argue—the resistance to the abolition of slavery and the absence of abolitionist movements in many of these societies (for Ottoman views on this, see chapter 4).

However, in recent years, the view that Third World slavery was mild and that slaves were well treated and socially assimilated has come under some new scrutiny. One of the strongest proponents of the opposite view is Jay Spaulding, who examined slavery in the northern Sudan under Ottoman-Egyptian occupation (from 1820 onward, locally known as the "Turkish Period"; in Arabic, al-Turkiyya).[25] Spaulding attributes to the occupying power a dramatic rise in the slave trade and in the use of slaves in agriculture and the military. Incidentally, this was the only place in the empire where an African slave army existed, which was mainly due to the "frontier situation" that prevailed in the Ottoman-Egyptian Sudan

24. Peter Kolchin, "Some Recent Works on Slavery outside the United States: An American Perspective," *Comparative Studies in Society and History* 28/4 (1986): 767–77; reference here is particularly to p. 773. For Philip Curtin's view, see his *The Rise and Fall of the Plantation Complex: Essays in Atlantic History* (Cambridge, 1990), p. 41.

25. Jay Spaulding, "Slavery, Land Tenure, and Social Class in the Northern Turkish Sudan," *International Journal of African Historical Studies* 15/1 (1982): 1–20, especially pp. 8–13.

under Mehmet Ali, Abbas, and Sait.[26] Spaulding criticizes the use of slaves as a form of "currency" for paying the soldiers, who then either exchanged them for food or sold them to the local population. As a result of this glut, prices declined sharply toward the end of the century. Unlike Ottoman practice, a form of joint ownership of slaves, including concubines, developed and was apparently sanctioned by local interpreters of Islamic law.

Spaulding strongly opposes the "comfortable interpretation" that slavery in the Ottoman-Egyptian Sudan was "a benign institution" and that "slaves or the offspring of slaves were integrated into northern Sudanese society at the family level through processes similar to marriage or adoption, culminating in manumission." His evidence leads him to conclude that a slave was considered a "talking animal" *(al-hayawān al-nātiq);* to prevent integration, slaves were given names that clearly distinguished them from free persons; to save money, in some districts dead slaves were not buried but rather left to scavenging animals or dumped in the river; government demands for slaves as taxes limited the ability of owners to develop "assimilative familial instincts"; slaves born in the household were commonly sold, contrary to the custom in other Muslin countries; manumission was rare, with a peculiar phenomenon that freed persons *(maʿtūq, maʿtūqa)* remained in a servile status, sometimes jointly owned by several people; and finally, "the weight of social pressure lay heavily against the assimilation of slaves or their children through marriage." Dismissing the claim advanced by a Sudanese writer that "a slave in the Sudan was above all a human being, a member of a society or a family,"[27] Spaulding brings as a counterexample the case of a female slave who in 1877 was sold five times in succession to different men, obviously for concubinage.

Concubinage is a sore point in the debate, since it is often seen as a channel of upward social mobility for female slaves, hence as an advantage over male slaves. Robertson and Klein criticize the argument that concubines were "not really slaves" because they enjoyed a privileged position. They maintain that this view emanates from

26. On military slavery, see Gerard Prunier, "Military Slavery in the Sudan during the Turkiyya (1820–1885)," in Savage, *The Human Commodity,* pp. 129–39.

27. Abbas Ibrahim Muhammad Ali, *The British, the Slave Trade, and Slavery in the Sudan, 1820–1881* (Khartoum, 1972), p. 75. For a comment on this work, see chap. 5, below.

a notion that "compulsory sexual relations somehow ameliorated rather than reinforced slavery for women." The authors believe that the opposite is true and that, in fact, concubinage reinforced and further manifested male dominance. They further argue that women were more easily assimilated into the slave-owning society than men because of their reproductive capacity and consequent absorption into the owners' families and because of their "submissive socialization," since "in many societies women were and are taught to obey men unquestioningly."[28] These observations are quite relevant to Ottoman slavery too, given the idealized image of *harem* concubinage. The relative protection accorded to *ümmüveled* (see above and, for details, chapter 2) and the social circumstances of elite concubines indeed led many observers to lose sight of the problematic predicament of the concubine in Ottoman society.

My last example of the difficulties with the simplistic view of the mild nature of Third World slavery comes from nineteenth-century Brazil. In line with the view on the "open" nature of Brazilian slavery, Gilberto Freyre argued that, owing to the nature of female domestic slavery and concubinage in Brazil during the first half of the nineteenth century, slavery there was mild.[29] Based on her thorough study of police records and other original sources from the capital city of Rio de Janeiro, Mary Karasch asserts rather that the opposite was true. She argues that frequent slave abscondence, high mortality figures, active resistance, and often harsh treatment—regular and punitive—"call into question previous generalizations on the 'mildness' of Brazilian slavery. . . . Even in the capital of the Empire of Brazil, where the best medical care existed, slave females died at early ages, and they did not bear enough children to sustain the city's slave population through natural reproduction."[30] While not denying that some slave women fared better and were even manumitted, Karasch is confident that the majority worked long hours in hard, menial, often

28. Quotations and views in this paragraph are from Robertson and Klein, "Introduction," pp. 6 and 8–9.

29. Gilberto Freyre, *The Masters and the Slaves: A Study in the Development of Brazilian Civilization* (New York, 1956).

30. Mary Karasch, "Anastacia and the Slave Women of Rio de Janeiro," in *Africans in Bondage: Studies in Slavery and the Slave Trade,* ed. Paul E. Lovejoy (Madison, 1986), p. 100.

unskilled jobs, under miserable conditions that cannot be described as "mild."

To sum up this discussion of the nature of non-American slavery, it is necessary to say a few words on the nature of Ottoman domestic—rather than *kul/harem*—slavery. As often happens, the truth in what I call "the good-treatment debate" lies somewhere in the middle. Whereas Spaulding's example of the concubine in northern Sudan who was sold five times was not common in the core areas of the Ottoman Empire, a great deal of what Robertson and Klein observe with regard to the position of female domestic slaves in African societies holds true for domestic slavery in Ottoman households. In northern Sudan as in other peripheral societies within the empire, the plight of slaves—and that of the urban poor and the peasantry in general—was not an enviable one. Yet in the core areas, most notably in urban elite households, the nature of bondage was closer to what historians of slavery elsewhere would call "mild," and the treatment of slaves was generally good. In those places, slavery was one of the mechanisms of incorporation into patronage networks, and slaves were not infrequently manumitted after several years of service, often remaining in the same household or a related one.

We should not, however, lose sight of the vulnerability and powerlessness of Ottoman slaves, especially bondwomen, vis-à-vis their owners: while social and legal norms militated against flagrant abuse, they could not prevent harassment and exploitation within the household. The following two chapters illustrate this point: chapter 1 discusses various aspects of *kul/harem* slavery, whereas chapter 2 deals with what could—and did—go wrong when norms and reality clashed.

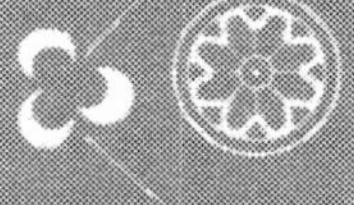

ONE

Kul/Harem Slavery

The Men, the Women, the Eunuchs

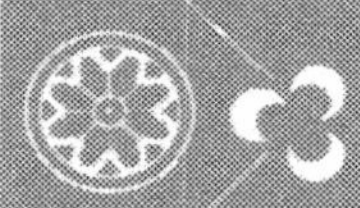

In large measure, the dynastic rule of the House of Osman was predicated on the sustained loyalty and continued state service of a dependent elite. The nucleus of that elite was provided by the *kul/harem* system, which produced the military commanders and civilian administrators who made it possible for the sovereigns to govern a rapidly growing and ultimately vast empire. By the nineteenth century, the *devşirme*-based corps of generals and governors had evolved into a diversified and more heterogeneous officeholding elite. Even the servile nature that had determined its identity from the inception of the Ottoman Empire has undergone some fundamental changes. This chapter begins with a brief discussion of the meaning of *kul/harem* slavery and then reviews the elements of that institution, which survived into nineteenth-century Ottoman society: (1) recruitment and socialization of both *kul*-type slaves and *harem* slaves (*câriye*s) and (2) the corps of the African eunuchs.

Of *Kul*s, *Câriye*s, and Slaves

The persistence of the opacity surrounding the servile status of Ottoman officialdom has spawned a scholarly debate over the classification of slaves. The result is still a rather blurred picture.

Hence, I need to digress briefly in order to clarify matters, before moving on to the situation which obtained in the nineteenth century. The controversy here is whether *kul*s should be considered "slaves" in the same category as Ottoman domestic and agricultural slaves.

The Ottoman situation resembles the realities that prevailed in Russia until the beginning of the eighteenth century, and in other ways it resembles those that prevailed there even later. An ambiguity similar to that surrounding *kul/harem* slavery existed with regard to the *kholopy*, and scholars have quibbled over whether that term should be translated "servants" rather than "slaves." Russian *kholopy* constituted about 10 percent of the population and were, in Peter Kolchin's words, "a diverse group" that included "high-status persons who served in administrative capacities as well as more numerous domestic servants, artisans, and agricultural laborers." In the seventeenth century, this category became internally more differentiated as *kholopy* merged with serfs and the number of high-status slaves declined.[1] These and other Ottoman-Russian parallels remain to be explored.

The noted Ottomanist Halil İnalcık stops short of arguing that military-administrative slaves were slaves in name only but states that there was much difference between them and "real" slaves. A somewhat different view is taken by Daniel Pipes and Orlando Patterson.[2] In his study of military slavery in Islam, Pipes argues that the designation of a person as slave in Islam refers only to that person's origins, not to his or her experience in later life. He then poses the question whether military slaves were "true slaves," that is, "persons in a state of legal and actual servility," or were merely "persons of slave origins."[3]

The notion of *control* is central to Pipes's concept: to qualify as a "true slave," a person must be both salable and lacking freedom

1. For Russian slavery, see Peter Kolchin, *Unfree Labor: American Slavery and Russian Serfdom* (Cambridge, Mass., and London, 1987), pp. 2–3 (for the quotation) and 385 n. 2 (with reference to the terminological controversy).

2. Halil İnalcık, *The Ottoman Empire: The Classical Age, 1300–1600* (New York, 1973), p. 87; and see also Bernard Lewis, *Race and Slavery in the Middle East: An Historical Inquiry* (New York and Oxford, 1990), p. 71; Daniel Pipes, *Slave Soldiers and Islam* (New Haven and London, 1981); Orlando Patterson, *Slavery and Social Death* (Cambridge, Mass., and London, 1982).

3. For Pipes's views cited in this paragraph and the next two, see Pipes, *Slave Soldiers and Islam*, pp. 15–23.

of action. He writes that "though everyone is subject to innumerable restrictions and limitations, the [true] slave . . . consistently lacks the power to make his own most important decisions." These include decisions regarding his or her whereabouts, occupation, marital status, and discipline. Military slaves, thus, differ from other types of slaves by their ability to gain control over their lives not only through manumission but also through the use of their own power base to liberate themselves and gain that control. Accordingly, "a military slave remains a true slave as long as his master controls him." Pipes concludes by rightly cautioning against dismissing military—what I call military-administrative—slavery as mere formality or legal fiction.

This concept enables Pipes to maintain that it was quite possible for a person to possess wealth, social status, and power while at the same time be considered a true slave. Conveniently for our purposes, his most striking example is that of Ottoman grand vezirs,[4] whom, he asserts, the sultans could execute or reduce "to a kitchen aide" at the "merest whim." Pipes's Ottoman point is picked up and expanded by Patterson in his *Slavery and Social Death*, but his radical definition of slavery is quite problematic in its application to Ottoman realities: "the permanent, violent domination of natally alienated and generally dishonored persons."[5] It is radical because of Patterson's insistence that it should be applied to all kinds of slaves, regardless of how elevated and powerful they might be.

Furthermore, in an example relevant to our discussion, Patterson argues that "Paul Rycaut's classic description of the Janissaries as men whom their master, the sultan, 'can raise without Envy and destroy without Danger' holds true for all slaves in all times."[6] When he subsequently delves into the specific case of military-administrative slavery in Islam, Patterson inevitably finds himself profoundly disagreeing with Halil İnalcık and other Ottomanists. In his analysis, the concept of *honor* is central, and the assumption that grand vezirs in the Ottoman Empire may have had considerable power but no honor is crucial to his argument. The only piece of evidence adduced

4. Throughout this book the spelling "vezir" will be used, rather than the English "vizier" or "vizir," to better approximate the Turkish word.

5. Patterson, *Slavery and Social Death*, p. 13; this is his preliminary definition, which is further developed in the later parts of the book.

6. Ibid., p. 8.

for this far-reaching claim is the refusal of a Muslim high court to admit the testimony of the powerful İbrahim Paşa, who served as grand vezir between 1523 and 1536, because he was a slave.[7]

In any event, one must never lose sight of the specificity of slavery in given historical situations. As is often the case for the specialist, the great appeal of a universal model tends to wear off almost as soon as the theory is applied in his or her scholarly territory. Thus, no matter how hard favorably disposed Ottomanists may try to set aside their preconceptions—and I have done my own best—it would be quite difficult for them to accept Patterson's, and even Pipes's, position. The historian's concern here is to convey and interpret the peculiar situation in which, for much of Ottoman history, powerful, highly honored personages throughout the army and bureaucracy, in Istanbul as well as in the provinces, labored under certain legal impediments resembling servile status. That some of Patterson's assertions might apply to early Ottoman history and the emergence of the *kul* system does not make them valid for the greater part of Ottoman history.

The overwhelming majority of high-ranking Ottoman officials of *kul* origins and training held their elevated, powerful positions *with all rights, privileges, and honors pertaining thereto*. It was uncommon for grand vezirs and other dignitaries—free or of slave origins—to be humiliated after their dismissal from office. *Kul*s were subject to the sultan's "whims" to the same extent as non-*kul*s, contrary to Pipes's view that they were necessarily more so. Rather, *kul*s of slave origins were often shielded by the intimacy and mutual reliance of the master-slave relationship in a way that free officials were not.

The problem with Pipes's position regarding the Ottoman *kul* system is his insistence that "grand vezirs," as a catchall category meaning "officeholders," were "true slaves" and not merely "of slave origins," to use his own typology. He himself, however, seems to be aware that much of post-sixteenth-century Ottoman history belies such a notion. To make amends, Pipes opines that during that period, Ottoman military slaves reached the point of "self-assertion" and passed into "domination," whatever that means.[8] He

7. Military slavery in Islam is discussed in ibid., pp. 308–14. The case of İbrahim Paşa is discussed on pp. 313–14.

8. Pipes, *Slave Soldiers and Islam*, pp. 20–21.

also provides some leeway by allowing that such slaves ceased to be "true slaves" when no longer (directly?) controlled by their masters. Thus, presumably, we could mitigate the "true slavery" of *kul*s who moved to the provincial administration, and maybe even of those who served in the central government, but we could not do so for those immediately under the sultan. Moreover, the condition of salability did not obtain with regard to officeholders unless they were of slave origins (the *kul* type), and even then it was rarely enforced.

In any case, the historical trend is clear. Even if the *kul* system yielded an all-slave military-administrative establishment in early Ottoman history—which is under debate—it soon came to include an ever-increasing number of freeborn men. As time went by, the "sultan's slaves" (*kul*s) became less *kul*-like. As we approach the nineteenth century, their bondage becomes more a symbol of their high status and less a practical fact of life. Their job insecurity then derives from their position as servants of an autocratic monarch, not from their formal servility. Even Carter Findley, who takes the servile status of officeholders almost literally, can cite only five cases over more than fifty years (1785–1837) in which highly prominent personages were treated as actual slaves when punished.[9] Be that as it may, the Gülhane Rescript of 1839 freed government officials from the last vestiges of bondage that attached to their status.

Kul-Type and *Harem* Slavery in the Nineteenth Century

HISTORIANS OF THE TANZIMAT devote little attention to the phenomenon of military-administrative, or *kul*-type, slavery, assuming perhaps that it was of no importance. However, what is sometimes overlooked, or just underestimated, is the fact that within the Ottoman elite, *kul*-type slavery was still very much alive in the second half of the nineteenth century. As noted in the Introduction, the major change that occurred in the practice was that the central government, and more specifically the Ottoman court, abandoned the *devşirme* as a system of recruitment, and the Palace School no longer served as a major agent of socialization. However, some constituent elements of *kul* slavery survived in both the central government and the provinces. Slaves in high and middle ranks of the army and

9. Findley, *Bureaucratic Reform in the Ottoman Empire,* p. 103.

bureaucracy were to be observed in both the central government and in Egypt, Tunisia, Algeria, and Iraq. In all core provinces, slaves served in government, although their number was small and steadily decreasing.

As readjustment to the changes that were occurring in the old *kul* system, there emerged, in the center and in many provinces, what can be described as a "*mamlūk*-type," or "*kul*-type," pattern of recruitment and socialization. The phenomenon that Metin Kunt identified in the provincial administration as the recruitment of slaves by prominent slaves *(kulların kulları)* was common from the seventeenth century onward and was an important element of the Ottoman grandee household *(kapı)*. In that system, dignitaries of state *(devlet adamları)* purchased young male slaves through agents and dealers, educated and trained them within the household, and socialized them into male elite roles. They would then attempt to place them into the army or the scribal service—later the bureaucracy—in the hope that they would accumulate power, attain influential positions, and, eventually, protect and promote their patron's interest. This career pattern coexisted with the recruitment of free men via *intisap* (social networks) and their socialization through the apprentice pattern.[10]

The cognate female pattern was embodied in the *harem* system. Similarly recruited, educated, and trained, these young slaves were socialized into elite female roles. Whereas the male slaves, heirs to the *kul* tradition, inhabited the public world of government life, female slaves inhabited the *harem* world and moved in the social network of elite households. Products of the two tracks often intermarried, since women who had been socialized in elite *harems* were the natural—almost the politically and economically required—brides for elite males of slave origins, as they also were for all other (i.e., free) male members of the elite. The currency, legitimacy, and respectability of *kul*-type and *harem* slavery in the Tanzimat period seem to have been somewhat underrated by scholars. The phenomenon is properly

10. See Metin Kunt, "Kulların Kulları," *Boğaziçi Üniversitesi Dergisi, Hümaniter Bilimler,* 3 (1975): 27–42. My own thoughts on the *mamlūk* pattern of recruitment and socialization are sketched in Ehud R. Toledano, "The Emergence of Ottoman-Local Elites in the Middle East and North Africa, 17th–19th Centuries," in *Essays in Honour of Albert Hourani,* ed. I. Pappé and M. Ma'oz (Oxford and London, forthcoming). See also Gabriel Piterberg, "The Formation of an Ottoman Egyptian Elite in the 18th Century," *International Journal of Middle East Studies* 22/3 (1990): 275–89.

noted, however, by Halil İnalcık in his article about Hüsrev Paşa (1756?–1855).[11]

Of Abaza (Abkhazian) tribal origins, Hüsrev himself was brought to Istanbul as a slave and entered into the household of Sait Efendi, chief of the corps of halberdiers in the sultan's bodyguard *(çavuş başı)*. He was later placed in the palace service but began his rise to the top as the protégé of Küçük Hüseyin Paşa, commander of the navy. During his long career, Hüsrev Paşa purchased and trained in his household more than fifty slaves, of whom about thirty made the elevated rank of *paşa*. He also succeeded in marrying them to daughters of sultans and members of top elite *harems*. İnalcık notes that this central political personage, who served in a great number of high government posts, including the grand vezirate, was the last representative of the old system. The Ottoman biographer Mehmet Süreyya notes that two of Hüsrev Paşa's slaves reached the highest office, that of grand vezir; one became minister of war; four were appointed cabinet ministers; one rose to the rank of field marshal; and many became generals.[12]

One of the most prominent of Hüsrev Paşa's slaves was the grand vezir İbrahim Edhem Paşa. He was bought by one of Hüsrev's agents when only one year old and taken to Hüsrev's mansion. There, the boy was adopted by Hüsrev's second wife and raised as her child, Hüsrev Paşa having no children of his own. Edhem did not know much about his origins, save for the scanty and dubious information related to him in his childhood. Hence, his biographers can only cite a number of conflicting stories. Because of the large number of orphans and abandoned children thus taken into Hüsrev's house, teachers were in residence and tutoring was done at home. When Edhem was nine years old, in 1827, Hüsrev Paşa—then commander of the navy—sent him with three of his other young slaves to Paris to be educated.[13]

The phenomenon of slaves in high office was well known not only to members of the Ottoman elite but also to European observers

11. Halil İnalcık, in *Islam Ansiklopedisi* (Istanbul, 1950), vol. 5, p. 613.

12. Mehmet Süreyya, *Sicill-i Osmani*, 4 vols. (Istanbul, 1308–15/1890–98), vol. 2, pp. 276–77.

13. A detailed biography of İbrahim Edhem Paşa is in Mehmet Zeki Pakalın, *Son Sadrazamlar ve Başvekiller* (Istanbul, 1942), vol. 2, pp. 403 ff. Information cited here is from pp. 403–4.

who acquired any familiarity with Ottoman society. Adolphus Slade, a British naval officer who visited the empire many times during the 1830s, asserts that "four-fifths of the ministers of the present sultan [Mahmut II, ruled 1808–39] were purchased slaves. How many of the pashas who rule the provinces sprung from the same origin I cannot say, probably great numbers."[14] Captain Charles White, a Briton who spent three years in Istanbul and knew Ottoman society well, writes that "slavery is often the road to the highest honours." He then names some of the highest dignitaries of the empire who were of slave origins and claims that "hundreds of others might be added."[15] Although the estimates given by these observers are clearly exaggerated, they do convey a notion that was familiar to members of the elite as well.

In provinces that gravitated toward some form of autonomy, like Egypt and Tunis, *kul*-type slavery—personified by the *mamlūk*s—was also part and parcel of elite life. The Ottoman-Egyptian elite during the long Tanzimat was Istanbul oriented and still a reflection of the Ottoman elite at the center.[16] Although its recruitment patterns were being gradually reoriented toward native, Arabophone, Egyptian sources, its high and middle ranks continued to flaunt a considerable number of ex-slaves. Nassau Senior, a prominent British economist who visited Egypt in the mid-1850s, conversed on the subject with Yusuf Hekekyan Bey, a high-ranking official in the Egyptian administration. After pointing out the slave origins of some of the cabinet ministers of Sait Paşa (ruled 1854–63), Hekekyan asserted: "In fact, Stephan Bey and Edhem Pasha are the only ministers that occur to me who have not been slaves—and I doubt their continuance in power. The *Liberti* will intrigue against the *Ingenui,* and drive them out."[17] This is obviously an overstatement, but again, it reflects common views in elite circles about the importance of and esprit de corps among ex-slaves.

14. Adolphus Slade, *Record of Travels in Turkey, Greece, &c. . . . in the Years 1829, 1830, and 1831*, 2d ed. (London, 1854), vol. 2, p. 243.

15. Charles White, *Three Years in Constantinople* (London, 1846), vol. 2, pp. 305–6.

16. On the Ottoman-Egyptian elite in the middle of the nineteenth century, see Ehud R. Toledano, *State and Society in Mid-Nineteenth-Century Egypt* (Cambridge, 1990), pt. 1.

17. Nassau W. Senior, *Conversations and Journals in Egypt and Malta* (London, 1882), vol. 2, pp. 117–19.

The importance of slaves in the army and administration of Tunisia under the Husaynid dynasty is well documented and analyzed in L. Carl Brown's work *The Tunisia of Ahmad Bey, 1837–1855*.[18] The phenomenon is manifested in the group of *mamlūk*s imported and trained by the ruling family and the households of its ministers. The importance of the *mamlūk*s within what Brown calls the "political class" is accentuated by the nineteenth-century decline of the military corps of the *kuloğulları*, the descendants of the Ottoman *kul* regiments that had occupied Tunisia in 1574. A *mamlūk*-type recruitment-cum-socialization is apparent also in Ottoman Algeria until the French occupation of 1830, and in Iraq well into the nineteenth century. In both Egypt and Iraq, a misapprehension of the Ottoman nature of *kul*-type slavery has led scholars to dub the local regimes that emerged in those provinces as "*mamlūk*."[19]

Alongside other tracks leading to social networks *(intisap)*, *kul*-type slavery survived well into the Tanzimat period. The amazing resilience of the *mamlūk* pattern not only ensured its survival over the centuries, long after the defeat of the Mamluk Sultanate at the hands of the sultan's *kul*s in 1517, but also rendered it attractive and viable even when competing against modern alternatives in the second half of the nineteenth century. Its counterpart, *harem* slavery, also weathered the changes of time as an efficient system of elite recruitment, marriage, and reproduction in a male-dominated world. In the following pages, I shall review and analyze some of the main features of *harem* slavery during the period under discussion here.

Slavery in its various forms has long fascinated the minds of the moderns, both scholars and nonscholars. This fascination becomes even more intense when we cross East-West cultural lines: the many travel accounts of Europeans and Americans who visited the lands of Islam rarely failed to comment on the phenomenon of slavery, with special reference to *harem* slavery. In most of these accounts, the need of both male writer and reader to satisfy their curiosity defied the inaccessibility of *harem*s to foreigners and produced descriptions which often belonged to the realm of sheer fancy. As recently shown, European women's accounts of the Ottoman *harem* were

18. L. Carl Brown, *The Tunisia of Ahmad Bey, 1837–1855* (Princeton, 1974), especially pp. 41–65.

19. Toledano, "Ottoman-Local Elites."

far more realistic, being based on eyewitness, participant-observer experiences.[20] To complicate the picture further, scholarly works have not always paid sufficient attention to the problem of terminology. Thus, non-Western slavery was depicted in terms loaded with meaning that was frequently too negative, being derived from Western experience with the practice, mostly that of the American South and the West Indies.[21] However, in recent years there have been a number of attempts to treat Islamic *harem* slavery in its own cultural context, a task made possible also by the availability of archival material, especially in Turkey's state archives and libraries, and by the existence of some insightful travel accounts.[22]

The *harem* system grew out of the need in Ottoman society to achieve gender segregation and limit women's accessibility to men who did not belong to their family. Households were divided into two separate sections: the *selamlık,* housing the male members, and the *haremlik,* where the women and children dwelt. At the head of the women's part reigned the master's mother or his first wife (out of a maximum of four wives allowed by Islam). The concubines were also part of the *harem,* where all the attendants were women. Male guests of the master were not entertained in the *harem.* An

20. Melman, *Women's Orients,* especially pp. 59 ff.

21. On the question of terminology, see Suzanne Miers and Igor Kopytoff, eds., *Slavery in Africa* (Madison, 1977), pp. 76–78 (the editors' introduction).

22. The most recent and comprehensive study of the Ottoman court is Peirce, *Imperial Harem.* For earlier studies, see Gabriel Baer, "Slavery and Its Abolition," in his *Studies in the Social History of Modern Egypt* (Chicago, 1969), pp. 161–89; Nada Tomiche, "The Situation of Egyptian Women in the First Half of the Nineteenth Century," in *Beginnings of Modernization in the Middle East,* ed. W. R. Polk and R. L. Chambers (Chicago, 1968), pp. 171–84; and my "Slave Dealers, Women, Pregnancy, and Abortion: The Story of a Circassian Slave-Girl in Mid–Nineteenth Century Cairo," *Slavery and Abolition* 2/1 (1981): 53–68, which is reproduced in a revised version in chap. 2, above). For a brief comment on the *harem* institution and an instructive comparison between Western and Eastern family structures, see Marshall G. S. Hodgson, *The Venture of Islam* (Chicago, 1974), vol. 2, pp. 140–46, 354–55. For accounts of Ottoman *harems* by British women, as distinct from the fantasy propagated by male accounts, see Melman, *Women's Orients,* especially pp. 59 ff., and consult also Melman's exhaustive lists of women writers on the *harem* on pp. 59–76, 318–35. For some of the better travel accounts, see Demetra Brown, *Haremlik* (Boston and New York, 1909); Melek-Hanum, *Thirty Years in the Harem,* 2 vols. (Berlin, 1872); Emine Foat Tugay, *Three Centuries: Family Chronicles of Turkey and Egypt* (London, 1963); Lucy Garnett, *The Women of Turkey and Their Folk-Lore* (London, 1891); Lucy Garnett, *Home Life in Turkey* (New York, 1909); and Lady F. J. Blunt, *The People of Turkey,* 2 vols. (London, 1878).

active and well-developed social network linked *harems* of similar status across Ottoman towns and villages; mutual visits and outdoor excursions were common. This system emanated from the top—the imperial household—whose lifestyle and structure were emulated by elite households to the extent they could afford it.

For the women who actually spent their lives in the *harems*, reality was, of course, far more mixed and complicated. The women who came into the *harem* as slaves (*câriyes*) were taught and trained to be "ladies," learning all the domestic and social roles attached to that position. As they grew up, they would be paired with the men of the family either as concubines or as legal wives. However, *harem* slaves' freedom of choice was rather limited, as was that of women in general in an essentially male-dominated environment. *Harem* slaves frequently had to endure sexual harassment from male members of the family.

The imperial *harem* was also the stage for behind-the-scenes politicking, which not infrequently influenced major court policies. At the helm stood the sultan's mother *(valide sultan),* who throughout the nineteenth century ruled over several hundred women and eunuchs.[23] The households of provincial governors and of elite members in the main urban centers, though smaller in size, were similarly structured. The non-elite groups could not afford to maintain such establishments and often had to relinquish the dual structure and separation altogether. Other forms would then remain: some sort of a divide, the veil, or the option of having the men of the family receive their male guests in an anteroom or outside the house.

Family politics, not sex, asserts Leslie Peirce, was the fundamental dynamic of the imperial *harem.* Sex was only one of a number of animating forces in the imperial *harem,* and it was much less important than other factors. She agrees with some of the more astute European observers that "the imperial *harem* was more like a nunnery in its hierarchical organization and the enforced chastity of the great majority of its members." She challenges the accepted view that sets a dichotomy between the public/commonweal/male and the private/domestic/female, arguing that in the Ottoman personalized

23. For the number of women in the imperial *harem* between 1552 and 1652, see Peirce, *Imperial Harem,* p. 122.

monarchical order, the legitimate and natural locus of politics was the sovereign's household and, more specifically, its innermost place—the *harem*. Authority was thus located in an inner circle, radiating outward gradually as one moved to the outer circles of the elite and society. In the sixteenth and seventeenth centuries, Peirce concludes, Ottoman society was dichotomized along distinctions of the privileged versus the common and the sacred versus the profane, which cut across gender.[24]

By the end of the nineteenth century, the imperial *harem* included between four hundred and five hundred female slaves, mostly Circassian, who resided in a number of palaces and were divided among the main *harem* compound and the suites of the members of the royal family. The *harem*'s population was only partially self-reproducing, because only the royal children continued to live on its various premises. Since many of the nonroyal women were given in marriage to state officials and consequently left the *harem*, the ranks had to be constantly replenished through purchase or gift. Such gifts and the marriage of *harem* women to high-ranking members of the elite were both part of the royal patronage-building mechanism. To provide personnel for the imperial and elite *harem* network, the traffic in Circassian girls was allowed to continue in spite of occasional British protests, though its volume had significantly dropped toward the end of the century. Thus, a few words about the nature of that specific branch of the Ottoman slave trade are in order at this point.

The mere hope of improving one's social and economic status through slavery created a somewhat peculiar situation in the Caucasian traffic. A seeming lack of contradiction between kinship and exploitation often led parents to willingly submit their daughters to the slave dealers to be carried off to Istanbul, Cairo, and the other great cities of the empire to serve in elite households. Trafficking in Circassian and Georgian slaves became temporarily illegal in 1854 as a result of British and French pressure during the Crimean War.[25] However, slave, family, dealer, buyer, and often the government itself (a duty of approximately 10 percent per slave was regularly imposed

24. Observations and quotations in this paragraph are from ibid., pp. 3, 6, and 7–9.

25. The grand vezir to the sultan, 28 Zilhicce 1270/23 Sept. 1854, and the enclosures, Başbakanlık Arşivi (Archives of the Prime Minister's Office; hereafter abbreviated BA)/İrade Tasnifi/Hâriciye/5553.

on the slave trade) all had a vested interest in the traffic, which soon conduced toward its renewal.

As the British were indeed told, the 1854 wartime prohibition, obtained under foreign pressure, was no longer considered by the Ottoman government to be in effect. In March 1858 the governor of Trabzon informed the British acting consul that he had been ordered not to impede in the future the passage of Circassian slaves through the area under his jurisdiction. This was after he had delayed the departure of some slaves to Istanbul in compliance with the acting consul's request. In December of the same year, the tax farmer *(mültezim)* of the Trabzon customshouse complained to the governor that he had difficulties collecting dues from the slave dealers. He asserted that although the new tariff sent to him specifically mentioned the duty on slaves *(pencik resmi),* the dealers had been told that it should be paid in Istanbul and not, as before, at the port of entry. In any event, it was "business as usual"; the trade was openly carried out and legally recognized by the authorities.[26]

As will be elaborated in chapter 3, the Russian expulsion of a very large free and slave population from the Caucasus in the late 1850s and early 1860s had a major impact on the Ottoman slave market. While reintroducing agricultural slavery into the sultan's domains, it also affected the traffic in young female slaves intended for elite *harems*. As before, these girls would be integrated into Ottoman society in various roles according to their looks and talents and as circumstances (or luck) determined. They were raised in the household and marked for either concubinage and marriage inside or outside that unit or were employed as skilled or unskilled domestic workers. After their settlement in the empire, Circassian parents continued to sell their daughters through slave dealers or, less frequently, directly to buyers. Although such dealings were largely conducted within the slave class—that is, slaveholders selling their slaves' children owing to the hardships and opportunities created by their forced dislocation—a growing number of freeborn children were also being traded and reduced to slavery.

26. For the contact of the acting consul with the governor of Trabzon, see Stevens to Lord Malmesbury (foreign secretary), 23.3.58, Public Record Office (hereafter abbreviated PRO), Foreign Office (hereafter abbreviated FO) 84/1060/126–27. The tax farmer's complaint is: the *mültezim* of the Trabzon Gümrük (customs) to the governor of Trabzon, 12 Kânun-ı sâni 1274/24.1.58, BA/İrade/Meclis-i Vâlâ/18167.

British sources and an Istanbul newspaper in the English language reported in 1872–73 that most steamers, many belonging to European companies, such as the Austrian Lloyd's Company, were regularly transporting Circassian slaves from Trabzon, Samsun, and other Black Sea entrepôts to Istanbul. It is unclear what, if anything, the Ottoman government did to stop the trade. When no coercion was involved, it seems that the traffic was allowed to go on undisturbed. The Penal Code of 1858 contained a number of clauses concerning kidnapping and enslavement, but the penalties were not too heavy. On 16 September 1867 these were amended to include further offenses and the penalties were somewhat increased, perhaps as a result of the growing number of cases of abduction and enslavement.[27]

In August 1870 Sir Henry Elliot, the British ambassador in Istanbul, wrote to the foreign secretary, Lord Granville, that he did not regard it possible to approach the Porte on Circassian slavery. He added: "With the knowledge not only that the wife of the Grand Vizier had been a Circassian slave, but that ladies in a still more exalted position had belonged to the same class, Your Lordship will understand that I should have been guilty of gross impropriety if I had gone to Aali Pasha and insisted upon the debasing consequences of an institution, which nobody can think more hateful than I do."[28]

This reference to Circassian *harem* slavery was made in the context of the traffic in young women, which was the aspect of Circassian slavery most familiar to foreigners. But in 1873 Elliot became aware of the widespread sale of whole slave families and, worse, of the breaking up of such families which occurred as a result of sale. This he found to be totally unacceptable, and he made a strong representation to Foreign Minister Halil Paşa, writing: "Je croirais très volontiers que l'on m'ait exagéré l'abus. Mais je puis malheureusement vous garantir qu'il existe dans les proportions qui non seulement justifient, mais qui demandent impérieusement que le sujet reçoive l'attention

27. For reports on transportation of slaves in European steamers, see Francis (consul general, Istanbul) to Elliot (ambassador, Istanbul), 29.11.72, PRO, FO 84/1427/218–19; U.S. consul in Malta to Lord Granville (foreign secretary), 1.1.73, quoting the *Levant Herald,* PRO, FO 84/1427/309–10. For the Penal Code of 1858, see Articles 203–6, *Düstur* (Istanbul, A.H. 1289), vol. 1, p. 582; and its amendment in Gregoire Aristarchi, *Législation ottomane* (Istanbul, 1873), vol. 2, p. 272.

28. Elliot to Granville, 10.8.70, PRO, FO 84/1324/108–10.

sérieuse du gouvernement."[29] In March 1873 the ambassador addressed Lord Granville again, describing the practice and asking for instructions. The matter was discussed at the Foreign Office in late March/early April.[30] W. H. Wylde, head of the Slave Trade Department, wrote:

> The state of things described by Sir H. Elliot in this Dispatch is one which ought not to be passed over in silence. However much we might have been inclined to shut our eyes to the so called Circassian and Georgian slave trade when girls were sold by their parents and thought it a great privilege to become inmates of Turkish Harems with the chance eventually of becoming the Wives of Turkish Officials, yet a totally new state of things is depicted by Sir H. Elliot which Lord Granville will perhaps think ought to be taken serious notice of. The Turkish Government and Authorities are not insensitive to Public Opinion in Europe, which might be brought to bear upon them by giving publicity to the iniquities of the Circassian Chiefs and Turkish Authorities as reported by Sir H. Elliot.[31]

Elliot was instructed by Lord Granville to remonstrate strongly against the practice and "to use every effort to procure its suppression." But Wylde's suggestion to bring the matter to the attention of the public was rejected. Later, Elliot described his attempts to induce the Ottoman government to act on this matter as unsuccessful.[32] What it meant was that the Ottomans still refused to allow any British interference, or even the appearance thereof, in Circassian slavery and slave trade. As will be shown in chapter 3, they certainly did act on the issue but kept the British in the dark as to developments and progress.

Thus, this type of traffic continued to be discreetly conducted; it was neither illegal nor considered dishonorable for the seller, the

29. Elliot to Halil Paşa, 21.1.73, PRO, FO 84/1370/42–43.

30. Elliot to Granville, 3.3.73, PRO, FO 84/1370/28–31. Elliot mentioned the Circassian issue again in a remonstrance regarding the slave trade in blacks from Benghazi (Elliot to Safvet Paşa, 14.4.73, PRO, FO 84/1370/47–49).

31. Minute by W. H. Wylde, 27.3.73, PRO, FO 84/1370/33–34.

32. Granville to Elliot, 14.4.73, PRO, FO 84/1370/7. Wylde's suggestion appeared in his minute but was struck out, probably by Granville: Elliot to Lord Derbey (foreign secretary), 16.8.74, PRO, FO 84/1397/173.

buyer, the slave, or the trader. As late as 1893, publicly endorsed receipts were being exchanged between trade partners, giving specific details of such deals. Among the papers of Deputy Minister of the Interior Ahmet Refik Paşa, there are several such documents attesting the purchase of some Circassian female slaves. One complete set of three documents refers to the purchase of a nineteen-year-old female slave by the deputy minister himself.[33] The seller confirmed that the woman belonged to the slave class and had been in his possession for many years. The transaction was witnessed by six persons, among whom were the deputy governor of the *nahiye* (small district), the village *imam* (prayer leader), and the village *muhtar* (headman). We should note that it was the Ministry of the Interior that handled many of the problems relating to the slave trade. Along with the Ministry of Police, it was responsible for the suppression of the traffic in Africans, and it occasionally coordinated matters concerning the trade in Circassians, as well as slavery among them. Yet the second-ranking official of this ministry did not even attempt to conceal the transaction.

This clearly demonstrates how various forms of what was legally one and the same institution, namely slavery, were in fact conceived to be different social phenomena and treated accordingly. African and Circassian slavery were considered to be totally different, and so were Circassian agricultural slavery and Circassian *harem* slavery. Although they may all appear to the outside observer as having a great deal in common, especially from a legal point of view, they were certainly quite distinct in Ottoman eyes. Since the reasons for this "bifurcated view" are elaborated in chapter 4, suffice it here to say that long-established practices and norms—and the stigma that came to be attached to them over time—assigned different places in Ottoman society to Circassian and to African slaves, to *harem* and to agricultural slaves. Because social realities were stronger, the fact that the Şeriat did not stratify slaves according to race or occupation could not, by itself, eliminate discrimination along these lines.

Let us turn now to the imperial *harem* in Istanbul in order to

33. Dâhiliye Müsteşarı Ahmet Refik Paşa Evrakı, three documents, 27 Şabân 1310/16.3.93, BA/Yıldız/K18/480/141/123/53; see also one document, 19 Teşrin-i evvel 1308/31.10.92, BA/Yıldız/K18/480/136/123/53.

examine some of the ways in which it procured female slaves during the early 1890s. If what characterized the purchases made by the deputy minister of the interior was the lack of secrecy in which they were effected, the same can hardly be said about the search conducted for the Palace by the chief secretary to Sultan Abdülhamit II, Süreyya Paşa. The Yıldız Palace archives contain a unique correspondence on the subject consisting of twenty-one letters and telegrams from the years 1891–92.[34] The correspondents were Chief Secretary Süreyya Paşa and the governor *(vâli)* of Konya, Hasan Hilmi Paşa. Most of the telegrams were coded, and great care was taken to maintain secrecy. Though neither earlier nor later documents of this nature are available at this point, it is possible that similar exchanges took place between the Palace and other provincial governors at other times as well.

The governor of Konya was asked to procure female slaves from among the Circassian refugees who had been settled in the province *(vilâyet)*. The Palace was looking for beautiful and healthy girls over fourteen years old who did not speak Turkish or have Turkish manners. Presumably, the reason was that the Palace wanted to give them the best possible Ottoman elite education in the tradition of the old *kul* system and to avoid lower-class "corruption" of their style. Such girls could be found, the Palace expected, among the newly arrived refugees from the Caucasus; but earlier arrivals were also acceptable, provided they possessed all the above-mentioned qualifications. The preferred features appear to have been blond hair and blue eyes.[35] So as not to violate the prohibition on trading in freeborn Circassians, the Palace expressed interest only in girls of slave status. In a few cases, however, freeborn and freed women were also offered by the governor of Konya, who argued that since a suitable amount of money had been paid for these girls, they could be

34. Twenty-one documents, BA/Yıldız/K35/2027/44/109. One of the letters in the file is from another province, the *vilâyet* of Sivas (İbrahim Zühdi to the *baş kâtip*[?] [chief secretary], 7 Muharrem 1310/1.8.92).

35. For palace requirements, see the *baş kâtip* to the *vâli* of Konya, decoded telegram, 23 Mayıs 1307/4.6.91; the *vâli* of Konya to the *baş kâtip,* 11 Zilkâde 1308/18.5.91; the *baş kâtip* to the *vâli* of Konya, 22 Teşrin-i evvel 1307/3.11.91; all in BA/Yıldız/K35/2027/44/109. On the *acemi* system, see İnalcık, *The Ottoman Empire,* pp. 85–87. On the preferred features of the slaves, see the *vâli* of Konya to the *baş kâtip,* 20 Kânun-ı evvel 1307/1.1.92, BA/Yıldız/K35/2027/44/109.

considered as belonging to the slave class.[36] But even so, the governor found it quite difficult to satisfy the needs of the Palace.

There were three reasons for the governor's problems in this respect. The first and second concerned the paucity of women who possessed the necessary qualifications. Especially hard to accommodate was the requirement that candidates be ignorant of Turkish language and culture. By the 1890s, the number of new immigrants had decreased substantially, while most of the earlier arrivals, having lived in the Ottoman Empire for twenty-five to thirty-five years, had already been Turkified, or Ottomanized, to a large degree. Difficulties in absorption, such as occurred, for example, in the province of Adana, offered an opportunity for recruitment, which indeed was seized upon by Hasan Hilmi Paşa when 250 families of immigrants were transferred to his province of Konya for resettlement.[37] But disappointment awaited him there too.

He soon discovered that beauty was not easy to find among recent arrivals. During the process of dislocation and settlement, the persons concerned endured great hardships, and they reached Konya in a most wretched condition. Under such circumstances, even beautiful girls retained very little of their original looks. To remedy that, the governor suggested that those girls he had selected as potentially attractive could still be taken into the *harem*. And, he observed, if they were well fed and properly cared for—and sent to the bath *(hamam)* twice a week—they would regain their beauty in no time. In the course of the correspondence, the governor became increasingly apprehensive about his judgment, as he had been rebuffed once by the sultan's chief secretary. In an exchange of telegrams, the latter advised him not to send two more slaves who had been bought if they were of the same quality as the last two he forwarded to the Palace.[38]

The third obstacle in the governor's way was the apparent refusal of some of the parents to sell their daughters. In one case, although a

36. The *vâli* of Konya to the *baş kâtip*, 29 Ağustos 1307/10.9.91, and 11 Teşrin-i sâni 1307/23.11.91 (letter and decoded telegram), both in BA/Yıldız/K35/2027/44/109.

37. The *vâli* of Konya to the *baş kâtip*, 20 Kânun-ı evvel 1307/1.1.92, BA/Yıldız/K35/2027/44/109.

38. Ibid.; and the *vâli* of Konya to the *baş kâtip*, 19 Eylûl 1307/1.10.91, BA/Yıldız/K35/2027/44/109. For exchange of telegrams, see the *vâli* of Konya to the *baş kâtip*, decoded telegram, 23 Şubat 1307/7.3.91; and the *baş kâtip* to the *vâli* of Konya, telegram, 25 Şubat 1307/9.3.91; both in BA/Yıldız/K35/2027/44/109.

large amount of money was offered, the parents could be persuaded to sell only after the intervention of the head of the refugee community in the area. In yet another case, money was not enough, the governor reported. Taking care not to implicate the imperial *harem* in any way, he was obliged to hint that the girls were intended for one of the large establishments in the capital; the parents then relented. In this context, it may be interesting to refer once again to the aforementioned receipts which were given to the deputy minister of the interior by the seller of one of the female slaves he had bought. The latter specifically noted in the document that arrangements should be made for the girl's parents to visit her once or twice a year.[39]

The evidence is insufficient to allow for any meaningful generalization regarding a possible change in the previously reported willingness of Circassian parents—mostly, though not exclusively, those belonging to the slave class—to sell their children to the highest bidder in the hope of bettering their own and their children's circumstances. If such a change indeed occurred, which is supported by the little evidence that is available, it probably came as a result of the changes in the lifestyle of the refugees brought about by their settlement in the Ottoman Empire. Most of the refugees became cultivators, and the attachment to the land introduced a certain stability into their lives, which they had lacked before in the Caucasus, especially during the long and arduous years of incessant war against the Russians. It is possible that slave families—the main source for the slave trade—who had secured manumission through *mükatebe* (for details of this practice, see chapter 3) became reluctant to sell their children again into slavery. When still in bondage, many parents—with the consent of their masters—sought to better their children's lot, as well as their own, by selling them to *harems* in the big cities. Having gained their freedom, they might have become less eager to do so. In addition, we should note that under normal circumstances of settlement, freeborn Circassians did not sell their children into slavery.[40] As pointed out, the governor of Konya also tried to purchase girls who belonged to

39. On the resistance of the parents, see the *vâli* of Konya to the *baş kâtip,* 7 Şubat 1307/19.2.91; and the *vâli* of Konya to the *baş kâtip,* decoded telegram, 19 Temmuz 1307/31.7.91; both in BA/Yıldız/K35/2027/44/109. For the deputy minister's receipts, see n. 33, above.

40. Ahmet Cevdet, *Tezâkir,* 4 vols., ed. Cavid Baysun (Ankara, 1953–67), vol. 1, p. 292; Lieutenant Herbert Chermside to Colonel Wilson (consul general, Anatolia),

the freeborn and freed classes; the refugees' reaction to that could, perhaps, be expected.

Displaying a great deal of energy and zeal, the governor conducted inquiries even beyond the limits of his jurisdiction. His searches spread into the provinces of Sivas, Ankara, and Bursa. However, because he met with only partial success, he decided to explore other ways to achieve his goal. One such way was suggested by the head of a large group of Circassian refugees, a thousand households, settled in the province of Konya. The man, who according to the governor had great influence over his people as well as good contacts in the Caucasus, offered to search the Samsun area and Russian-held territories. He said he would take with him two pictures of girls whose beauty fulfilled the governor's requirements and bring back with him girls of comparable, or even greater, beauty. Although the governor wrote to the Palace in favor of the plan, there is no information as to what, if anything, ever came of it.[41] In any event, an alternative course was soon adopted.

Owing to the existence of cultural, at times including linguistic, barriers between Ottomans and Circassians, the governor wanted to engage the services of a trustworthy Circassian who could conduct the search on his behalf. He found such a man in the *miralay* (rank equivalent to a colonel) Mehmet Bey. After serving in the 1877–78 war against Russia, Mehmet Bey worked in settling refugees in the province of Konya, thus acquiring the necessary experience in dealing with them. The governor promised him a promotion to the rank of *mirliva* (equivalent to brigadier general) if he could find suitable girls for purchase. Indeed, his knowledge would be especially useful, the governor wrote, in determining whether or not the girls were of slave status. The governor added that in Russia a number of Circassian slaves had been manumitted by the Russian government for a partial manumission fee (*bedel-i cüzi;* the rest of the fee having been paid by the Russian government). After their immigration into the empire, they were considered by the Ottoman government to be

---

15.3.81, PRO, FO 84/1596/93–99 (this very interesting and perceptive report displays a great deal of knowledge about Ottoman slavery and the slave trade).

41. The governor's searches outside Konya are recorded in the *vâli* of Konya to the *baş kâtip,* 29 Ağustos 1307/10.9.91, BA/Yıldız/K35/2027/44/109. For the headman's suggestion, see the *vâli* of Konya to the *baş kâtip,* 7 Şubat 1307/19.2.91, BA/Yıldız/K35/2027/44/109.

freed persons. Slaves whom the Russians had not manumitted tried to exploit the situation and also present themselves as free. Some of the ownership disputes which resulted were resolved by Mehmet Bey. Within a year after sending to Istanbul a number of girls who had been selected and purchased through the endeavors of Mehmet Bey, the governor recommended to the Palace, as promised, that Mehmet Bey be promoted to the rank of *mirliva*.[42]

The high prices paid by the Palace for these slaves and the small number ultimately procured indicate that by the early 1890s this kind of slave trade (i.e., in Circassian women intended for *harem* service) was being pursued only on a very limited scale. It is unlikely that more than fifteen or twenty young women were purchased in 1891 for the imperial *harem*, surely the largest customer in the empire. Although slaves reached the Palace in other ways too—notably as gifts from elite women who had reared and trained them since early childhood—and taking account of the existence in Istanbul and other cities of sizable *harems* in addition to the imperial one, still the total number of acquired slaves was considerably lower than in previous decades.

As will be argued in chapter 3, the completion of the process of settlement and the gradual manumission of refugee slaves through government-funded and encouraged *mükatebe* were the main factors in reducing the volume of the Circassian slave trade and in driving prices up. The generally worsening economic conditions in the empire during the last decades of the nineteenth century, which also affected the wealthy and powerful classes, made the possession of a Circassian female slave, even more than before, a luxury. As long as the imperial household continued to serve as a model to be imitated by the elite, and as long as that household continued to maintain Circassian *harem* slavery, it was up to market forces and economic realities to

42. The *vâli* of Konya to the *baş kâtip*, decoded telegram, 22 Mayıs 1307/3.6.91; and letter, 29 Ağustos 1397/10.9.91; both in BA/Yıldız/K35/2027/44/109. Mehmet Bey's promotion is requested in the *vâli* of Konya to the *baş kâtip*, 1 Kânun-ı sâni 1308/13.1.93, BA/Yıldız/K35/2027/44/109. The *vâli* used this opportunity to request a personal favor: he solicited the *baş kâtip*'s intercession in behalf of his brother, who wished to be transferred from the position of battalion commander (in the Gendarmerie) at Kayseri to the equivalent position at Teke. An earlier request, supported by the *vâli* of Ankara, had been addressed to the *serasker* (commander of the army) but had produced no results. This time, he suggested that the *baş kâtip* talk about the matter with the head of the Gendarmerie Commission (Jandarma Komisyonu).

determine the extent to which the practice would persist. The same applied also to the use of eunuchs in elite *harems*, which was governed by similar considerations and market forces.

The African Eunuchs in the Nineteenth Century

PERHAPS THE MOST CURIOUS and intriguing aspect of *harem* slavery has always been the employment and role of eunuchs. Eunuchs were not an Islamic innovation, but as with slavery itself and other borrowed institutions, Islam endowed the use of castrated men with its own special character. White and black eunuchs—as they were designated by contemporary Ottoman terminology—guarded the women and maintained contact between them and the outside male world. That position of middlemen gave them special political influence, which they amply exploited in various pre-nineteenth-century periods, as will be discussed further below. Even when their political power had waned, they still retained great economic and social influence due to their control of important assets, such as the Holy Cities Endowment in Cairo. By 1903, long past their political heyday, there were still no fewer than 194 African[43] eunuchs in the service of the ruling Ottoman family.

Medieval Islamic military slavery and the role of the eunuchs in it have received proper attention in modern scholarship, but the same can hardly be said about *harem* slavery in the Ottoman Empire, especially with regard to the social—as distinct from the political—role filled by eunuchs.[44] For the history of eunuchs in medieval Islam we owe our knowledge mostly to David Ayalon's studies, which also provide an indispensable foundation for the understanding of the place of eunuchs at the Ottoman court. Of course, Ottoman eunuchs

43. I chose this term to denote their geographic and ethnic origins.

44. For the medieval period see, mainly, David Ayalon, "The Eunuchs in the Mamluk Sultanate," in *Studies in Memory of Gaston Wiet* (Jerusalem, 1977), pp. 267–95; and David Ayalon, "On the Eunuchs in Islam," *Jerusalem Studies in Arabic and Islam* 1 (1979): 67–124. Some references to the Ottoman imperial eunuchs in the fifteenth and sixteenth centuries can be found in Peirce, *Imperial Harem;* the role of the imperial African eunuchs in seventeenth- and eighteenth-century Cairo is discussed in Jane Hathaway's *The Politics of Households in Ottoman Egypt: The Rise of the Qazdağlı Bayt* (Cambridge, 1997); a recent work on eunuchs in some Muslim societies is Shaun E. Marmon, *Eunuchs and Sacred Boundaries in Islamic Society* (Oxford and New York, 1995).

did not occupy any significant military position comparable to that of the eunuchs in the Mamluk Sultanate of Egypt, but Ayalon's two other observations hold true for the Ottoman Empire as well: (1) all eunuchs were slaves, and all were imported from outside the empire; (2) an especially close relationship existed between master/mistress and eunuch, for not only were the eunuchs a foreign element in society, but unlike other slaves, in most cases they did not form alternative family ties by marriage.

Information about the Ottoman eunuchs comes from works by five authors: Uzunçarşılı, Gibb and Bowen, Penzer, and Uluçay.[45] Penzer relied on European sources; Gibb and Bowen, on the well-known account of d'Ohsson (eighteenth century) and on Tayyarzade Ata's chronicle (mid-nineteenth century). Uzunçarşılı added more chronicles and some archival material, while Uluçay used Uzunçarşılı and Penzer with some additional documents. Except for Uluçay, no writers ventured in their treatment of the African eunuchs into the Tanzimat period (1839–76). And none of these writers made any reference to the single most important archival source for the history of the African eunuchs: the *Register of the Biographies of the Imperial African Eunuchs*. Although I have been able to locate at the archives of the Turkish Prime Ministry only one such register, dated 6 May 1903, it is quite possible that others were compiled for earlier periods.

The register of 1903 is contained in the Yıdız Collection, which includes the documents housed in the Yıldız Palace, the abode and governing headquarters of Sultan Abdülhamit II (1876–1909).[46] It lists 194 biographies of the African eunuchs owned by the Ottoman imperial family and serving, or retired, at the time. The biographies vary in length and detail, with greater attention paid to the senior members of the Eunuchs' Corps (Ocak). Information provided usually includes the date of the eunuch's registration as belonging to the imperial household; the Ottoman province into which he had been imported and whence he reached Istanbul; some indication as to how he entered the Ocak, that is, whether given as a present or purchased; information about his previous service, in case the eunuch had not

45. İsmail Hakkı Uzunçarşılı, *Osmanlı devletinin saray teşkilatı* (Ankara, 1945); H. A. R. Gibb and Harold Bowen, *Islamic Society and the West* (Oxford, 1969), vol. 1, pt. 1; Norman H. Penzer, *The Harem* (Philadelphia, 1936); Çağatay Uluçay, *Harem ii* (Ankara, 1971).

46. BA/Yıldız/XXI/11–140.

reached the *harem* directly after entering the empire; in which section of the imperial household or in which princely suites he served; in which of the imperial palaces he served; whether he had ever been manumitted; and, finally, if at any stage of his career he ever retired.

What the register does not tell us is how and from where in Africa the eunuch was recruited, or where the operation of castration took place. No indication of the eunuch's age at registration or at any other time is provided. Finally, there is no information in the register about the eunuch's property or about the lucrative and prestigious *waqf* (Turkish *vakıf*) endowments they traditionally supervised. Still, the register is an excellent and rare source for the history of the African eunuchs at the Ottoman court and thus forms the basis of the present study. The necessary background information not provided by the register was culled, for the most part, from the abovementioned studies by Uzunçarşılı, Uluçay, Gibb and Bowen, and Penzer, as well as directly from the chronicles used by them.

Following Burton's translation of *A Thousand and One Nights,* Penzer cites three modes of castration: removal of both penis and testicles; removal of penis alone (reproductive capability retained without the means); removal of the testicles alone.[47] Almost all the eunuchs at the Ottoman court belonged to the first category. It is quite clear that an operation of such a nature had far-reaching effects, both physical and psychological. With the medical methods and unhygienic conditions of premodern times, mortality was high, especially as a result of pus clogging the urethra.[48] Throughout their lives the survivors suffered hormonal and psychological disorders and were said to have developed peculiar characteristics and an eccentric social behavior. This has special significance since senior eunuchs had access to power and during certain periods of Ottoman history exercised it to influence the course of political events.

Although it is hard to adduce direct evidence, most writers believe that eunuchs were often motivated by a deep sense of bitterness and sought to avenge the "unnatural crime" perpetrated on their persons by "society," or what we might call today "the system." The rise

47. Penzer, *The Harem,* p. 143.

48. Ayalon, "On the Eunuchs in Islam," p. 281. Burckhardt, on the other hand, minimizes the death rate; see his *Travels in Nubia,* as quoted in Lewis, *Race and Slavery in the Middle East,* pp. 76–77.

to power of the African eunuchs at the Ottoman court occurred during the second half of the sixteenth century and lasted, with vicissitudes, well into the eighteenth century. Some Ottoman historians refer to parts of the early seventeenth century as the "Sultanate of the African Eunuchs,"[49] attributing the decline and fall of the empire to the "corrupting role" played by the eunuchs at the court, which is associated with the rising influence of the *harem* women in Ottoman politics. The first half of the seventeenth century was also known as the "Sultanate of the Women," because the influence and political involvement of *harem* women and eunuchs rose dramatically during this period.

The great majority of the eunuchs whose biographies are listed in the register served exclusively during the reign of Abdülhamit II. In that period, with its strong emphasis on personal access to the sultan for the conduct of state affairs,[50] two of the head eunuchs were recognized as having attained high standing in the government. Since much of the eunuchs' actual impact on court politics was of the informal kind, it is not normally reflected in the official correspondence and, hence, hard to gauge. Eunuchs still performed their usual palace duties, which according to Abdülhamit's daughter were "to lock and unlock the doors of the imperial *harem* every evening and morning, to take shifts guarding the doors, to watch those entering and leaving, and not to allow anybody from the outside in."[51] They performed similar services at the various princely suites as well.

A question for which we cannot yet provide a satisfactory answer is where the African eunuchs were castrated. For the Mamluk period, Ayalon found one such location in Ethiopia, outside the borders of the sultanate.[52] Dr. Louis Frank, in a report written in 1802, states that these operations were performed in the Upper Egyptian village of Abu Tig. The Swiss Arabist J. L. Burckhardt adds the village of Zawiyat al-Dayr near Asyūt in Upper Egypt, where Coptic monks regularly "manufactured" eunuchs at the time of his travels there in 1813 and 1814. He also mentions a place west of Darfur whence some eunuchs

49. In Turkish, Kızlar Ağaları Saltanatı. See, e.g., Uluçay, *Harem ii,* pp. 120–26, where he surveys in detail the many highly influential African eunuchs.

50. For the structure of government during the reign of Abdülhamit II, see Findley, *Bureaucratic Reform in the Ottoman Empire,* pp. 221–90.

51. Ayşe Osmanoğlu, *Babam Abdülhamid* (Istanbul, 1960), p. 85.

52. Ayalon, "The Eunuchs in the Mamluk Sultanate," pp. 280–82.

were being imported into Egypt, but most were sent to the Holy Cities in the Hijaz.[53] Uzunçarşılı claims that most eunuchs were sent to the imperial *harem* by the governors of Egypt and were, presumably, also castrated in that province. He then cites Raşit's chronicle, where it is stated that the grand vezir of Sultan Ahmet III ordered the governor of Egypt in 1715 to put an end to the castration of Ethiopians in Egypt and the surrounding area.[54] However, the vezir died a while later and his order was never implemented.

I could not find any specific indication that during the second half of the nineteenth century, young boys were being made into eunuchs on Ottoman territory. The fact that the anti–slave trade conventions signed between Britain and both Egypt (1877) and the Porte (1880) included clauses prohibiting castration is not sufficient proof that such operations were actually still being performed within the empire. Importation of eunuchs lingered, nevertheless, well beyond the conclusion of these conventions. In Egypt, too, eunuchs continued to play a role in the governor's household, which was the closest imitation of the sultan's court. A book published in 1892 in defense of Islamic slavery noted the influence and prestige possessed by high-ranking eunuchs in Cairo. Foremost among these were the head eunuchs who served the mothers of two Egyptian governors, Abbas Paşa and Ismail Paşa.[55]

During the years of their long residence in Istanbul, the Ottoman sultans and their extended families did not stay in one palace. In the nineteenth century, changes of residence within the capital, and the considerable construction and expenditure attending every such move, were more frequent than in previous centuries. Following the fall of Constantinople in 1453, Sultan Mehmet the Conqueror built the Old Palace (Eski Saray), where the main campus of Istanbul University is now located.[56] The New Palace, better known as Top

53. The accounts of Frank and Burckhardt are cited in Lewis, *Race and Slavery in the Middle East,* pp. 76–77. On eunuchs in the great mosques of Mecca and Medina, see ibid., p. 75.

54. Uzunçarşılı, *Osmanlı devletinin saray teşkilatı,* p. 172.

55. Ahmad Shafiq, *Al-Riqq fī-l-Islām,* trans. from French by Ahmad Zaki (Cairo, 1892), pp. 98–99.

56. For concise information about the palaces of Istanbul and previous Ottoman capitals, see Uluçay, *Harem ii,* pp. 1–4. For a recent innovative approach, see Gülru Necipoğlu, "The Formation of an Ottoman Imperial Tradition: The Topkapı Palace in the Fifteenth and Sixteenth Centuries" (Ph.D. diss., Harvard University, 1985).

Kapı Sarayı, was completed in 1478. Until the reign of Sultan Murat III (1574–95), this palace served as the center of government, though not as the sultan's residence. From Murat III's time until the opening of Dolma Bahçe Sarayı in 1853, the Ottoman sultans resided with their *harems* at Top Kapı.

The Old Palace continued to house the women of nonreigning sultans and to serve as a detention place for *harem* inmates who, for political or other reasons, were banished from Top Kapı. In addition to their main residential palace, the sultans also maintained other palaces and mansions in and around the capital. In the nineteenth century, among the best known and most used of these were Beşiktaş and Çirağan, favored by Mahmut II; Dolma Bahçe of Abdülmecit, Beylerbeyi, renovated by Abdülaziz; and Yıldız, the abode of Abdülhamit II. Princes and princesses had their suites in some of these palaces, while the imperial *harem* was located where the reigning sultan resided. According to our register, in 1903 imperial eunuchs resided at four palaces: Yıldız (main *harem*), Beşiktaş, Top Kapı, and Çit (an imperial mansion). It is not always clear where each of the princely suites was located.

At the beginning of the twentieth century, there were 31 eunuchs serving at Yıldız with the immediate entourage of the sultan, his mother, and his wives. The auxiliaries to the main *harem* in Beşiktaş, Top Kapı, and Çit had 19, 6, and 18 eunuchs respectively. The remaining 120 were divided among thirteen princes and eleven princesses, whose suites were located in the various wings of Yıldız and Beşiktaş, as well as in a number of royal mansions in and around the capital. The largest suite, that of the crown prince, employed 10 eunuchs, as did the suite of Abdülhamit II's eldest daughter. Lesser members of the Ottoman imperial family normally employed half that number of eunuchs.

According to the recruitment and socialization system used in corps formation within the Ottoman elite, the eunuchs attended a "school for eunuchs," where they began their career at the palace.[57] Like the Janissary recruits in previous centuries, and the Caucasian female slaves throughout the nineteenth century, the newly acquired African eunuchs had to be introduced to high court culture and palace etiquette. Under strict discipline, they were taught the norms of elite

57. Uluçay, *Harem ii,* p. 118.

culture along with the practical side of their duties. The young ones were allowed to play with the young slave girls of the *harem*, who were also being trained and educated. Three retired eunuchs, one of high rank, are listed in the register as assigned to the school, presumably to supervise and guide the young recruits. "Graduates" began as *harem* eunuchs with the rank of *en aşağı*, meaning literally "the lowest."

The structure of the corps of the African eunuchs underwent several changes through the centuries of its existence, ascent to power, and decline. On the basis of the sources available to them, modern scholars have tried to reconstruct the hierarchy of the corps and to sort out the various titles assigned to eunuchs in the Ottoman court. Penzer attached no special significance to the meaning of titles, merely ranking them in descending order; on the other hand, Uzunçarşılı, Uluçay, and Gibb and Bowen attempted to relate the meaning of titles to actual function but could not settle all questions of rank and position.[58] All, it seems, relied on mid-nineteenth-century and earlier sources, giving us only a general structure of the institution as it came to be by the beginning of the twentieth century. Earlier versions of the *Register of the Biographies of the Imperial African Eunuchs* still remain to be located and explored. The register of 1903 throws more light on the problem of title and rank, although it, too, leaves a few questions unanswered.

Of the 194 African eunuchs listed in the register, 35 bear a title of some seniority which distinguishes them from the rest. Apart from the head African eunuch, whose biography is not included in the register, we find ten different titles in actual use. In most cases, these no longer had any relation to the services performed by the eunuchs who bore them; some of the titles seem to have signified a rank and came to the holder with seniority and promotion. Thus, in the period under discussion, one could be a head eunuch of a prince or princess with the rank of *hasıllı, önünce, ortanca,* or without any of these ranks. The other titles, however, appear to have entailed some specific responsibilities, though not necessarily, or precisely, those discharged by the original bearer of the title in earlier centuries.

58. Penzer, *The Harem,* p. 132; Uzunçarşılı, *Osmanlı devletinin saray teşkilatı,* pp. 172–74; Gibb and Bowen, *Islamic Society and the West,* pp. 329–31; Uluçay, *Harem ii,* chap. 2.

The remaining 159 eunuchs were not distinguished by any title or position. If we follow the chronicler Ata, considered the best authority on Palace structure, we ought to assume that they belonged to the two lowest categories of eunuchs: *en aşağı* ("the lowest") and *acemi ağa*.[59] We may also note that certain positions previously filled—some even by eunuchs who appear in our register—were left vacant at the date of recording. This may be explained by changes in protocol or by minor structural alterations made to suit the preference of high-ranking officers of the corps.

Perhaps the data most indicative of the vigor and strength of the institution of royal slavery are the dates on which eunuchs were admitted to imperial service and their names entered into the register. Such dates are provided for 189 of the 194 eunuchs whose biographies we have. As will be shown later, many of the eunuchs had served in elite households, whether in Istanbul or in the provinces, before reaching the Ottoman court. Some of these men had long years of such service on their records, while others came to the *harem* directly from the province into which they had been freshly imported. Therefore, the registration date does not help much in determining a eunuch's age. Nevertheless, we can cull interesting information about recruitment patterns and the "maintenance" of the eunuch population.

One would expect that by the turn of the century, after almost fifty years of official prohibition against trading in African slaves, the number of eunuchs being entered into the register should have declined, reflecting the gradual demise of the institution of *harem* slavery. Nonetheless, the picture is quite different: the closer we approach the register's closing date, the larger the number of eunuchs entered. Whereas between the years 1865 and 1875, only 17 eunuchs were registered, we note close to 50 new entries for the years 1880–90. During the last ten years of registration (1893–1903), no fewer than 100 eunuchs were put on the imperial payroll. The longest-serving eunuch was registered way back in 1849, and the last eunuchs presented to the Ottoman family were registered in 1901. Of course, we have no indication of recruitment past the closing date of the register. This pattern clearly reflects the fact that the demand for eunuchs at court survived into the twentieth century, and that it was possible to obtain African eunuchs as late as 1901, if not later.

59. Tayyarzade Ahmet Ata, *Tarih-i Ata* (Istanbul, 1874), vol. 1, pp. 257–69.

It is difficult to determine the exact places of origin of African eunuchs. The most we can do is to state the provinces from which the eunuchs were brought into the capital, but not the areas in Africa where they had actually been captured or purchased. For 114 of the 194 eunuchs, we have a clear indication of the province of origin; in the remaining biographies, this information is lacking. Perhaps it is not surprising that the Arabian Peninsula and Egypt supplied 103 of the 114 eunuchs, or more than 90 percent. Roughly half of those (50 eunuchs) came to Istanbul from the Hijaz, 27 came from the Yemen, and 26 came from Egypt. The remaining 11 men were brought from the North African slaving province of Tripoli (6), Iraq (2), Tunis (1), the Sudan (1), and Aleppo (1; more likely via Aleppo).

Clearly, there is a correlation between the provinces from which most of the African eunuchs were imported and the provinces in which the slave trade was most active. It is plausible to assume that most of the Africans traded at the Hijazi, Yemeni, and Egyptian marts were captured or bought in western Sudan, the Nile basin, and other East African regions, including Ethiopia. To reiterate, in all probability they had already been castrated by the time they reached Ottoman territory.

How were the eunuchs acquired? Eighty-two of the biographies provide interesting information about the nature of this branch of the traffic. Only 10 of these 82 eunuchs were actually purchased by the imperial Ottoman family; the rest were given as presents to various members of the imperial household. Of those purchased, it is recorded that 3 were bought from slave dealers in the capital and its vicinity, 3 were bought at Medina by a Palace official, 1 was bought at Jidda, and 1 was purchased in the Yemen by a member of the military, who later sold him to the Palace. It is of interest to note that one of the eunuchs, purchased from a slave dealer near Istanbul, was said to have been manumitted before. He was very likely as interested in the deal as were the parties who concluded it.

The overwhelming majority of the African eunuchs were not purchased but were given as presents. Here we have information about 72 cases, which reveals the nature of the practice. In the upper echelons of Ottoman society, as in the lower classes, presents were an important, legitimate means of securing the goodwill and concomitant cooperation or intercession of powerful persons and of people with access to such persons. Because eunuchs were expensive, difficult to obtain, and highly sought after, they were especially suited to attract the favors of the royal family. Thus, we find among the high personages who presented eunuchs to the Ottoman sultan and his immediate relatives the khedive of Egypt and members of his family, grand vezirs, governors-general of the Hijaz and Tripoli, not a few *şerif*s of Mecca (guardians of the Holy Cities), army generals, and other high functionaries.

There are also a few cases in which eunuchs had been presented to high officials who later gave them to the imperial family. One such eunuch was given by the governor of Tripoli to the grand vezir Âli Paşa, and another was given by Khedive Ismail of Egypt to the grand vezir Fuat Paşa, the two most prominent reforming grand vezirs of the third quarter of the nineteenth century. All eunuchs presented as gifts were received long after the slave trade in Africans had been prohibited in 1857. As slaveholding remained legal, no specific regulation prevented the transfer of slaves from one family to another, nor was it illicit to travel with one's own household slaves.

Not for all the African eunuchs—whether purchased or given as presents—was the imperial court the first place of service. Only forty-seven biographies make it clear that their subjects had never engaged in any service prior to their registration as palace eunuchs. At least the same number had served in provincial households, mostly those of governors and *şerif*s of Mecca. Twenty-four eunuchs had been employed by military families in the provinces, often families of generals or of other high-ranking officers. Fifty-five eunuchs had served in elite households in Istanbul before joining the royal *harem*. Among such households were those of grand vezirs, cabinet ministers, and other dignitaries. Some eunuchs who had served in the provinces accompanied their masters to the capital and continued to serve them there. Many of the officials purchased or received their eunuchs long after slave trading had been prohibited; some, such as ministers of the interior, were actually in charge of enforcing that prohibition.

Another revealing aspect of the institution is the lack of mobility of the African eunuchs within the imperial Ottoman family after their registration. If one takes the basic unit of service to be the "princely suite" *(daire)* and counts every movement into such a unit or out of it as one transfer, the remarkable stability in the service patterns of African eunuchs emerges. Of course, the longer the eunuch's life, the better his chance of being moved, mostly as a result of the death of his master or mistress. Nevertheless, over 55 percent of the eunuchs were never transferred; 23 percent were transferred once; 12 percent were transferred twice; 5 percent were transferred three times; 2.6 percent were transferred four times; two eunuchs were transferred five times; and one eunuch was moved between suites six times. This may be taken as an indication of the personal attachment of masters and mistresses to their eunuchs, and of the eunuchs' loyalty to their owners.

Two interesting phenomena in the careers of the royal eunuchs were manumission and retirement. Regarding twenty-seven eunuchs, or roughly 14 percent, it is said in the register that at one point in their service they were manumitted. Each of these eunuchs had been freed before his name was entered into the register. It is likely that their manumission had no real effect on their careers, since the wealth and prestige which attached to the position of palace eunuchs ensured that no coercion was needed on the part of their masters. This rendered almost irrelevant the fact that legally they were no longer slaves. The physical damage inflicted upon them could not be remedied by a mere certificate of manumission; their employment and prosperity were practically guaranteed by their handicap.

Retirement, too, had a curious angle to it when applied to the royal eunuchs. In all probability, retirement was related to the eunuch's age and his physical condition. Nevertheless, it was not always final, and quite often a retired eunuch would be reappointed to an active position. At the signing of the register, ten eunuchs were listed as retired. Another fourteen had been reassigned to active duty after having retired earlier. Retired eunuchs continued to reside in the various palaces of the Ottoman family, but it is not clear if they had any duties. On the other hand, the three retired eunuchs assigned to the school of eunuchs were, presumably, entrusted with the training of the young and newly acquired members of the corps.

Members of the Eunuchs' Corps labored under the constraints of dual loyalty, a phenomenon that the imperial register only further emphasizes. It is clear that a eunuch owed allegiance both to his royal master or mistress and to the senior officers of the corps. If he was not attached to a particular princely suite, his situation was less awkward, but otherwise, he had to maintain a delicate "balance of loyalties." His position and influence depended on the manipulation of information because he was inextricably woven into the intricate network of court politics.

Clifford Geertz's observation concerning the centrality of access to information in the bazaar is even more apt with regard to the Ottoman court.[60] Information about personal and political connections was guarded with great zeal by those who possessed it, and people who did not have such information strove most diligently to obtain it. And at the court, personal and intimate information was in itself politically significant. Thus, the eunuchs were advantageously positioned at the crossroads of the traffic in sensitive information, privy to the innermost secrets of many court figures. Serving as a conduit for such information was one of their main tasks at the palace. They were trusted, suspected, and manipulated at the same time, but if deft, they often benefited in the process.

A great deal of the political influence of the African eunuchs depended on the status acquired by the head eunuch. Although at the end of the nineteenth century the "Sultanate of the African Eunuchs" was but a faded memory, two of the head eunuchs attained the high rank of vezir during the reign of Sultan Abdülhamit II.[61] Thus, they were placed officially near the top of the government structure and had considerable influence and prestige. Nevertheless, the eunuchs' position at the turn of the century, as before, was predicated upon their access to the sultan and the other powerful figures in the imperial Ottoman family. This was even more so during the highly personal government of Abdülhamit II. The importance of the royal personage whom the eunuch served determined the level of political business transacted at that particular princely suite. This, in turn, decided the significance of the information the eunuch could obtain and, consequently, his influence. Since promotion was also determined by the highest-ranking officers of the Eunuchs' Corps, personal and political information must have circulated within the corps, serving to attract favors and patronage from the senior eunuchs.

The changes brought about by the reforms of the nineteenth century affected almost all spheres of life in the Ottoman Empire. How-

60. Clifford Geertz et al., *Meaning and Order in Moroccan Society* (Cambridge, 1979), pp. 124–25.

61. Stanford J. Shaw and Ezel Kural Shaw, *History of the Ottoman Empire and Modern Turkey* (Cambridge, 1977), vol. 2, p. 214.

ever, it is perhaps a reflection on the depth and efficacy of these reforms that one of the most central and traditionally sensitive institutions in Ottoman society hardly showed any signs of transformation: the basic structure of the sultan's household, the model of elite emulation, remained much the same. Not only did the traditional segregation of women persist at the imperial court, but *harem* slavery continued to be the rule of the house. Although, as noted above, it became increasingly difficult to obtain slaves of any kind or color, the royal family still clung to the old ways—so much so that it continued to replenish its Eunuchs' Corps, acquiring no fewer than one hundred new recruits in the last decade of the nineteenth century.

In sum, *kul/harem* slavery survived at the core of the Ottoman elite until the demise of the empire and the fall of the House of Osman in the second decade of the twentieth century. In sociocultural terms, the royal household was still a model of emulation for the elite, retaining its position at the center of social networking within the elite. Within that center, various forms of bondage persisted as part of the *kapı,* or imperial and elite household: *kul/harem* servitude, *kul*-type slavery, and the use of eunuchs. Only the abolition of the sultanate, and the physical removal of the royal family from Turkey, finally brought the practice to an end. The following chapter will look at the other side of life in the *kul/harem* world—from the perspective of the slaves themselves.

TWO

The Other Face of *Harem* Bondage

Abuse and Redress

With modifications, the *kul/harem* system described in chapter 1 prevailed throughout the Ottoman Empire. But in few of the provinces, and in none of the Arab ones, was the Istanbul model imitated more fully than in Egypt. Cairo continued to be the second most important Ottoman city, and the Ottoman-Egyptian elite maintained strong social, cultural, economic, and political ties with Istanbul. Members of the prominent households in both cities were linked to one another either by family relations or through social networking. Hence, the realities that will unfold in the following pages are not just peculiar to Cairo but could happen—and not infrequently did happen—in Istanbul and in the other large urban centers in the empire.

My purpose in this chapter is to concretize, personalize, and humanize the discussion of *kul/harem* slavery through the story of a woman who actually experienced what it meant to be a Circassian slave in an elite household. Her story also serves to point out that realities often deviated from the norm, and that those deviations were also part of the historical record of Ottoman slavery. While we should note the privileged position of *kul*s and *harem* women, we must not overlook the unhappy side of their lives. Thus, the story around which this chapter revolves comes "from within" Ottoman society and is told in great part by the young woman herself and by the people who touched her life in Cairo during the middle years of the nineteenth century.

However, before we proceed to let the records of the Cairene police and court speak for themselves, we need to situate the events that will unfold here in their historical context. Thus, I shall first briefly discuss the position of Egypt as an Ottoman province and slavery in it, and then present the records with as few interruptions as possible. Following the records, and in order to fully appreciate the broader meaning of the information contained therein, I shall look into the "worlds" inhabited by the men and women who played a role in the life of Şemsigül, the Circassian slave who is at the heart of this chapter. We shall learn something about the world of the slave dealers, the competition among them, and the ethics of their trade; then we shall briefly review issues such as life in the world of women, contraception, pregnancy, and abortion.

Under Mehmet Ali Paşa (ruled 1805–48),[1] Egypt experienced a period of military and economic expansion. In order to realize his desire for autonomy and regional hegemony, Mehmet Ali launched an ambitious, Western-oriented reform program that exhausted the country's human and material resources. When Mehmet Ali's ambitions threatened the integrity of the Ottoman Empire in 1840–41, his forces were pushed back from Syria, and his regional "empire" was dismantled by European military and diplomatic intervention. However, his family was invested with the hereditary government of Egypt and continued to rule it until 1952. The 1840s and 1850s were a calm period in which Egypt slowly recovered from the *paşa*'s forced-march modernization policies.

The middle decades, under the aging Mehmet Ali (1840–48), Abbas (1848–54), and Sait (1854–63), were a period of political and economic contraction.[2] As part of the Ottoman war effort, Egypt participated in the Crimean War (1853–56); but except for that episode, these were peaceful and prosperous years, and relations with the central government were improved considerably. Despite

1. On Mehmet Ali Paşa, see Ehud R. Toledano, "Muhammad ʿAli," *Encyclopædia of Islam*, 2d ed. (Leiden, 1991), vol. 7, pp. 423–31.

2. For a discussion of the Ottoman character of nineteenth-century Egypt and an account of Egypt during the middle decades of the century, see Toledano, *State and Society*, pt. 1, especially pp. 22–23.

its political separatism during the reign of Mehmet Ali, there can be little doubt of the Ottoman character of Egypt in the nineteenth century. Though the "Founder of Modern Egypt" in the eyes of many, Mehmet Ali was culturally and socially an Ottoman *vâli* (governor of a *vilâyet,* or province). Perhaps the most Ottoman of his successors was his grandson Abbas Paşa; it was during Abbas's reign, in 1852, that Şemsigül was brought as a young slave woman from Istanbul to Egypt, where she would spend her adult life.

Gabriel Baer estimates the number of slaves in Egypt during the 1850s at between 20,000 and 30,000, with almost half of them in Cairo alone, but Ralph Austen does not consider slave population estimates for Egypt to be very reliable. The total population of Egypt at the time is put at 5 million, of whom 276,000 resided in Cairo. The number of slaves imported into the country fluctuated according to changing economic conditions and needs: in the 1830s about 10,000 slaves were imported annually, in the 1840s the annual number was 5,000 slaves, in the 1850s it fell to 3,500 slaves, but in the 1860s, following the cotton boom, it rose again to 10,000 slaves a year.[3]

Slavery in the *vilâyet* of Egypt differed from slavery in the rest of the Ottoman Empire in two ways. Unlike the situation prevailing in other parts of the empire, both military and agricultural slavery were practiced in Egypt during various times in the course of the nineteenth century.[4] African slaves, mostly from the Sudan, were employed as soldiers in the armies of all Egyptian governors from Mehmet Ali to Ismail (ruled 1863–79), though from the 1820s onward the slave army operated only in the Ottoman-Egyptian Sudan. Male slave labor was occasionally used on large cash-crop estates, but slaves

3. The most recent analysis of the slave trade volume and slave population size is provided by Ralph Austen, "The Mediterranean Islamic Slave Trade out of Africa," pp. 218, 232–33. For the slave population, see also Baer, "Slavery," pp. 167–68. Figures for the general population of Egypt and Cairo are taken from Justin McCarthy, "Nineteenth-Century Egyptian Population," in *The Middle Eastern Economy*, ed. Elie Kedourie (London, 1976), pp. 30, 33.

4. Baer, "Slavery," pp. 164–66. For the agricultural slavery practiced by the Circassian refugees, who were forced out of the Caucasus by the Russians in the 1860s and resettled in the Ottoman Empire, see chap. 3, below. The best and most recent account of Mehmet Ali's army is Khaled M. Fahmy, "All the Paşa's Men: The Performance of the Egyptian Army during the Reign of Mehmed Ali Paşa" (D.Phil. diss., Oxford University, 1993). For the cotton economy in Egypt, see Roger Owen, *Cotton and the Egyptian Economy, 1820–1914* (Oxford, 1969). For military slavery in the Ottoman-Egyptian Sudan, see Prunier, "Military Slavery in the Sudan," pp. 129–39.

never rivaled the Egyptian free peasants (the *fallāḥīn*) as a workforce. During times of increased agricultural activity, such as the cotton boom of the 1860s, the use of slave labor rose significantly. A small number of African male slaves also worked as attendants in wealthier families or as assistants to artisans, shopkeepers, and merchants. On the whole, it seems that the number of male slaves of all kinds in Egypt was higher than in the rest of the empire.

But most of the slaves in Egypt at the time—as in the other domains of the sultan—were African women serving as domestics and engaged in menial jobs in urban households. In Egypt, even the lower-middle strata could afford to own at least one African slave and often did so. White female slaves, like Şemsigül, were a minority in nineteenth-century Egypt. Some of them served as domestics, but others entered the *harems* and were socialized into the Ottoman-Egyptian elite.

Most of our information about "daily life" in Ottoman Egypt comes from state archives—Ottoman and foreign—and from travelers' accounts. Official documents have a tendency to "dehumanize" history and deal mostly with bureaucratic matters, finances, and the state apparatus. Travelers, on the other hand, often lacked the tools—such as language fluency and knowledge of the local culture—necessary to form and convey a deeper-than-surface impression. Hence, as already noted above, life in the *harem* was often romanticized in contemporary travel accounts by European women,[5] and to many Western men, its elusive mystery was a rich source of fantasy. For Egypt, there is an even greater paucity of accounts from within *harems*. Even Edward Lane, who devoted to the "Hareem" a whole chapter in his *An Account of the Manners and Customs of the Modern Egyptians,* is almost silent on female life within the *harem.*[6] Fortunately, however, a unique document survives from the Cairo of Abbas Paşa that throws light on some features of the Ottoman-Egyptian *harem* system; it forms the centerpiece of this chapter.

The Arabic and Ottoman Turkish collections at the Egyptian National Archives (Dār al-Wathā'iq al-Qawmiyya) are still only partially exploited by scholars.[7] They offer a wealth of information on all, but

5. On this literature, see Melman, *Women's Orients*, especially pp. 59 ff.

6. Edward W. Lane, *An Account of the Manners and Customs of the Modern Egyptians* (1860; reprint, New York, 1973).

7. For a detailed listing of collections, see Helen Rivlin, *The Dār al-Wathā'iq in 'Abdīn Palace at Cairo as a Source for the Study of the Modernization of Egypt in the Nine-*

mostly on the socioeconomic, aspects of life in nineteenth-century Egypt. The Registers Section, as distinct from the separate Documents Section, is divided into five subsections referring to the various branches of the government. The fourth subsection, marked L, covers records of the local government; its second subdivision, marked 2, contains the records of the Egyptian police (Dabtiyyat Misr). The Turkish registers of the police are fullest and most orderly for the reign of Abbas Paşa (1848–54). It is among the police investigation reports that the story of the Circassian slave Şemsigül is filed.[8] The Council of Police, located at the Citadel (the seat of the *vilâyet*'s government), drew up an investigation report (*jurnāl,* from "journal") for each case it reviewed. The reports were then sent, with recommendations, to be adjudicated by the Egyptian Council for Judicial Ordinances (Majlis al-Ahkām al-Misriyya), a kind of administrative court.

The police reports are one of the most interesting and important sources for the study of Egyptian social history. They contain testimonies given by people from the lower strata about their daily lives. Since many of these people were illiterate, they did not leave any written records, and the only way they can "speak" to us is through their literate investigators. Testimonies were recorded in their original language, that is, either in Ottoman Turkish, literary Arabic, or colloquial Egyptian Arabic. Many of them are quite detailed and their content is not limited to the offenders' world but provides a much fuller picture of life among the lower strata.[9] Şemsigül's story was the subject of police report number 13, sent to the administrative court on 12 July 1854. The report, in Ottoman Turkish, covers nine handwritten pages of thirty-five lines each; it begins with the testimony of the slave woman herself. While we have a number of accounts of *harem* life written by elite women—stories of Circassian slaves turned grand ladies—records like the one before us are

---

teenth Century (Leiden, 1970); Egyptian Ministry of Culture, National Archives, "Lists Regarding the Organization of Registers at the Archives" (an unpublished, experimental catalog in Arabic, Feb. 1970). Two recent works which utilize such material are Juan R. I. Cole, *Colonialism and Revolution in the Middle East: Social and Cultural Origins of Egypt's 'Urabi Movement* (Princeton, 1993); and Toledano, *State and Society.*

8. L/2/67/4, Investigation Report No. 13, pp. 44–54 (reference is transliterated from Arabic into Ottoman Turkish).

9. For examples of how this material can be used, see Toledano, *State and Society,* pt. 2.

rare.[10] Hence, in the following pages, I shall translate large portions of her testimony and those of others involved in her story. As indicated above, this will be followed by an excursion into the worlds of the slave dealers and the women.

Şemsigül's Story

Şemsigül was born in the late 1830s or early 1840s in the Caucasus, which was then under Ottoman control. Slavery was still common among the tribal federations of Circassia, where a special stratum of agricultural slaves had existed for centuries (for an account of slavery among the Circassians, see chapter 3). Şemsigül was brought to Istanbul by a relative or by a slave dealer, who offered her for sale in the Ottoman capital. As noted above, the extreme poverty of Circassian slave families and the dire conditions among free members of the lower strata forced them to sell their young children to slave dealers, who carried them off to Istanbul and other urban centers. Parents who did so believed that they were thus improving the chance of their offspring to attain better living conditions and, possibly, entry into the Ottoman elite. As we consider how they ultimately fared, we should weigh the loss of family and legal freedom (for those who had not been born slaves) against the possibility that they might thereby have gained access to a better life.

The other main figure in our story is Deli Mehmet, the slave dealer who bought Şemsigül in Istanbul with the intention of placing her in one of the Ottoman-Egyptian elite *harem*s, a position that only a relatively small number of white women enjoyed. He was based in Cairo and operated on the Mediterranean and Red Sea

10. Some of the better accounts of *harem* women are Melek-Hanum, *Thirty Years in the Harem;* Tugay, *Three Centuries;* Brown, *Haremlik.* We also have accounts of European women who spent much time in such *harems*: Blunt, *People of Turkey;* Garnett, *The Women of Turkey;* Garnett, *Home Life in Turkey;* Grace Ellison, *An Englishwoman in a Turkish Harem* (London, 1915). On this literature, see Melman, *Women's Orients*, especially pp. 59–76, 318–35. The few other stories of female slaves that have been published to date come mostly from Africa: see, e.g., the papers included in Robertson and Klein, *Women and Slavery in Africa*, pt. 3 ("The Slave Experience: Case Histories"), especially Edward A. Alpers, "The Story of Swema: Female Vulnerability in Nineteenth-Century East Africa," pp. 185–219; see also Terence Walz, *Trade between Egypt and Bilād as-Sūdān, 1700–1820* (Cairo, 1978), pp. 215–21, for a full translation of a legal case involving a female slave rejected by the buyer after her pregnancy had been discovered.

routes, as well as on the long-distance route to India. The portion of Şemsigül's life about which we have information covers a little more than two years, 1852–54, beginning at the time when she came into the possession of Deli Mehmet, when she was in her mid- to late teens. The events described below took place in Istanbul, on a boat crossing the Mediterranean, in Cairo, and at Tanta, a market town in Lower Egypt. In order to reconstruct the undocumented chapters of her life with reasonable confidence, we have to rely on what we know from other sources and similar cases.

On 30 June 1854, Şemsigül appeared before police investigators in Cairo and gave the following testimony.

QUESTIONS: When did you come to Cairo? Who was the person who brought you? Where did you stay when you arrived? To whom were you given by the person who had brought you here?

ŞEMSIGÜL: I came here two years ago. The person who brought me from Istanbul is the slave dealer Deli Mehmet. When I arrived, I was sold to the palace of Mehmet Ali Paşa [son of Governor Mehmet Ali Paşa].

QUESTIONS: Was the person who brought you over to Mehmet Ali Paşa's palace Deli Mehmet? How long did you stay there? Where did you go afterward?

ŞEMSIGÜL: The person who sold me to Mehmet Ali Paşa is Deli Mehmet. I stayed there for about five months. Afterward, the aforementioned [Deli Mehmet] took me from the palace. I [then] went to the house of Mustafa [another slave dealer].

QUESTION: Since Deli Mehmet had sold you to the household of Mehmet Ali Paşa, and since you stayed there for five months, why did he take you from there and why did you go to Mustafa's house?

ŞEMSIGÜL: After I had stayed at Mehmet Ali Paşa's palace for five months, it was suspected that I was pregnant. A midwife was brought in to examine me, and she verified that I was indeed pregnant. So they summoned Deli Mehmet and returned me to him. He then took me and brought me to the house of Mustafa.

QUESTION: By whom did you become pregnant?

ŞEMSIGÜL: I became pregnant by Deli Mehmet.

QUESTIONS: You state that you became pregnant by Deli Mehmet. Where, then, did he have sexual relations with you? And since you became pregnant, why did he sell you [this being illegal]?

Şemsigül: In the boat, on the way here, he forced me to have sexual relations with him; he continued to sleep with me until he sold me. Before the sale, I told him: "Now you want to sell me, but I have missed my period, and I think that I am pregnant by you." When I asked him later what would happen, he did not listen but went away, brought back some medicines, and made me drink them [to induce an abortion]. Finally, he sold me to the palace.

Question: Your answer is [now] well understood. When they said at the palace that you were pregnant, they returned you, and you went to Mustafa's house. But now, you need to explain how many days you stayed there and what was the state of your pregnancy.

Şemsigül: When I left the palace, I went to the house of Mustafa and stayed there for about ten days. While I was there, Deli Mehmet's wife came to the house and cursed me, as she also did Mustafa. Finally, when she wanted to hit me, Mustafa's wife prevented her from doing so. When Mustafa saw the woman's rudeness, he sent me to the house of Deli Mehmet. When I got there, Deli Mehmet's wife brought in a private midwife and demanded that she perform an abortion on me. At that, the midwife said: "This [woman's] pregnancy is well advanced, and now there is a big child in her stomach [which] cannot be aborted." Having said that, she left, but the woman [Deli Mehmet's wife] insisted, saying: "I shall put an end to this pregnancy." Later, her husband, Deli Mehmet, came. She said to him: "Let us beat this slave and end her pregnancy," [to which] Deli Mehmet replied: "I am not going to beat [her]." But the woman would not stop. She fetched a clothespress, hit me with it several times on my stomach and back, and [then] beat me with a mincing rod. At that point, one of the neighbors, a peasant woman, came to the house. When she saw the cruelty with which I was being treated by Deli Mehmet's wife, she pitied me and went to the house of Selim Bey. When she told [them] about the beating and the pain inflicted upon me, the wife of the said dignitary heard the peasant woman, got up, and came in person to the house of the said Deli Mehmet. When she saw my suffering, she had mercy on me and said to Deli Mehmet's wife: "I shall take her and perform the abortion." She then took me to her house but left my condition as it was. When[ever] Deli Mehmet's wife would come and ask [about the pregnancy], they [the people at Selim Bey's house] would lie to her, saying: "We are giving her medicine [to induce an abortion]." I stayed there in that way for about three months. When the child was expected to come into the world, Deli Mehmet's wife came and stood at the bedside. As he was born, she took the child to another room and passed him through her shirt to mark that she was adopting him. To me she said that he died. Later, she went to her house, brought in a wet nurse for the child, and gave [the baby] to her [care]. One day, Selim Bey's wife brought the baby [home] secretly and showed him to me. After twenty days, I went to the house of Deli Mehmet and stayed there for about twenty days, but they did not show me my baby. Finally, they gave me in trust to Timur [another slave dealer] in order to be sold at the Tanta fair, so I went with him to Tanta.[11] A few buyers came and looked me over but did not buy. Ultimately, I returned from Tanta and stayed at the house of Timur. Deli Mehmet took me there and gave me to [name not clear], where I stayed for three months and about ten days. Later, he returned from India and brought me to the house of the agent of Yegen İbrahim Paşa [to be inspected for sale by] an Indian who was going back to India. Since an agreement was not reached with the Indian, and Deli Mehmet wanted to go to the Hijaz, he took me again to the house of Mustafa the slave dealer, on the condition that he sell me to a foreigner [someone not living in Egypt]. He himself went to the Hijaz, and I stayed at Mustafa's house. Because Mustafa had become aware of Deli Mehmet's position [regarding my having borne him a child], he did not show me to any buyers. When Deli Mehmet returned from the Hijaz, he took me [from Mustafa's house] and sold me to Timur. I stayed there [at Timur's house] for about two and a half months.

QUESTIONS: Did you, at any stage from the beginning [of the story], inform the slave dealer Timur, or anyone else, that you had been pregnant and that you were badly beaten? If you did not, why?

ŞEMSIGÜL: As a slave, I was afraid to say anything about my suffering, so I did not tell Timur [or anyone else].

The next witness summoned by the police on the same day, 30 June 1854, was Ali Efendi, head of the Slave Dealers' Guild. The

11. The annual fair at Tanta was the largest in Egypt, attracting in the first half of the nineteenth century from 100,000 to 150,000 visitors annually, the number increasing to half a million in the 1860s and 1870s (Baer, "Slavery," pp. 138–39, 176).

point to note in his testimony is the position and authority of the guild head. His testimony describes what we might today call a preliminary hearing. The *shaykh* was empowered not only to listen to the parties but also to take action to redress grievances. The following is what he told his interrogators about the procedure he had followed.

QUESTIONS: How was the slave named Şemsigül—who had become pregnant by Deli Mehmet and had borne him a child—sold to Timur? What offense was committed [thereby]? You must also make clear to the said slave where her child is.

ALI EFENDI: On the morning of the third day of Bayram [a Muslim high holiday], Timur sent the slave named Şemsigül to my house. Later, he himself came and said: "The slave I had sent you is a slave who must be freed after her master's death [because she had borne him a child] and [therefore] her sale is illegal [according to Islamic law]. [But] having no previous knowledge of that, I bought her from Deli Mehmet and took a promissory note [in return]. [Thus,] there is now a [legal] dispute between us." [So] I sent for the said Deli Mehmet and had him brought in. When I explained to him Timur's statement, he denied [all], claiming that the said slave [Şemsigül] had not been pregnant, nor was she entitled to the legal status of "mother of her master's child" [the child is considered free, and the mother, as mentioned above, cannot be resold and becomes free upon the master's death]. So I called in the said slave and asked her about the whole matter. According to her report, she had become pregnant by the said Deli Mehmet and borne him a child. She [also] reported her suffering in this regard [from Deli Mehmet and his wife]. Nevertheless, Deli Mehmet denied everything. It was suggested to him to take an oath to that effect, at which he declared: "I swear [to it]." The slave was then asked: "Do you have proof or witnesses that you were pregnant?" She stated: "Mustafa and his wife know that I was pregnant, and Selim Bey's wife and the servants of that household know that I gave birth." It was then again inquired of Deli Mehmet: "Will you accept [the consequences] if the said Mustafa testifies that the slave was indeed pregnant and gave birth?" Deli Mehmet replied: "[If so,] I shall manumit her." Based on this declaration, the said Mustafa was summoned and interrogated about the matter. He corroborated the slave's assertion. As it became clear from Mustafa's testimony that [Şemsigül] had borne Deli Mehmet a child, I took the promissory note from Deli Mehmet, returned it to Timur, and detained the slave at my place [pending police investigation and likely manumission].

We now come to the main culprit, Deli Mehmet. His tactics changed several times, only exacerbating his credibility problem. In his testimony to the police, he at first denied all; then he stated that he did not remember Şemsigül or the circumstances of her importation and sale; then he claimed that in Istanbul he had had a concubine named Şemsigül and that she had borne him a son who died a few months later and that she, too, had died since. Finally, he admitted that he had brought Şemsigül from Istanbul and sold her to the household of Mehmet Ali Paşa for sixty purses (about three hundred Egyptian pounds) and later to Timur for only half that amount.

DELI MEHMET: Afterward, Şemsigül stayed at the palace [of Mehmet Ali Paşa] for about two months. Since the said slave was not on friendly terms with the *harem* ladies of the said paşa, I was summoned to the palace, given back Şemsigül, and told to provide another white slave in her place. I took Şemsigül, and since she had misbehaved and claimed that she was pregnant, I asked her whom was she pregnant by. She replied that she had alleged to have been pregnant only to get herself out of the paşa's house. Until the question of her pregnancy could be verified, I left her in trust at Mustafa's house, [where] she stayed for about a month. [It turned out that] she was not pregnant, and when she menstruated, the said Mustafa notified me. So I removed her from there, and she spent some time at our house.

At one point, Deli Mehmet stated that if Mustafa confirmed Şemsigül's version, he would have nothing further to say on the matter. He then appealed to the mercy of the police, without, however, accepting responsibility for the offense imputed to him.

At another stage of the interrogation, Deli Mehmet was asked to produce the papers issued to him in Istanbul for traveling by steamer to Egypt. The police expected that, according to practice, the document would contain the names and sex of his family members and the number, type, and sex of the slaves he was transporting. But, perhaps not surprisingly, Deli Mehmet failed to locate the certificate among his documents at home. Therefore, a fellow traveler and slave dealer, Uzun Ali, was summoned and reported that Deli Mehmet had on board approximately thirteen white female slaves and two white male slaves. The witness had not seen among them any female slave with a child. That testimony undermined Deli Mehmet's story about the "other" Şemsigül, the concubine he claimed to have brought with him from Istanbul with a child. The credibility of the witnesses and the compatibility of their testimonies led to one, clear conclusion, which police investigators did not fail to realize.

Thus, on 11 July 1854 the police department concluded its investigation of the Şemsigül affair. In the report submitted to the administrative court, the police accepted Şemsigül's story and rejected Deli Mehmet's version. Mustafa's testimony was pivotal in forming the view of the investigators, who believed they had established the basic facts of what had happened. Their report concluded: "The police department informed [Deli Mehmet] that he must abandon his deceptive assertions and tell the truth. When asked: 'How do you answer [now]?' he here [at police headquarters] affirmed: 'I have no answers but those which I have [already] given.' "

On the following day, the report was forwarded to the administrative court, and a week later, the court gave its decision. Although I could not locate the actual ruling in the Egyptian archives, we know from the police records that after the court ruling had been studied by the police, the matter was referred to the grand *müfti* (Arabic *muftī*) of Egypt. In such cases, a legal opinion was usually solicited from the *muftī*. The probable outcome of a case such as Şemsigül's was that the slave would be manumitted and the slave dealer punished, according to circumstances. To enforce manumission, an Islamic court ruling was desirable, for which purpose, too, the case was probably referred to the grand *muftī*. It is likely that Deli Mehmet received some punishment in addition to the loss of a valuable slave. It was rare for the court to rule against a police recommendation, especially after elaborate investigation backed by a lengthy report, as in this case.

How did this story reach the police and court? The circumstances are fairly clear, though the motives of the characters involved are not. Some two and a half months after the slave dealer Timur had bought Şemsigül, an unidentified man informed him that a while back she had borne Deli Mehmet a son. When Timur asked her about it, she confirmed the story. Realizing the legal situation, he immediately went to the head of the Slave Dealers' Guild. It was this official, after internal investigation, who turned the whole matter over to the police. At this point, we must consider Deli Mehmet's claim during the investigation that the whole affair was instigated by his competitors in order to hurt his business.

It is impossible to know what the motive of the unidentified man who provided Timur with the incriminating information was, but malice should not be precluded. Timur had to protect himself from possible litigation, so it is not difficult to see why he went to the head of the guild. The *shaykh* might have been able to resolve the matter inside the guild but chose not to. He might have wanted to show the authorities that he was loyal and honest or to enhance his own standing within the guild. It is also possible that he might have had it in for Deli Mehmet and seized the opportunity. We should note, however, that the risk of harboring the culprit and concealing the information from the police was considerable, given the fact that a number of people already knew about the situation. Şemsigül herself must have been made aware of Deli Mehmet's precarious position and could have used the story at one point or another to pull him down.

What happened to Şemsigül afterward must be left to the imagination. In some ways, her manumission would make her less secure and more vulnerable to harsh economic and social realities. This is not to say that there was no element of oppression in *harem* life. Female slaves in an Ottoman-Egyptian elite *harem* were restricted in their freedom of movement, association, and choice of partners. In the power relations with the adult male members of the family, slave women did not have the upper hand, though they could sometimes negotiate a highly influential position within the household. While concubinage was hardly an ideal arrangement for women like Şemsigül, it was socially respectable and, if a child was born, also legally binding on the man. However, especially for women, but for men too, freedom had its own disadvantages: limited choices, deprivation, and oppression.

The act of manumission did not usually entail severance of owner-slave relations. Rather, the mutual dependence would continue under patronage without bondage (*walāʾ* in Arabic), and the slave would remain attached to the manumitter's household. Manumitted slaves, male or female, often remained within the family compound and were expected to render such services as were required of them. This they provided in exchange for the social and economic protection an elite household afforded. Patronage ties were often maintained even if the slave left the master's house, frequently in order to get married. Şemsigül was probably manumitted by court order with Deli Mehmet's reluctant acquiescence. Obviously, she could not expect any assistance from him. If she could not secure alternative patronage immediately upon manumission, she faced the danger of falling out of society's accepted frameworks for an unmarried woman, which could bring upon her want and destitution.

Şemsigül probably sought patronage from the house of Selim Bey, whose wife had offered her protection during the last phase of her pregnancy and in whose house she gave birth. The women's world would then take her in and prevent her from drifting toward the margins of society. If she could secure patronage, she would probably live in the household compound, perform services, and gradually negotiate her position in that milieu. It would be the patron's responsibility then to marry her off well and see to it that she settled down properly.

We shall probably never know how the story of Şemsigül actually ended. What happened to her depended on circumstance but also on her resourcefulness. We do know that she was courageous enough to state her case and stick to it despite the pressures that were undoubtedly put on her. We also know that during her pregnancy, when she was most vulnerable and virtually defenseless, most women with whom she came into contact showed her compassion. And, not least important, although as a woman and a slave she belonged to a doubly disprivileged social group, Şemsigül did ultimately receive justice in the courts, although her baby was not returned to her. Given these propitious circumstances, there are grounds for cautious optimism that Şemsigül's story ended well.

The World of the Slave Dealers

THE SLAVE DEALERS WERE the active element that made the traffic work. In general, they operated between the sources supplying the slaves and the purchasers of slaves in the Ottoman Empire. But there were different kinds of dealers and it was quite rare to find a dealer who would regularly go all the way to the Sudan, Lake

Chad, Ethiopia, or the Caucasus to buy slaves and then sell them in Cairo, Damascus, or Istanbul. Rather, most slave dealers specialized in one of two types of trade: there were source dealers, who went to the areas where slaves were captured and sold to traders and then drove the slaves, over sea or land as the case was, to the market towns and trading entrepôts; then there were the market dealers, who operated in the cities and towns of the empire, buying from source dealers and selling to slaveholders. This division resulted from the tremendous difficulties involved in organizing and financing a full-scale expedition from market to source and back again.

Another division was that between dealers in African slaves and dealers in white, mostly Circassian, slaves. In Egypt, the dealers in Sudanese goods were known as the *jallāba;* they also controlled the trade in African slaves.[12] Their trade was not considered respectable or prestigious, and the guild in which they were organized was listed among the "cursed and impious." On the other hand, dealers in white slaves were a highly esteemed lot. They were called *esirci* (pronounced in Turkish *esirji*), a term which in Egypt often appeared as *yasīrgī* (pl. *yasīrgiyya*). There is precious little information about this group, to which our document might be able to add somewhat. Şemsigül's investigation report mentions six slave dealers in various capacities, and their connections, modes of operation, and professional organization are given some attention.

All the slave dealers mentioned in the report were men. This does not mean that women did not engage in the trade. At the same period in Istanbul, women took part in the sale of white female (and occasionally male) slaves. Some were professional slave dealers; others were elite ladies who bought young Circassian and Georgian girls, raised and educated them, and then sold them as slaves in their early teens. It is therefore possible that women practiced slave trading also in Cairo during the mid-nineteenth century. All the dealers in our document spoke Turkish with their interrogators, though they had the option to address the Council of Police in Arabic if they so wished.

12. For the *jallāba* and the trade between Egypt and the Sudan, see Baer, "Slavery," pp. 172–73; and Walz, *Trade between Egypt and Bilād as-Sūdān,* pp. 77 ff. (social background of the *jallāba*) and pp. 173–214. Walz also gives a full translation of a legal case involving a female slave rejected by the buyer after her pregnancy had been discovered (pp. 215–21). See also Janet J. Ewald, "The Nile Valley System and the Red Sea Slave Trade, 1820–1880," in Clarence-Smith, *Indian Ocean Slave Trade,* pp. 71–92.

This is not conclusive evidence but is a suggestive indication that they were probably not Arab. They could have come from any ethnic group within the Ottoman Empire, though often we find dealers in white slaves to be of Circassian, Albanian, Lâz (Muslim Georgian), or Turkish origin. All of our dealers had Muslim names and there is no reason, on the basis of other sources as well, to doubt that they were Muslim. Christians and Jews rarely engaged in the sale of slaves in the empire during the second half of the nineteenth century.

There is ample evidence that dealers in African slaves also traded in other items and that the slave trade was intertwined in the general commercial network of the Middle East and the Mediterranean.[13] There is also evidence that dealers in Circassian slaves in various parts of the empire also combined slave trading with other kinds of commerce.[14] Nevertheless, there is no mention of such practice in our investigation report. The report, however, does yield information about the slave trading network and its operation. The dealers in white slaves who appear in the document seem to have engaged in long-distance traffic. That is, they themselves went out to major markets such as Istanbul, the Hijaz (where many Muslim pilgrims assembled every year), and even to India. They also traded in closer slave markets, peddling their human merchandise in Cairo and at the annual fair in Tanta. Such dealers brought their slaves from Istanbul—where the slaves had been transported from the Caucasus by other dealers—in small batches on board sailboats. When regular steamer services were established in the third quarter of the century, they used these as well, though with greater caution.

Most of the white female slaves living in Ottoman-Egyptian elite *harems* were imported in this very profitable trade by such dealers, who used to cross the Mediterranean several times a year. In one of these trips, Deli Mehmet brought from Istanbul to Cairo thirteen female and two male slaves. On such trips the dealer was required to have traveling papers *(yol tezkeresi),* in which were recorded the names of the slaves he was transporting with him. These papers were used by the government to assess customs duties. Duties were

13. See Walz, *Trade between Egypt and Bilād as-Sūdān;* Baer, "Slavery," pp. 174–75; Toledano, *Slave Trade,* chaps. 1–2.

14. Toledano, *Ottoman Slave Trade,* chap. 2.

calculated at approximately 10 percent of a government-estimated average price of a white slave (9 percent of price + 10 percent of that amount).[15]

Dealers in white slaves normally conducted their business in their own private homes, where customers would come to inspect the slaves, or in the houses of the very wealthy, where they would take a few slaves for examination on order. This mode of operation was preferred to the public exposure of slaves at the marketplace or in open caravanserais. It was more discreet and respectable, for the social position of the clientele in that type of trade was much higher and the expected intimacy of master-slave relations was far greater, since many white female slaves were intended for concubinage. Nevertheless, Şemsigül was taken by one of the dealers, Timur, to the fair at Tanta and shown there to several customers. But then we must remember that she was no longer a virgin, and if the story of her pregnancy ever got out—as indeed it did—the whole sale would be annulled. The loss of virginity lowered her price, and the risk element increased the need to sell her as soon as possible. Even so, there is no indication that she was publicly exposed at Tanta; she was probably offered for sale by Timur in his tent or other facility, if he had any at the fair.

The guild of dealers in white slaves was considered a highly respected corporation and was listed together with the prestigious merchant guilds of Khān al-Khalīlī, the Cairene bazaar.[16] At the head of the guild was the *shaykh,* here a certain Ali Efendi. As part of the state system of urban control, the guild head acted to ensure that members complied with the Şeriat-based ethical code of the Slave Dealers' Guild. Obviously, both the law and guild practice derived from Ottoman-Egyptian elite values and reflected freeborn, Muslim, male supremacy.

When Şemsigül's case was reported to Ali Efendi, he immediately summoned the concerned parties and held an investigation. He thus found the culprit and cited him for violation of the guild's code. Ali also had the executive power to impose a sanction: he annulled the

15. Ibid.

16. Baer, "Slavery," p. 174. On guilds in nineteenth-century Egypt, see Gabriel Baer, *Egyptian Guilds in Modern Times* (Jerusalem, 1964); Toledano, *State and Society,* pp. 225–30; and Cole, *Colonialism and Revolution,* pp. 164–89.

deal and caused the papers exchanged between Deli Mehmet (seller) and Timur (buyer) to be returned. In its investigation report, the Council of Police stated that cases involving slaves should immediately be brought to the attention of the police, which normally looked into them without delay. In reality, however, despite enforcement of the code by both the guild and the authorities, the slave dealers developed their own mode of operation, which deviated—albeit not drastically—from the practiced code *(usul)* of the guild.

Much in that business depended on mutual trust between members of the trade, who often—as in the case before us—helped each other in carrying out deals. Timur and Mustafa took care of Şemsigül while Deli Mehmet was in India and later in the Hijaz. There is mention of some sort of recordkeeping, perhaps beyond the exchange of the sale papers *(sened)* in which the details of the deal were written: when Deli Mehmet was told by the Council of Police to produce the traveling certificate issued to him for the Istanbul-Cairo trip on which Şemsigül was imported, he said he would have to search for it among his "papers." He then went home but—not surprisingly—returned with nothing. It was quite common for records not to be complete, if at all extant, because information about one's financial situation and business was most zealously guarded from officials, friends, and even family. This was done to evade taxes or avoid competition and was deeply ingrained in Mediterranean bazaar culture,[17] though by no means alien to other cultures. It was practiced even more persistently in sensitive and discreet professions such as slave dealing.

This conveniently leads us to the competition that existed within the Slave Dealers' Guild, a subject also alluded to in our investigation report. When Deli Mehmet had to explain why a fellow slave dealer with whom he had conducted business (i.e., Mustafa) testified against him, he mentioned jealousy and competition. In his own words: "When someone in the [Slave Dealers'] Guild becomes an importer of slaves [as distinguished from mere market dealer], and if then he turns rich, the rest of the guild detest him. Consequently, when complaints such as this [Şemsigül's] are launched, these [guild members] give false testimonies [against the rich importers]." As for Mustafa's testimony, said Deli Mehmet, it was given "solely for this reason, since he [Mustafa] is one of the poor [slave dealers]."

17. See, e.g., Geertz et al., *Meaning and Order in Moroccan Society,* pp. 124–25.

Very little information is available about the relations between the slave dealers and their slaves. Legally, the slaves were the property of the dealers, and the dealers could dispose of them according to the prescriptions of the Şeriat. Slave dealers as such have no legal status and are considered by Islamic law as legal masters or mistresses. Here, I am mostly concerned with the sexual aspect of the relations between male slave dealers and their female slaves. Ownership allowed the slave dealer sexual access to his female slaves, but they then became his concubines (*odalık*, known in Western literature as "odalisk"). As the law did not require the slave's consent, it condoned rape if the woman refused to have sex.

That reality belies attempts to portray concubines as "not really slaves" or as socially privileged by having (forced or voluntary) sexual relations with their masters. As Claire Robertson and Martin Klein point out for Africa, compulsory sexual relations did not ameliorate, but rather reinforced, slavery for women; concubinage undergirded male dominance and further manifested it.[18] A striking example of the enormous hazards of female slave vulnerability in sexual matters is provided by Claude Meillassoux, who relates that Saharan slave owners used to claim that venereal disease could be cured by having sexual relations with a young virgin slave. As if the story itself is not horrible enough, Meillassoux's comments only aggravate it by their amazing insensitivity toward the plight of the real victims in this case—the female slaves. He writes: "This particularly ignoble custom revealed a complete lack of concern for the *fertility* of the young slaves or for *their future partners*" (my emphases).[19] What should have come first, of course, is concern for the health and well-being of the young slaves themselves, well ahead of the rather instrumental concerns for their fertility or for the plight of their future (male) sex partners, who in all likelihood would not bother to obtain their consent or care about the consequences.

As already noted, concubines received some protection from the law if they did get pregnant, thereby assuming the status of *ümmüveled* (Arabic *umm walad*). An added constraint on the sexual access of dealers was provided by economic realities: a virgin was

18. Robertson and Klein, "Introduction," in *Women and Slavery in Africa*, pp. 8–9.
19. Claude Meillassoux, *The Anthropology of Slavery: The Womb of Iron and Gold* (Chicago, 1991), pp. 79–83; the quotation is from p. 82.

worth far more than a nonvirgin; abortion could result in the slave's death, which no dealer wanted; and finally, dealers did not want any restrictions on their ability to dispose of their slaves, such as would result from pregnancy or fatherhood, unless of course they meant to attach the slave to their own household permanently.

In addition, we may wish to consider the fact that slave importers, such as Deli Mehmet, spent a great deal of their time traveling in the company of young female slaves, their own families normally remaining in the home base. This combination of months-long journeys and the availability of women, under legal sanction, often led to the situation described in Şemsigül's testimony. In an already unequal power situation, the law provided no protection for the slave because it did not require her consent, thereby allowing rape in case of resistance. Male slaves, too, were exposed to sexual harassment, abuse, and rape by dealers and masters, although the Şeriat strictly prohibited homosexual relations. Custom, however, was more lenient and turned a blind eye on it. Market dealers who operated mostly in the cities had less sexual access to their slaves because the slaves were normally kept within the household, where a wife would often be present and in charge of the *harem*.

Pregnancy, Abortion, and the World of Women

THE POLICE REPORT under review mentions four women with distinct roles and a few other women in the background. It is a story about a woman, her plight, her suffering, her intimate life, but it also opens a window onto the "world of women" in mid-nineteenth-century Cairo.[20] We should bear in mind that it is told from a male perspective, which has to be filtered in order to get the full picture. Thus, it is not surprising that except for the main figure, Şemsigül, the other women who appear in it do not have names: they are described

20. Having lagged behind the remarkable growth during the 1980s of works on women in Western history, the study of the history of Middle Eastern women has made great strides in recent years. The list of recent works is rather too long to be cited here, which is in itself indicative. A conference on "Women in the Ottoman Empire," organized by Madeline Zilfi at the University of Maryland in mid-April 1994, attracted a large audience and presented some of the excellent work being carried out in the field. A good place to begin is Nikki R. Keddie and Beth Baron, eds., *Women in Middle Eastern History: Shifting Boundaries in Sex and Gender* (New Haven, 1991).

either as "the wife of," "the peasant woman," or "the midwife." This lack of individuated identity stands in stark opposition to the fact that all the men in the story are named.

As already noted, *harems* in Ottoman cities formed a social network which was almost a system unto itself. Women interacted with other women, entertained and were entertained by each other, helped each other and competed among themselves, stood together vis-à-vis the men's world and, not infrequently, sought to influence the course of events in that world. On the highest level, such activities affected politics and the affairs of state.[21] On lower levels, daily life was, to a great extent, shaped by this dual structure of society.

In Şemsigül's story we have some of the components mentioned here. Her story concerns the threat of the concubine-master relationship to the position of the legitimate wife and the latter's jealousy and revenge as she attempted to put an end to Şemsigül's pregnancy. It reveals the solidarity among women and the compassion displayed by the peasant woman, who told Selim Bey's wife about Şemsigül's plight, and by Selim Bey's wife, who came to save the young woman from Deli Mehmet's wife and later safeguarded her pregnancy. We also have the wife of the slave dealer Mustafa, who at her own home protected Şemsigül from the wrath of Deli Mehmet's wife. A professional woman—the midwife *(ebekarı, daya)*—appears on a few occasions, which brings us to the intimate aspect of relations between the sexes and their consequences: pregnancy and abortion.

Although we have no information about whether Deli Mehmet or Şemsigül attempted to prevent pregnancy, we know that methods of contraception were known and practiced at the time. It is likely that sex partners—married or not—applied such methods in order to prevent unwanted pregnancies. Earlier and contemporary Islamic lawbooks even discuss various methods of contraception. Thus, for example, Ibn ʿĀbidīn (died in 1836), one of the great interpreters of the Sharīʿa in the nineteenth century, cites various opinions regarding methods of contraception and tends to condone the use of coitus interruptus.[22]

21. See Peirce, *Imperial Harem,* pp. 153–228, especially pp. 229–65.

22. Ibn ʿĀbidīn, *Radd al-Muhtār ʿala al-Durr al-Mukhtār* (Beirut, n.d.), vol. 2, pp. 379–80; on methods of contraception, see Basim F. Musallam, *Sex and Society in Islam* (Cambridge, 1983).

As we shall see, legal discussions of contraception and abortions reflect a male perspective that treats the well-being of the woman, if at all, as secondary. This is especially true in the case of female slaves. Thus, some legal authorities required the consent of both sex partners to the use of contraceptive measures, which seems to have been ignored when a female slave was involved. Other doctors of law mentioned the need for a reason to avoid pregnancy, procreation being strongly favored as a rule. Others considered contraception to be legitimate in the event of anticipated hazard to the fetus, such as might result from a long journey or, especially, if the birth was expected to occur in a non-Muslim territory (Dār al-Harb). If the husband intended to divorce his wife at some point in the future, attempts to prevent pregnancy were also legitimate.

Abortion was well known in premodern Islamic societies, including Ottoman Egypt. From its inception, Islamic law dealt with abortions, but, again, mostly from a male perspective. Most jurists tended to allow abortions during the first four months, or 120 days, of pregnancy. They believed that before the end of that period the fetus did not possess a human soul. The dissenting view maintained that there was life in the womb from the moment of conception and, thus, prohibited abortion, regardless of the wishes or well-being of the pregnant woman. Some of those who believed abortion was legal in the early months of pregnancy required that a sufficient reason be produced for allowing it, in order to clear the pregnant woman of potential murder charges. If, for example, a woman was believed to be unable to breast-feed the child after birth, and if the man lacked the means to hire a wet nurse, this constituted for some jurists a legally acceptable cause for abortion. However, it seems that the consent of the father was, generally, not required for abortion during the first four months after conception. Şemsigül's case, of course, was quite different, as the attempts to terminate her pregnancy were made against her express will.

Şemsigül's concerns and considerations were rather complex and ultimately led her to struggle against the attempts to abort her fetus. It is certainly possible that she simply wanted to have the baby, not realizing that this would tie her to Deli Mehmet—if he so wished—for the rest of his life, for she would only be manumitted upon his death. If she had the baby and remained in the household, she would constitute a real threat to the status of Deli Mehmet's wife, especially if the latter had no children of her own or if she had only daughters. If Şemsigül's child was a boy, the threat would be greater still, given the cultural preference for boys. Additional children would normally reduce the share of the wife's children in the father's inheritance. Thus, beyond jealousy and hurt, there were material reasons for the violent reaction of Deli Mehmet's wife to Şemsigül's pregnancy.

Şemsigül might have come to see Deli Mehmet—and even his wife—as a lesser evil, fearing that a new master might bring new and unforetold calamities. It is also possible that she had realized that since she was no longer a virgin, the chances that buyers would be interested in her for marriage or concubinage-leading-to-marriage were slim. That meant that she would rank low on the social ladder of any *harem* and have a more difficult life. In such circumstances, it would make sense to have the baby, remain in Deli Mehmet's possession, and fight for her status within it, possibly through having more children.

Another angle of our story demonstrates the importance of midwives in the women's world of the time, for they performed a major gynecological and social role during pregnancy, birth, and early maternity. A midwife was called to examine Şemsigül in the palace and verify whether she was indeed pregnant. Then again, when Deli Mehmet's wife wished to stop the slave's pregnancy, she invited a midwife to her house. As mentioned, the woman stated that the pregnancy was too advanced and that an abortion would have endangered Şemsigül. Midwives were a very important part of preindustrial society both in Europe[23] and in the Middle East. Their knowledge was based on experience and did not, until a later period, require official schooling or licensing. Their role made them privy to the most guarded secrets of family life in the community.

The thoroughness of their training and the effectiveness of the examinations they performed on patients are debatable. In France of the ancien régime, there was reluctance to perform autopsies on women who died in the early stages of pregnancy, and vaginal examinations of patients were rare.[24] In Egypt, midwives, like all

23. See, e.g., Mireille Laget, "Childbirth in Seventeenth and Eighteenth-Century France: Obstetrical Practices and Collective Attitudes," in *Medicine and Society in France: Selections from the Annales*, ed. R. Foster and O. Ranum (Baltimore, 1980), pp. 157–67.

24. Ibid., p. 140.

other professions, were organized in a special guild. The midwives' guild continued to exist throughout the nineteenth century, and a decree of 12 October 1889 exempted it, along with other guilds of women, from the professional tax.[25] Organization into guilds enabled both the government and the members of any recognized trade to exercise professional supervision for the maintenance of standards and ethics.

In *An Account of the Manners and Customs of the Modern Egyptians* (1860), Edward Lane describes the role of the midwife in birth ceremonies. A few days before an expected delivery, the midwife conveyed to the house of the pregnant woman the "delivery chair" *(kursī ʾl-wilāda),* which was her own property. The specially built chair would serve the patient at the time of birth and was ornamented appropriately for the occasion. On the seventh day following the birth, the family celebrated the event in a traditional ceremony. The mother, attended by the midwife, was seated once more on the delivery chair "in hope that she may soon have occasion for it again." During the night preceding the seventh-day ceremony, a decorated water bottle filled with water was placed by the sleeping baby's head. The midwife would take this bottle and place it on a tray, which she then would present to the women, who were expected to put coins on the tray to remunerate the midwife. Lane also claims that the wealthy families used to maintain a midwife on a permanent basis within the household to care for the women of the *harem.*[26]

For centuries, Muslim jurists debated the question of whether the midwife should be paid by the husband or by the wife.[27] According to Muslim law, as also expressed in article 443 of the Ottoman Civil Code (the Mecelle), the physician, and for that matter the midwife, are hired by contract to perform a service. It is especially in emergencies that an ambiguity may arise as to who hired—and should therefore pay—the physician. Normally, the woman paid all her own expenses, including medical treatment, but Ibn ʿĀbidīn took a different stand: he imposed the midwife's fees on the husband,

25. On the exemption of the midwives' guild from the professional tax, see Baer, *Egyptian Guilds,* pp. 33, 171.

26. Lane, *Manners and Customs of the Modern Egyptians,* pp. 163, 503–5.

27. Yaakov Meron, "Medical Treatment Viewed by Moslem Law," in *International Symposium on Society and Law,* ed. H. Karplus (Jerusalem 1972; Amsterdam, 1973), pp. 43–44.

arguing that the man is responsible for the child's maintenance and that it is the child who derives the greater benefit from the midwife's services. This view still left open the question of an aborted, or incomplete, pregnancy.

When Mehmet Ali was governor of Egypt, especially between the years 1825 and 1848, various attempts were made to introduce European concepts of public health into the country. It is not entirely clear how successful those attempts were, and there is evidence of the many obstacles that were thrown in the way of medical reform during that period. Nevertheless, a change was effected in the definition and role of midwives as part of Clot Bey's (1793–1868) great contribution to the development of Egyptian medicine and medical education. Until the early 1830s, midwives in Egypt acquired their knowledge through apprenticeship and experience. A school for women doctors and midwives was established in Cairo in 1829, and the first class consisted of thirteen African slaves, since the idea was not readily embraced by the population and candidates were hard to recruit. Women "doctors," or *hakīma*s, were trained to attend maternity cases and replace traditional midwives, and female medical aides—circulating in villages or working in health centers in the cities—administered vaccinations to women and verified female deaths.[28]

Only a limited amount of work has been done on the effects of pregnancy, abortion, and birth in the preindustrial societies of the Middle East. The difficulties involved in trying to reconstruct the emotional and psychological world of women who lived then are quite obvious. With the help of an excellent article by Mireille Laget and of Şemsigül's story, we can begin to explore that vast field. About the France of the ancien régime, Laget writes that

> in the mass of nameless families the woman was incapable of separating copulation from "generation." She was beyond ignorance,

28. On the problems generated by the health reforms, see Lavern Khunke, *Lives at Risk* (Berkeley, 1990). On the *hakīma*s, see ibid., pp. 186–87, 268; and Lavern Khunke, "The 'Doctress' on a Donkey: Women Health Officers in Nineteenth-Century Egypt," *Clio Medica* 9 (1974): 193–205. A recent feminist critique of Clot Bey's attitude to women's medicine (also including a reference to midwives) is Mervat Hatem, "Colonizing Women's Bodies: A Poststructuralist View of the Health and Education Professions as Forms of Governmentalities in 19th-Century Egypt," paper delivered at the conference "Women in the Ottoman Empire: History and Legacy of the Early Modern Middle East (1650 ff.)," University of Maryland, 17–18 Apr. 1994.

in the realm of the "unthinkable." She was submissive, "illiterate and treated harshly." . . . she was worn out by many confinements and sometimes by service as a wetnurse; and she was treated with contempt if she was indigent. She lived through her time of waiting in a state of exhaustion and anxiety. I am speaking here of the exhaustion resulting from pregnancies and miscarriages repeated every year or two, as well as of the anxiety of women who were pregnant outside the social norms. Women in their forties had been unable to avoid ten or twelve pregnancies, even by means of late marriage or abstinence. By the end of their fertile years, they were at the threshold of old age, often suffering the incurable consequences of poorly handled confinements. As for the women whose children were illegitimate, the disapproval of society made them into hunted creatures who tried to hide their pregnancy or to "kill their fruit." Servant girls [were] seduced by their masters, girls [were] impregnated by passing strangers or soldiers, rarely consenting but always accused. . . . Women would simulate a fit of coughing in order to contract their muscles and keep the child from moving or assert that they suffered from dropsy. The glory of motherhood, though still sung in church, had ceased to be a moral, religious, and artistic ideal. . . . One must be very careful not to attribute the mentality of today's women to women who lived two centuries ago.[29]

Laget tends, however, to go along with the view that in less-developed societies, the period of labor was shorter and the pain experienced less intense. She asserts that in conditions deemed "closer to nature," births rarely took more than two hours and women suffered considerably less.[30] I suggest that mid-nineteenth-century Cairene society was probably neither as close to nature as, perhaps, that of the aboriginals of Australia nor as burdened by guilt and fear as the French society described by Laget. In Cairo at the time discussed here, reproduction was seen as propitious and decreed by God, and there is no reason to doubt the joyous nature of the ceremonies and celebrations attached to it, as described by Lane. Yet, in that milieu, as in others elsewhere, infant mortality, children

29. Laget, "Childbirth in France," p. 142.
30. Ibid., p. 147.

deformed as a result of mismanaged delivery, miscarriages, mortality of the mother during pregnancy or birth, and unwanted children were all part of life. People accepted these calamities when they befell a member of their own family and praised God if their dear ones were spared the agony. Women and men did not know a better life and learned to cherish and celebrate moments of happiness.

Even by the yardstick of her own society, Şemsigül's plight was not a happy one. Surely there were other women who suffered as she did, and yet others who endured more. But ultimately, custom and the law prevailed over Deli Mehmet's cruelty, his wife's vengeance, and the complicity of fellow slave dealers. The code of the Slave Dealers' Guild was applied by the head of the guild, the police took action to investigate and punish the offender, and the courts adjudicated. Thus, even in a preindustrial, gender-segregated, male-dominated, strictly hierarchical society, justice was extended to a powerless, suffering female slave.

In any event, the story analyzed and contextualized in this chapter complements the discussion of Ottoman *kul/harem* slavery offered in chapter 1. Without wishing to argue that Şemsigül's story was typical of most *harem* slaves, I do maintain that her experience was familiar to many of the women whose lives spanned the spectrum of poverty in childhood, uprooting in adolescence, and *harem* realities in youth and adulthood. We now move to explore yet another facet of Ottoman slavery, agricultural bondage, which though considerably removed from *kul/harem* urban life, is not entirely divorced from it. The nexus is to be found in the fact that many of the young Circassian girls and boys sold into *kul/harem* slavery came from rural origins in the Caucasus, where agricultural slavery was common and whence it was imported into the Ottoman Empire in the second half of the nineteenth century.

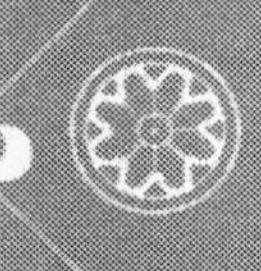

THREE

Agricultural Slavery among Ottoman Circassians

As already mentioned, agricultural slavery was not common in the Ottoman Empire.[1] Agricultural land was state domain, which the sovereign assigned to a dependent elite in return for military and administrative services rendered to the dynasty. The ruling elite appropriated the surplus via a variety of revenue assessment and collection mechanisms, relying on a free peasantry to till relatively small plots, produce for subsistence, and provision the urban centers of the empire. In such a system, slave labor was rare, localized, and short term, and gang cultivation did not exist at all. These realities were changed in the late 1850s and early 1860s with the introduction of a large agricultural slave population from the Caucasus.

Agricultural slavery was common among the Circassian population of the Caucasus. The Circassians were only nominally Muslim,

1. Ömer Lûtfi Barkan, "Le sêrvage éxistait-il en Turquie?" *Annales ESC* 11 (1956): 54–60. Agricultural slavery had existed on a small scale in the fifteenth and sixteenth centuries but gradually disappeared later. The two notable exceptions occurred in nineteenth-century Egypt (see Baer, "Slavery," p. 165) and Çukurova (in eastern Anatolia). Throughout this chapter I shall use the term "agricultural slavery" in order to avoid confusion with different practices—notably serfdom—in other societies. Agricultural slaves had the same legal status as all other slaves. Customary law, especially that of the Circassians, reflected some of the social differences among slaves in various occupations, but this had no effect on Islamic law in the Ottoman Empire.

and their institution of slavery was rooted in local custom rather than in the concepts and practices of the Şeriat, though both Circassian and Ottoman institutions emanated from a concept of a broadly conceived state of dependence. A landed stratum of leaders, commonly referred to in Ottoman and European sources as *emir*s (pl. *ümera*) or *bey*s, ruled Caucasian society through a tribally based sociopolitical structure. A large number of bonded peasant families belonged to their *bey*s, fulfilling an array of roles beyond mere cultivation of the land. In times of peace, the slaves cultivated the *bey*'s land; in war, they fought under his command; and it was their children, mostly the girls, who were sold to local slave dealers for the Ottoman market. This system seems to have features in common with Russian serfdom, but it resembles even more the East African coastal type of agricultural slavery described by Frederick Cooper in that it reflects an all-encompassing relation of dependency rather than just the linkage to menial labor.[2]

Given those social realities, it is hardly surprising that when the Ottoman government decided to take in the Circassian refugees, it allowed the slaveholding *bey*s to enter the empire with their slaves and refrained from interfering in their affairs. However, once on Ottoman territory, these slaves were treated according to the rules of the Şeriat, which recognized only one slave status without distinguishing between the various socially determined types of bondage. Circassian broad-base agricultural slavery thus became an internal social problem with which the Ottoman government would have to deal for the rest of the century.

Unlike the prohibition of the African slave trade—which owed a great deal to British pressure—reforms concerning Circassian slavery were, for the most part, the result of Ottoman initiative. Motivated by internal considerations, the Porte moved gradually and with caution during the last third of the nineteenth century to de facto abolish agricultural slavery among the Circassian refugees. But to understand this process, we should first review the events in the Caucasus during the period following the Crimean War.

2. For Russian slavery, see Kolchin, *Unfree Labor,* pp. 1–7, and the chapters on Russian serfdom; for Frederick Cooper's views, see his *Plantation Slavery on the East Coast of Africa* (New Haven, 1977), p. 261. American slavery seems to have less in common with the Circassian phenomenon because it was labor centered, was not indigenous, and organized cultivation differently.

After the Crimean War, the Russians intensified their efforts to subdue the Caucasus, committing greater resources and changing their strategy.[3] A systematic military advance aimed at clearing populated areas and resettling them with reliable elements—what might today be called "ethnic cleansing"—replaced the prewar approach of dealing only with pockets of resistance where they existed. The success of this strategy in the eastern Caucasus, which culminated in the defeat of the famous leader Şamil in 1859, was followed by its application in the western Caucasus in 1860.[4] Circassians in conquered territories were given the choice of emigrating either to the interior of Russia or to the Ottoman Empire.

In December 1863 the tribal federation of the Abaza surrendered, and 150,000 of them were ordered to leave the Caucasus by the following spring. Four months later, the last Circassian tribe—the Ubikh—was defeated and ordered to emigrate; the Russians reportedly offered the lands to the Azov Cossacks and to government employees who had served in the Caucasus ten years or more.[5] Military operations in the Caucasus ended in May 1864, but the flow of refugees continued into 1866.

Transportation of the Circassians became a major problem, and the Russian government, obviously interested in speeding up the process, took an active part in it. The Russians were said to have contracted two merchants of Kerch to transport refugees to Samsun at a rate of five rubles per person—three to be paid by the government and two by the Circassians themselves in money, cattle, or produce. Although the Russians offered to pay five rubles per person for steamer transportation, shipowners in Odessa and Istanbul refused to get involved in what became a chaotic operation.[6]

The Ottoman government negotiated some arrangements with the

3. Marc Pinson, "Ottoman Colonization of the Circassians in Rumili after the Crimean War," *Études Balkaniques* (Sofia) 3 (1972): 71.

4. On events in the northern Caucasus at the time, see Moshe Gammer, *Muslim Resistance to the Tsar: Shamil and the Conquest of Chechnia and Daghestan* (London, 1994).

5. R. C. Clipperton (consul, Kerch) to Lord John Russell (foreign secretary), Confidential, 21.12.66; C. H. Dickson (consul, Sohum Kale) to Russell, Confidential, no. 3, 13.4.64; both in PRO, FO 87/424.

6. Clipperton to Russell, Confidential, 13.4.63; Clipperton to Russell, Confidential, 10.5.64; both in PRO, FO 87/424. In November 1860, when emigration had not yet reached its mass proportions, the British consul at Sohum Kale reported that ships of

Russians and sent vessels to carry the Circassians to various ports on the Black Sea. Refugees intended for settlement in Rumelia were taken to Constanţa and Varna; those intended for Anatolia entered through Trabzon and Samsun. Much to the Russians' delight, few refugees were settled in border areas. The receiving ports were ill-equipped and could not cater to the basic needs of the refugees. Food shortages, lack of sanitation, inadequate medical facilities, and ineffective quarantine combined to exacerbate the already great suffering of the refugees. Smallpox, typhus, and dysentery took a heavy toll; mortality estimates varied from two hundred to three hundred persons per day.[7]

The available sources differ as to the number of Circassians who entered the Ottoman Empire between the years 1855 and 1866. Most of the Ottoman estimates are considerably higher than the Russian figures and run between 595,000 and 1,008,000, with one surprisingly low figure of 395,000. The Ottoman government estimated in 1867 that among the Circassian refugees there were more than 150,000 persons of slave status.[8] Although this figure may be too high, it is clear that the number of slaves was very large indeed.

When the British ambassador in Saint Petersburg brought up the matter with Prince Gorchakov, the Russian foreign minister, in March 1864, the prince observed that the estimate of 300,000 refugees was greatly exaggerated. Russia, said the foreign minister, regretted this emigration, but the Circassians had rejected the government's offer for their resettlement on Russian territory. The Ottoman Empire, he added, would nevertheless benefit from the Circassian immigration, which would increase its military manpower potential. It is open to challenge whether this was valid even as a long-term prediction, but the short-term problems created by the Circassian expulsion certainly outweighed the benefits. The prince was probably well aware of that. Despite repeated Ottoman pleas during 1864, the Russians refused to

---

the Russian Steam Navigation and Trading Company regularly transported Circassian emigrants to Trabzon (Dickson to Russell, Confidential, 17.11.60, PRO, FO 87/424).

7. Sir Henry Bulwer (ambassador, Istanbul) to Russell, no. 54, 12.4.64, PRO, FO 87/424; Pinson, "Ottoman Colonization," pp. 73–74, 83–84; Clipperton to Russell, Confidential, 10.5.64, PRO, FO 97/424; Stevens (consul, Trabzon) to Russell, 4.8.63, PRO, FO 84/1204/224–25.

8. The grand vezir to the sultan, 24 Zilkâde 1283/30.3.67, BA/İrade/Meclis-i Mahsus/1407. On the class structure of Circassian society, see Chev. Taitbont de Marigny, *Three Voyages in the Black Sea to the Coast of Circassia* (London, 1837), pp. 47–50.

halt the expulsion; though Prince Gorchakov claimed that an order to this effect had been issued, the Ottomans reported that the inflow of refugees continued unhampered.[9]

The Immigration Commission and the Slaves

FACED WITH THE HOST of problems created by the Circassian and, earlier, the Tatar and Nogay population inflow, the Ottoman government decided on 5 January 1860 to establish the Immigration Commission (Muhâcirin Komisyonu, sometimes called Muhâcirin Idaresi, which less literally might be rendered as the Refugees Commission). Headed by the former governor of Trabzon and including mostly sub-cabinet-level officials from the various concerned ministries, the commission was charged with coordinating all Ottoman efforts to cope with the refugees' problems.[10] Owner-slave relations were included in the commission's mandate, and as we shall see, it indeed intervened in many of the disputes that occurred. The government's decision to subject owner-slave matters not only to the jurisdiction of the Şeriat courts but also to the rulings of the commission constitutes a clear breach of the exclusivity of the owner-slave relationship. That breach significantly eroded the hold of agricultural slavery among the Circassian refugees and became one of the main devices employed by the Ottomans to ultimately abolish that component of the institution.

In the early 1860s, the Immigration Commission dealt primarily with four types of problems concerning slavery and the slave trade:

1. The most important task of the commission was to supervise and facilitate the settlement of the refugees and to provide them with

9. For a discussion of the migration estimates, see Pinson, "Ottoman Colonization," p. 75n. İnalcık quotes the figure 595,000, which is the same as that mentioned by Ubicini, a resident of Istanbul in the nineteenth century (Halil İnalcık, "Čerkes—iii. Ottoman period," *Encyclopædia of Islam,* 2d ed. [Leiden, 1960], vol. 2, p. 25). For British-Russian contacts on the issue, see Lord Napier (ambassador, Saint Petersburg) to Russell, no. 255, Confidential, 17.8.64, PRO, FO 97/424; Pinson, "Ottoman Colonization," p. 77.

10. For events leading to the decision to create the Immigration Commission, see Ahmet Cevat Eren, *Türkiye'de göc ve göcmen meseleleri* (Istanbul, 1966), pp. 39–61. Only a few documents relating to the commission's actions on Circassian slavery and slave trade have survived or are presently accessible at the Ottoman archives. The most useful among these are the registers—or précis books—in which the correspondence addressed to the commission was recorded. However, it should be borne in mind that the information is as yet incomplete, and the conclusions here are, therefore, tentative.

the necessary means to cultivate the land and to establish their homes. Slave families followed their masters' households and often formed extended groups that had to be settled on one estate. The allocation of land for such purposes and the occasional need to relocate these extended units were among the problems that the commission was called upon to resolve.[11]

2. Then came the settlement of disputes that erupted among the refugees between master and slave.[12] Many such disputes revolved around assertions by individual slaves that they were actually free and did not belong to the slave class. Cases of runaway slaves were also reported to the commission by slave owners. In some instances, the commission was asked to compel slaves by issuing orders to obey their masters *(itaat)*. Crimes committed by slaves, especially murder and robbery, were laid before the commission, and its intervention was solicited. Conversely, abused slaves sought redress by petitioning the commission. The commission did not, however, act as a court; it supplemented court action either by enforcing court orders or by acting when and where the courts were ineffective.

3. The mass Circassian refugee influx created conditions that were conducive to excesses and abuses committed by privileged refugees against their weak and poor compatriots. Sensing the inability of the Ottoman government to enforce the law strictly in that period of transition, such individuals would sell into slavery persons who belonged to the free classes but who could not—under the circumstances—effectively resist them. Others also took advantage of the situation. Captains of the transporting boats were said to exact passage fee "in kind," that is, by taking refugees' children (one child per thirty passengers, according to one report), whom they would later sell as slaves. It is difficult to estimate how common these practices actually were, but scattered evidence exists which indicates that both individuals and groups among the Circassian refugees were subjected to them.

11. E.g., entries 101 (for the year 1278/1861–62); *fevkalâde* 2, 259 (for the year 1279/1862–63); petitions 26, 31, 271 (for the year 1281/1864–65); 29 (for the year 1282/1865–66); all in BA/Babı Âli Evrak Odası (hereafter abbreviated BAEO)/Muhacirîn Komisyonu/vol. 758.

12. E.g., entries 66, 126, 179, 403 (for the year 1278/1861–62); *fevkalâde* 2, 209 (for the year 1279/1862–63); 190 (for the year 1280/1863–64); 167, 282 (for the year 1281/1864–65); *fevkalâde* 1, petition 7 (for the year 1282/1865–66); all in BA/BAEO/Muhacirîn Komisyonu/vol. 758.

Complaints about such incidents were referred to the commission, which tried to prevent their recurrence. In 1862, for example, the commission ordered the manumission of a freeborn refugee who had been brought from Amasya to Istanbul by a woman who sold him there into slavery. Orders were then sent to Amasya to prevent such cases. Another measure taken for this purpose was a restriction imposed on the sale of slaves among the refugees. A number of applications by slave owners for exemptions to allow them to sell their slaves—usually because of economic need—were submitted to the commission. One such application was made in 1861 by the governor of İzmir, who asked that slave sales by Circassian refugees settled in the *sancak* (district) of Aydın be allowed to resume.[13]

4. In addition to these three kinds of activities—which concerned primarily, though not exclusively, slave families engaged in agriculture—the commission also dealt with problems related to the slave trade in individual refugees that was being pursued by slave dealers.[14] Extensive correspondence concerning the status of refugee women bought by certain slave dealers occurred between the commission and the office of the *şeyhülislam* (the head of the Islamic legal hierarchy), which handled the Şerî (legal) aspect of the problem. In Istanbul in September 1864, when eighty-five slaves aboard a Russian ship were found to be ill, presumably with smallpox or typhus, the case was referred to the commission. On 12 December 1865 the commission was petitioned in regard to the admission of two male slaves to the preparatory vocational school in Tophane. The two became the property of the Treasury (Beytülmal) after the death of the woman slave dealer Nâzir Hatun, to whom they belonged.[15]

13. For children as passage fee, see Bulwer to Russell, 31.8.64, PRO, FO 84/1225/166–67; *Anti-Slavery Reporter*, 3d series, vol. 12 (1964), p. 198, quoting the *Levant Herald* of 17.8.64. Examples of selling freeborn into slavery are in entries 179, 371 (for the year 1278/1861–62); 91, 167, 218 (for the year 1281/1864–65); *fevkalâde* 1 (for the year 1282/1865–66); all in BA/BAEO/Muhacirîn Komisyonu/vol. 758. See also enclosure 2, *Emirname-i Sâmi*, 19 Sefer 1281/24.7.64, BA/İrade/Meclis-i Mahsus/1407. For manumission in Amasya, see entry 371 (for the year 1278/1861–62), BA/BAEO/Muhacirîn Komisyonu/vol. 758. For applications to the commission to allow sale, see entries 133, 256, 358 (for the year 1278/1861–62), BA/BAEO/Muhacirîn Komisyonu/vol. 758.

14. This activity overlapped with that in category 3.

15. Correspondence with the office of the *şeyhülislam* in entry 24 (for the year 1281/1864–65), BA/BAEO/Muhacirîn Komisyonu/vol. 758, mentions the existence of sixty-seven enclosures. For sick slaves aboard a Russian ship, see entry 111 (for the year

There are indications even before 1864 that the Immigration Commission tried to restrict in some measure the refugees' freedom of movement within the empire in general, and into Istanbul in particular. The effectiveness of this policy is hard to judge, but stricter measures were needed in 1864 due to the overwhelming wave of refugees entering the empire following the collapse of Circassian resistance in the Caucasus in May of the same year. In July 1864 the governor of Trabzon was ordered not to send any more refugees to the capital. Probably around the same time, for an exact date has not been established, the commission moved also to prohibit the entry of slaves into Istanbul and tightened its control over their movement in general.[16]

Although no record of such instructions has been found, a report *(mazbata)* drawn up by the commission on 17 April 1865 reiterated a "previous prohibition" against slaves' entering Istanbul, thereby confirming that earlier orders to that effect had indeed existed. Government officials and the head of the Slave Dealers' Guild (Esirciler Kethüdâsı) were to be informed that, unless for an essential personal purpose, no slave would be permitted to enter the city. Slaves going to the capital for such purposes should carry documents, endorsed by government officials, attesting to that fact. No permits of passage *(mürur tezkeresi)* would be issued to slaves wishing to leave Istanbul unless they carried identity papers *(ilmühaber)* provided by the Immigration Commission. The *mazbata* was marked "urgent" and was sent to the High Council for Judicial Ordinances; a day later it was enacted and entered in the registers of the Imperial Council (Mühimme Defterleri).[17] The need to reissue the prohibition may be taken as an

---

1281/1864–65), BA/BAEO/Muhacirîn Komisyonu/vol. 758; for the admission of two male slaves to school, see petition 14 (for the year 1282/1865–66), BA/BAEO/Muhacirîn Komisyonu/vol. 758. The British ambassador reported in August 1865 that the commission was preparing a new program of relief, under which an asylum would be established for children whose parents were in great destitution, so as to prevent their being sold into slavery. In the asylum, boys would be taught a trade, and girls would be trained for attendance in *harems* (Bulwer to Russell, 10.8.65, PRO, FO 84/1246/125–26).

16. For restrictions of movement, see entries 60 (for the year 1278/1861–62) and 139 (for the year 1279/1862–63); both in BA/BAEO/Muhacirîn Komisyonu/vol. 758. Entry 34 (for the year 1281/1864–65) refers to the existence of earlier orders restricting the entry of slaves into Istanbul. For the order to the governor of Trabzon, see Pinson, "Ottoman Colonization," p. 73.

17. Entry 34 (for the year 1281/1864–65), BA/BAEO/Muhacirîn Komisyonu/vol. 758. In another entry (37, for the year 1282/1865–66), the Slave Dealers' Guild is referred to as having been abolished. A circular to the governors of all provinces, signed by the

indication that previous attempts to control the movement of slaves in and out of Istanbul were not entirely successful.

In the coming years, the Immigration Commission handled a growing number of applications from Circassians who wished to move their slaves from one place to another within the Ottoman domains. Again, it is difficult to assess how effective the control was, but in October 1865 the commission deemed it necessary to issue yet another order prohibiting the entrance of slaves into Istanbul.[18]

The reasons for this policy are not entirely clear. Restriction of the movement of slaves was meant to give the government means for controlling the traffic in slaves, which it could implement as it saw fit. These measures could also be employed in the service of slave owners for the purpose of tracking down runaway slaves, again if and when the government chose to use the restriction in that way. Finally, this policy could have been motivated by a specific desire to check the movement of agricultural laborers into the cities, where they would swell the ranks of the urban poor, and often unemployed, and might join criminal elements. In any event, this increased influx—especially into Istanbul—also caused the government to formulate a clearer policy in general on the question of slavery and the slave trade among the Circassian refugees.

Restrictions on Slave Trading in Circassians

ON 24 JULY 1864 THE GOVERNMENT issued an instruction to its officials which laid down ground rules for dealing with the problems of slavery and the slave trade among the Circassian refugees.[19]

grand vezir Âli Paşa on 19 July 1871, seven weeks before his death, also said that the guild had been abolished (Aristarchi, *Législation,* vol. 5, p. 36). In the latter, it is implied that the abolition took place when the Istanbul slave market was abolished. In any case, it continued to function unofficially.

18. For restrictive measures, see also Bulwer to Russell, 31.8.64, PRO, FO 84/1225/166–67. For examples of applications to move slaves, see entries 124, petition 21, 255, 261, petition 36 (for the year 1281/1864–65); 29, petition 6, 80 (for the year 1282/1865–66); in BA/BAEO/Muhacirîn Komisyonu/vol. 758. The new prohibition against entering Istanbul is in entry 84 (for the year 1282/1865–66), BA/BAEO/Muhacirîn Komisyonu/vol. 758; the *mazbata* was sent to the High Council for Judicial Ordinances on 12 Cemaziyülevvel 1282/3.10.65.

19. Enclosure 2, *Emirname-i Sâmi,* 19 Sefer 1281/24.7.64, BA/İrade/Meclis-i Mahsus/1407. For additional material on the internal slave trade in Circassians, see also Erdem, *Slavery in the Ottoman Empire,* pp. 113–24.

The free but poor refugees, the government said, were compelled, out of sheer want, to sell their children into slavery. Some shameless and base people, in collusion with slave dealers, were taking advantage of the situation, gathering and enslaving a large number of freeborn boys and girls. The established practice was, the instruction continued, that when children were discovered who had been taken from their parents by deception, they were returned to them by the authorities after proper investigation. However, it was well known that fraud and trickery were often used to evade such measures taken to retrieve the children, and many complaints about that had reached the government. "Free refugees were being traded regularly and without impediment like sacrificial lambs" (*ahrar-ı muhacirîn âdeta bimuhaba kurbanlık koyun gibi satılıp alınmakta*), the instruction stated. It then went on to denounce and prohibit the practice.

The selling of free men and women into slavery was prohibited by the Şeriat, the government asserted. Moreover, it was inhumane to violate the rights of helpless persons who came to the empire seeking refuge and relying on the sultan's compassion. The miserable life they were forced to lead would make them regret ever having come to the country; it gave Islam "a bad name." Therefore, no further sales of free persons would be allowed, and offenders would be severely punished, the government declared. However, if parents sold their children out of their own free will, the sale—though clearly against the Şeriat—would be valid, and the right of ownership and usage would not be affected. But parents should be warned, the instruction concluded, that by so doing they would incur the wrath of God. Incidentally, the sale of relatives into slavery was known also in certain African societies; Claire Robertson and Martin Klein observe in this regard that "it was, in a sense, the very lack of opposition between *kinship* and *exploitation* that often allowed slavery to exist" in the first place.[20]

The prohibition sought to stem forced reduction to slavery and to discourage all slave trading. Further instructions established a procedure to verify the status of persons claiming to have been forcibly enslaved.[21] Upon appearance before a Şerî court, attempts

20. Robertson and Klein, "Introduction," p. 7.

21. The grand vezir to the sultan, 24 Zilkâde 1283/30.3.67, BA/İrade/Meclis-i Mahsus/1407.

would be made to establish whether the plaintiff was a free person or a slave. If the plaintiff failed to produce satisfactory evidence attesting to his or her freedom but asserted that he or she had relatives at his or her original place of residence who could testify to that effect, he or she would then be sent to that place, where the investigation would be resumed. This complicated procedure was often abused, or simply ignored, by the courts. The following test case was used in 1867 to amend it.

Early in 1866, a slave dealer was caught by the police in Istanbul as he was about to sail to Egypt with five Circassian boys, four of whom claimed to be free.[22] The boys, said to be from seven to eleven years old, had been brought to the capital from towns in eastern Anatolia and sold into slavery by members of their own families. At the Şerî court, they failed to prove that they were free, but they nevertheless insisted that they could find witnesses in their hometowns who would back their assertion. Contrary to the established procedure, instead of pursuing the investigation, the court issued a statement affirming that the boys were of slave status. Thus the court was used—probably not uniquely—by the dealer to frustrate the government's efforts to prevent the enslavement of free persons. Faced with that situation, the Council of Ministers decided to change the procedure.

In a report dated 30 March 1867, the council ruled that testimony concerning personal status could be given by relatives in their places of residence and communicated to the court through the local authorities.[23] This was clearly aimed at helping the enslaved; some officials were prepared to go even further.

Basing his decision on the prohibition of July 1864, Osman Paşa, a member of the High Council for Judicial Ordinances, ruled in September 1866 that individuals held as slaves by refugee slaveholders or by slave dealers would be considered free if it could be established that their relatives were free.[24] An official of the Ministry of Police wrote in

22. Enclosure 4, Zaptiye Müşiriyeti (signed Mehmet) to Osman Paşa (member of the High Council for Judicial Ordinances), 19 Rebiülevvel 1283/31.7.66; enclosures 6–9, statements by slave dealer and the slaves, 21–29 Sefer 1283/5–13.7.66; in BA/İrade/Meclis-i Mahsus/1407.

23. The grand vezir to the sultan, 24 Zilkâde 1283/30.3.67, BA/İrade/Meclis-i Mahsus/1407; memo from the Porte to the president (of the High Council for Judicial Ordinances?), 29 Ramazan 1283/4.2.67, BA/Âyniyat/vol. 1136.

24. Correspondence on the matter is in enclosure 3, Osman Paşa to the High Council for Judicial Ordinances, 21 Rebialâhir 1283/3.9.66; enclosure 4, Zaptiye Müşiriyeti

July 1866, in a letter to Osman Paşa, that even if an individual was a slave, it was illegal to separate him or her from parents and relatives, and he or she should be returned to them. Osman Paşa concurred in this view and suggested that all slave dealings among the refugees be deferred until the process of settlement was completed. It is doubtful whether such a policy could have been enforced, since this transition period created the greatest economic need for selling slaves. Constant mobility and the lack of proper registration and means to impose law and order offered many opportunities for effecting sales.

As in other societies where slavery was practiced, separation of slave families usually occurred through the sale of one or more members of the family or through the sale of the whole family but to different buyers. In an attempt to maintain the unity of slave families, the established customs among the Circassians strongly militated against such practices.[25] But the fact that the Council of Ministers had to address itself to the matter indicates that the hardships of expulsion eroded the old and established customs. Refugee slaves resisted, as much as they could, any attempt to effect involuntary separation, and the unrest among them was partially caused by this issue. The government was not unsympathetic toward the slaves' position but had to contend with strong opposition from the Circassian slaveholders and other conservative elements, which often prevented effective action on its part. The following case illustrates this point.

Four people, two men and two women, held in common ownership eleven Circassian male and female slaves.[26] The eleven formed an extended family: a middle-aged woman, her son, his wife, and their four children; and the woman's two married sons and two unmarried daughters. The owners' ways parted and they decided to divide the slaves among them. Six of the slaves were to remain in Tekfurdağ, where they had resided, and five were to accompany their masters to Istanbul. Even the smaller nuclear family, consisting of the married couple and their four children, was to be split up, two of the children

(signed Mehmet) to Osman Paşa, 18 Rebiülevvel 1283/31.7.66; both in BA/İrade/Meclis-i Mahsus/1407.

25. Enclosure 1, *mazbata* of the High Council for Judicial Ordinances, 22 Cemaziyülâhir 1284/21.10.67, BA/İrade/Meclis-i Vâlâ/25956.

26. The grand vezir to the sultan, 1 Cemaziyülâhir 1284/30.9.67, BA/İrade/Meclis-i Vâlâ/25956; the Porte to Osman Paşa (member of the High Council for Judicial Ordinances), 8 Cemaziyülâhir 1284/7.10.67, BA/Âyniyat/vol. 1136, no. 675.

remaining with their grandmother and three of her children. The slaves protested against the deal and demanded to be reunited in Tekfurdağ. The owners, however, obtained a Şerî court order enjoining the slaves to obey their masters. The total value of the slaves was assessed at 20,000 *kuruş*, but they did not have that much money and therefore could not purchase their freedom. The matter was brought before the Immigration Commission.

On 26 August 1867 the commission referred the case, along with its own recommendations, to the High Council for Judicial Ordinances.[27] The commission stated that to comply with the owners' demand to separate the slaves, though backed by the court's ruling, would be "contrary to observed principles of conduct and the Şerî command to heed the slaves' cry for help" *(usul-ı merîye ve üseranın istimâ-ı feryadi hükm-i Şerîye mugayır)*. Taking into consideration the perseverance demonstrated by the slaves and the failure of the parties to conclude a manumission contract *(mükatebe)*,[28] the commission proposed that the Treasury pay the 20,000 *kuruş* and secure the manumission of the whole family.

The High Council for Judicial Ordinances accepted the commission's views, stating that under the circumstances justice demanded both that the court order not be followed and that the slaves should not be set free against their masters' will.[29] The sultan, acting on the recommendation of his grand vezir, agreed to pay the necessary amount, and the slaves were given their freedom. The government's support of the slaves on the issue of "family splitting" was mainly motivated by the need to appease them and prevent rioting but was also influenced by Şeriat-enjoined piety and compassion on the part of the sovereign. As in other, similar cases, however, the Şerî courts had ruled for the slaveholders, clearly opposing forced manumission or sale. During the Tanzimat period and later, this was not a unique

27. Enclosure 2, the Immigration Commission to the High Council for Judicial Ordinances, 25 Rebiülâhir 1284/26.8.67, BA/Âyniyat/vol. 1136, no. 675.

28. The *mükatebe* (Arabic *mukātaba*) is an Islamic legal procedure whereby the owner and the slave voluntarily conclude an agreement to enable the slave to gain his or her freedom in exchange for a set payment, the form and amount of which are decided by the parties. The slave is manumitted when the payment is completed.

29. Enclosure 1, *mazbata* of the High Council for Judicial Ordinances, 22 Cemaziyülâhir 1284/21.10.67; the grand vezir to the sultan, 1 Cemaziyülâhir 1284/30.9.67; and the *baş kâtip* to the grand vezir, 2 Cemaziyülâhir 1284/1.10.67; all in BA/Âyniyat/vol. 1136, no. 675.

instance of the courts adopting a conservative stance. This attitude led the reformers to seek adjudication in non-Şerî administrative councils or courts. As for slavery, state generosity could perhaps solve some isolated cases, but it could not take the place of a coherent and decisive policy.

No doubt the story told above would be familiar to students of most slave societies, as the issue of splitting up slave families was one of the most distressing to the slaves. It was, however, an issue over which the slaveholders often expressed sympathy, and when their pecuniary loss was not too significant, they let it be balanced by the gratification they derived from not inflicting separation on husbands and wives, parents and children, brothers and sisters. But as the rather exemplary case of Thomas Jefferson shows, even highly acclaimed democrats allowed self-interest to override their humanity. Tremendous misery was occasioned by the liquidation of Jefferson's estate after his death in 1826, when some 130 slaves were auctioned to the highest bidder, with the separation of families occurring as a result.[30] This would not be a typical Ottoman scene, and as demonstrated above, the state did not condone it and, when feasible, stepped in to prevent it.

Splitting up slave families did occur in Ottoman society, albeit on a much smaller scale and only among Circassian agricultural slaves. Not infrequently parents voluntarily sold their children, though the psychological consequence was the same. However, once children reached the age of ten or so, their working life began and their labor value usually precluded their sale; this was a common phenomenon in many slave societies, such as the Antebellum United States.[31] It should be noted here that the separation of families in general—that is, not only slave families—became a serious problem during the Circassian influx into the Ottoman Empire. In 1865, the Immigration Commission issued instructions to the governors of the provinces that received and absorbed the refugees.[32] Article 14 of these instructions

30. See, e.g., Lucia Stanton, "'Those Who Labor for My Happiness': Thomas Jefferson and His Slaves," in *Jeffersonian Legacies*, ed. Peter S. Onuf (Charlottesville, 1993), pp. 147 ff.

31. See, e.g., ibid., pp. 150–51.

32. Enclosure 2, the High Council for Judicial Ordinances to the *vâlis*, *mutasarrif*s, and *kaymakam*s of the provinces that absorbed refugees, 12 Cemaziyülevvel 1282/13.10.65, BA/İrade/Meclis-i Vâlâ/24269.

provided for the reunion of families that had been separated and settled in different places owing to the circumstances of expulsion. For this purpose, the commission recognized only the nuclear family as eligible, including the family's slaves.

Orders concerning slavery and the slave trade among the Circassian refugees were occasionally reiterated as the government tried to bring the situation under control; slave dealers were caught and imprisoned for violations of these orders.[33] However, this was not enough to eliminate the practice, and because the injured group received only partial satisfaction, discontent and anger among its members increased. On the other hand, the government went far enough in its measures to antagonize the slaveholders, who opposed any interference with their right of ownership over their slaves. Thus, rather than satisfying all, the government's half-measures satisfied none. Exacerbated by this policy, the already existing tension soon led to open hostilities.

Violence and a Change in Government Policy—the *Mükatebe*

On 9 September 1866 the governor of the province of Edirne reported to the grand vezir that in the village of Mandira violent clashes had erupted between Circassian slaveholders and their slaves. The issue was the slaves' status. A few policemen were sent to stop the fighting, but they were barred from entering the village. When the authorities learned about this, they immediately dispatched more policemen under the command of a *binbaşı* (rank equivalent to major). This time, the police managed to control the situation and put an end to the skirmish, but the dispute that had caused it remained unresolved. The slaves demanded to be freed, and the slaveholders refused to manumit them. The governor reported that he had sent one of his staff officers to the village to mediate between the factions. He was concerned, however, that with four hundred households of refugees—all armed—fighting could be resumed at any time. Therefore, the governor suggested that the

33. For examples of repeated orders, see entries 34 (for the year 1281/1864–65); 84 (for the year 1282/1865–66); both in BA/BAEO/Muhacirîn Komisyonu/vol. 758. For arrest of slave dealers, see BA/İrade/Meclis-i Vâlâ/24924 and 26185.

villagers be disarmed, and he asked the grand vezir to authorize this move.[34]

This incident was not an isolated case, and the situation greatly alarmed the Ottoman government. The immediate effect was to stop the practice that had probably upset the Circassian slaveholders most—that is, the issuing of manumission papers by some Şerî courts to children of parents belonging to the slave class. This practice was apparently encouraged by the government even against the will of the masters, but in the face of violent opposition the Porte was obliged to retract its orders on the matter.[35] Two reasons were given for the change of policy.

One was that the slave owners considered the offspring of their slaves as their own property, and the government was reluctant to tamper with old and established Circassian practices; this particular view, we may note, was not in conflict with the Şeriat. The large number of refugees and the "savage and vile" nature of the majority of them were blamed for the difficulties. The other reason was legal: it was contrary to the Şeriat to effect manumission without the master's consent unless ill-treatment could be proved. The government had adopted the policy of manumitting children of slaves probably because it miscalculated the violent opposition such a policy would generate. In an effort to accommodate both sides, the authorities now decided that, when slaves complained, attempts would be made to reconcile the parties and induce them to conclude a *mükatebe*. But the Porte also realized that a more thorough review of the whole issue was necessary.

On 30 March 1867 the Council of Ministers discussed the recommendations of the Immigration Commission and the High Council

34. Enclosure 5, telegram from Mehmet Hurşit Paşa, governor of Edirne, to the grand vezir, 21 Eylûl 1285 (5:10 p.m.)/1.10.69, BA/İrade/Meclis-i Mahsus/1407. It is not known what was done in this case, but a later document may shed some light on the fate of the villagers. In a government report of 4 June 1879, the Circassians of the village of Mandira are mentioned as having been moved to Anatolia and given land for settlement there; they were forbidden to return to Rumelia (*mazbata* of the Council of Ministers, 13 Cemaziyülâhir 1296/4.6.79, BA/İrade/Meclis-i Mahsus/2926). It is possible that the relocation took place after further clashes, but it could be unrelated to these events altogether.

35. The Porte to the president (of the High Council for Judicial Ordinances?), 29 Ramazan 1283/4.2.67, BA/Âyniyat/vol. 1136. For other violent incidents, see enclosure 1, *mazbata* of the High Council for Judicial Ordinances, 5 Zilkâde 1283/11.3.67, BA/İrade/Meclis-i Mahsus/1407; Blunt, *People of Turkey*, vol. 1, p. 150.

for Judicial Ordinances on slavery and the slave trade among the Circassian refugees.[36] The Circassian *emirs* traditionally held some of their people as slaves, the council observed, and they continued to do so after their entry into the empire. As Muslims, and like all Ottoman subjects, the Circassian refugees were entitled to the full benefits of Ottoman citizenship, one of which was freedom. Nevertheless, the council ruled, the mere act of migration could not abrogate Circassian slavery, an old, well-established institution. Because the number of slaves in the refugee population was estimated at over 150,000, measures had to be taken that would ensure that disputes over personal status were resolved in a peaceful manner.

Since earlier attempts to restore slaves to freedom without their owners' consent had been met with strong and often violent opposition, the ministers advocated the conclusion of a *mükatebe* as the best possible solution. Being a voluntary contract, the *mükatebe* had the advantage of securing the manumission of the slave while providing a fair compensation to the owner. However, in order to induce a slaveholder to conclude such a contract, the compensation (*bedel-i ıtk,* "manumission fee") had to be worthwhile. The slaves themselves could hardly be expected to come up with the necessary fee, so leaving the matter at that would have been tantamount to perpetuating the stalemate. Aware of this, the ministers decided that the government would have to bear the cost of its proposed reform policy. In this respect, the attitude of the Ottoman government was not unique; in many other areas, various kinds of compensation were granted to powerful slave-owning elites—presumably to offset their expected economic losses—in order to secure the liberation of slaves and abolish the institution.[37]

With the Ottoman Treasury in chronic deficit and heavily in debt to foreign creditors, all the government could offer as compensation was land. During the period of settlement, land was allocated to the refugees for cultivation, and with government approval, adjacent lots were given to slave families for the same purpose. The authorities, the Council of Ministers noted, had been treating the slaves as free

36. The grand vezir to the sultan, 24 Zilkâde 1283/30.3.67, BA/İrade/Meclis-i Mahsus/1407.

37. Stanley L. Engerman, "Slavery and Emancipation in Comparative Perspective: A Look at Some Recent Debates," *Journal of Economic History* 46/2 (1986): 330.

refugees, and gradually some of them were manumitted. The ministers proposed now to continue this policy and to allow the slaves to use these government lands as their manumission fee. To facilitate that, a method of assessing the value of the land and that of the slaves would be devised. The land would then be transferred to the slave owner as a full or partial compensation, according to the *mükatebe;* after which, manumission would be granted. Slaves who gained their freedom in this way could, with the consent of their former masters, remain on the land and continue to cultivate it.[38] However, if the freed slaves wished to leave the estate, they could do so. In this way, the ministers observed, the land would be tilled and inhabited, many slaves would be manumitted, and the slaveholders too would be satisfied. It was nevertheless made clear that such an arrangement would not be imposed by the government on the refugees; officials were to be sent to explain the proposed policy to the leaders of the Circassians, get their reaction, and report it to the Porte.

This decision of the Council of Ministers was a setback for the slaves. A *mükatebe* could not be imposed on a slave owner who had not flagrantly mistreated a slave; the policy also gave greater leverage to the Şerî courts, before which such procedures were normally conducted. Apparently, the government was unable to overcome the strong opposition of the Circassian slaveholders, or possibly, it simply preferred to avoid a direct, and undoubtedly bitter, confrontation with them. The readiness with which the Şerî courts were issuing orders supporting the position of slaveholders against the claims of their slaves put the government in a difficult situation. In both cases cited above (that of the five boys who demanded their freedom and that of the family who resisted separation), as well as in others, the courts impeded the authorities' actions which were meant to benefit the slaves.[39]

This may be indicative of a general mood in religious circles, one which upheld the legality of slavery because it was sanctioned by Islam. The government, it should be stressed, was consistently careful

38. Although this provision was not mentioned in the council's report, it becomes apparent from a later *mazbata* on the issue (see draft of minutes of the Council of Ministers, 19 Rebiülevvel 1299/8.2.82, BA/Meclis-i Vükelâ Mazbata ve İrade Dosyaları/vol. 225).

39. See, e.g., the Porte to the Immigration Commission, 21 Sefer 1286/2.6.69, BA/Âyniyat/vol. 1136, no. 210.

in emphasizing that slavery, as distinct from the slave trade, was not to be interfered with. The Persian Gulf *ferman* (decree) of 1847, the prohibition of the Circassian and Georgian slave trade in 1854–55, and the *ferman* of 1857 against the traffic in Africans come to mind in this context. It was only the institution of agricultural slavery among the Circassians that the Porte was trying to dismantle, and in the face of strong opposition, it proceeded gradually, with great caution, and somewhat diffidently.

It is interesting to note that in documents of the Council of Ministers concerning the abovementioned *fermans* of 1847 and 1854, the term used to denote slavery in the context of abolition was neither *esaret* nor *kölelik* but rather the less common *rıkkiyet,* the term usually employed in Şerî legal language. This was, perhaps, an indication of how much slavery was still being considered within an Islamic context at the time. Religious and conservative opposition, which had played an important role in shaping government policy with regard to the African slave trade,[40] was probably also behind the decision of the Council of Ministers to prefer the procedure of the *mükatebe* to more drastic measures and to make the application of the procedure contingent upon its acceptance by the refugees' leaders, most of whom were slaveholders.

In the absence of the determination, or perhaps the ability, to formulate and implement a clear policy in regard to Circassian slavery and slave trade, there was no peace among the refugees. Consequently, the authorities were often obliged to extinguish fires whose outbreak they had failed to prevent.

More Violence, the Slaves, and the Draft

Several times during 1872 the Ottoman government received information that groups of Circassian slave dealers in various parts of Anatolia were conspiring to continue the traffic despite government orders which restricted the trade and even suspended it altogether for a while. Authorities in the provinces of Sivas, Konya, and Adana were instructed to investigate and halt such activities. Similar allegations were being investigated in the province of Sinop in the same year. In the province of Hüdavendigâr and the *sancak*s of

40. See Toledano, *Ottoman Slave Trade,* p. 99 n. 12.

Canik and Lâzistan, reports regarding the establishment of secret societies (sing., *cemiyet-i hafiye*) to promote the slave trade were investigated and found to be without foundation.[41]

In August 1874 it was reported that in the area of Çorlu, a town in the province of Tekfurdağ and not far from Istanbul, a large number of Circassian slaves had organized and demanded their freedom. The slaveholders, also Circassian refugees, refused to grant manumission unless it was purchased by the slaves; they tried to impose their will on the recalcitrant slaves by force of arms. On the Porte's orders, the governor of Edirne moved immediately to subdue the slaveholders. He brought troops and four field-guns to Çorlu and read to the *emirs* an instruction from the Porte enjoining them to lay down their weapons and to accept the government's terms. These terms conformed to the general policy as formulated in the abovementioned decision of the Council of Ministers. Accordingly, the slaves were to be manumitted and the masters compensated by gaining ownership over the lands previously occupied and cultivated by the slaves. The exact value of the slaves and their plots, as well as the ways of making up the differences between land value and slave value where such existed, was to be determined by an ad hoc commission. If the government's demands were not met, the governor warned, the army would attack. The slaveholders surrendered their arms and accepted the Porte's mediation.[42]

In the settlement that followed, the slaves were liberated and removed—some 250 "*araba* [carriage] loads" of them—from Çorlu

41. Orders to check activities can be found in entries 211, 215, the Porte to the Immigration Commission, 28 Sevval 1288/10.1.72; 237, 239, the Porte to the Immigration Commission, 3 Zilkâde 1288/14.1.72; in BA/Âyniyat/vol. 1136. For the Sinop investigation, see entry 127, the Porte to the Immigration Commission, 24 Rebiülâhir 1289/1.7.72, BA/Âyniyat/vol. 1136. Secret societies are mentioned in entries 237, 239, the Porte to the Immigration Commission, 3 Zilkâde 1288/14.1.72; 255, 256, the Porte to the Immigration Commission, 12 Zilkâde 1288/23.1.72; in BA/Âyniyat/vol. 1136.

42. Depuis (vice-consul, Edirne) to Elliot, 12.8.74, PRO, FO 84/1397/180–81. This arrangement was reported by the British vice-consul in Edirne in a somewhat confusing manner. The first dispatch asserted that no compensations would be paid by the slaves themselves, but the second dispatch (Depuis to Elliot, 28.8.74, PRO, FO 84/1397/184–85) mentioned that a special commission would determine the amounts to be paid by the slaves. This was probably a result of the vice-consul's ignorance of the Council of Ministers' decision of 30 March 1867, as his reports do not indicate any awareness of the fact that this was not a unique settlement but rather part of a broader policy based on precedents and formulated to deal with a large number of cases.

to other parts of the province. They were to be distributed among the villages in the interior, one family per village, and allotted land for cultivation. About ninety of the most belligerent slaveholders were arrested. Another fire was put out, but the unrest caused by master-slave relations continued to demand the government's attention in other parts of the empire.

In 1878–79 more groups of Circassian slaves claimed their freedom, and some even asked for permission to return to the Caucasus.[43] The legal ambiguity which enveloped the status of the refugee slaves must have served the interests of the Ottoman government, for no serious attempt was made to clarify matters, say by issuing an imperial *ferman* which would set the basic guidelines. Decisions were being made to resolve specific cases, but when some government officials or local authorities tried—somewhat timidly, it appears—to interpret such decisions as having general applicability, the Porte moved to block their efforts. The confusion that necessarily resulted does not seem to have affected the situation too adversely and might have actually served the Porte's ends best. To illustrate this point I will examine a few cases.

In September 1878 the province of Kastamonu addressed the Council of State (Şura-yı Devlet) in regard to a problem of ownership which arose among the refugees.[44] A number of Abaza refugees who had come to Kastamonu fifteen and twenty years earlier claimed ownership over a group of other Abaza refugees who had recently moved into the empire from Sohum. The recent arrivals asserted that the Russian government, presumably acting in lieu of the absent owners, had concluded *mükatebe* agreements with them and handed them certificates of manumission. This seems to have been a happy marriage of Russian and Islamic practices, since the Russian state, which was accustomed to owning serfs, took over effective ownership from the expelled Circassian owners and then agreed to act as a Şerî slaveholder and manumit the slaves. In consequence of this action, the slaves claimed to be free and to owe nothing to their

43. See, e.g., entries 89 (29 Şabân 1295/18.8.78) and 168 (12 Sevval 1296/29.8.79), BA/BAEO/Muhacirîn Komisyonu/vol. 758. The request to return is in entry 196 (22 Zilkâde 1295/17.11.78), BA/BAEO/Muhacirîn Komisyonu/vol. 758.

44. Draft of minutes of the Council of Ministers, 19 Rebiülevvel 1299/8.2.82, BA/Meclis-i Vükelâ Mazbata ve İrade Dosyaları/vol. 225 (reference to the letter from the province of Kastamonu, 22 Ramazan 1295/20.9.78).

former Circassian masters. Although legally open to challenge—a non-Muslim government assuming the role of master over Muslim slaves, contracting with them as such, and manumitting them—the procedure was accepted by the Council of State, which in a ruling dated 24 October 1878 rejected the claims of the former masters.

The council stated that "persons who immigrated to the Ottoman Empire should be considered free *[hür],*" which clearly implied general applicability. It was indeed taken to mean exactly that by no less an authority than the Porte itself. Early in 1879 the local authorities in the provinces of Trabzon and Sivas were being confronted with strong demands from Abaza slaves to be freed from bondage, and the central government was called upon to help settle the dispute.[45] Basing its decision on the Council of State's ruling, the Porte apprised the governors of these provinces that all refugees were in fact free and that it was therefore illegal to claim them as slaves. The governors were ordered to ensure that no improprieties were resorted to by the former slaveholders and that the freedom of the slaves was guaranteed. However, it seems that this policy ran into difficulties, which, in February 1882, caused the government to review its position.

The Ottomans expected that the Circassian refugees would contribute to the manpower potential of the imperial army. They were granted a twenty-five-year exemption from military service but encouraged to enlist as volunteers.[46] Several cavalry units were formed for them, and many indeed agreed to serve in the sultan's forces. The military offered food, shelter, clothes, and a way of life which many Circassians preferred to farming. But, after some time, these units had to be disbanded because of the unruliness of the refugees, who resisted discipline and, reportedly, even killed some of their Ottoman officers. The army drafted only free men, including slaves who had gained their legal freedom. However, the government soon found out that this arrangement left out a large number of potential soldiers.

Early in 1882, military authorities in the province of Sivas attempted to register the refugee slaves in the draft lists which were

45. The Porte to the Ministry of Justice, 12 Nisan 1295/25.4.79, BA/Âyniyat/vol. 1011, no. 148.

46. Pinson, "Ottoman Colonization," pp. 80–82. Pinson mentions a twenty-year exemption, but, according to Ottoman sources, the exemption was for twenty-five years (see the province of Kastamonu to the Cabinet, 22 Ramazan 1295/20.9.78, BA/Meclis-i Vükelâ Mazbata ve İrade Dosyaları/vol. 225).

being drawn up in the province at the time.[47] The slaveholders, of course, opposed the move, since it would have deprived them of their right of ownership over their slaves from the time of the men's entry into the army. The Council of State, to which the matter had been referred, acknowledged that a blanket conscription, regardless of personal status, was bound to create problems between master and slave and needed careful consideration. The Sivas authorities were therefore instructed to postpone action until a decision was reached by the Council of Ministers.

The Council of Ministers discussed the issue in detail on 8 February 1882. Already at the outset, the council affirmed its support for the procedure of *mükatebe* as the only way to redress the grievances of slaves and to grant them their freedom. The ministers ruled that the decision of the Council of State regarding the Abaza slaves from Kastamonu applied only to that case. The declaration that all refugees were actually free was based on error. The Ministry of the Interior was instructed to clarify that point to the Immigration Commission and to ensure that the erroneous statement was corrected. Having laid down this basic principle, the council proceeded to decide the question of the draft.

Here, the ministers confirmed the policy which granted the refugees a twenty-five-year exemption from military service and stated that a thorough investigation should be conducted in each case to establish the length of time elapsed from the date of the refugee's entry into the empire. Refugees' children born in the Ottoman Empire were to be drafted upon reaching the age of twenty. In addition, the council went on to establish an important principle.

Since in most places slaves had been given separate land near that allotted to their masters, it was "only natural," the ministers argued, that, after twenty-five years, they too would join the army. According to previously formulated guidelines, a *mükatebe* would then be concluded and the land cultivated by the slave would revert to his master to cover, wholly or in part, the manumission fee. The council noted that even if the slave remained indebted to his master—the value of the land that he and his family cultivated falling short of his own market value—he first had to serve his term in the army, since "defending one's country is the highest of all duties."

47. BA/Meclis-i Vükelâ Mazbata ve İrade Dosyaları/vol. 225.

The debt could be paid to the master after the manumitted slave had completed his service. The specific case of drafting the Circassian slaves in Sivas was referred to the Council of State for further deliberation.

It appears that in its decision on the draft, the council wished to achieve two goals at once. On the one hand, the ruling made a large number of slaves eligible for military service; on the other hand, it devised a mechanism for speeding up the manumission of the whole Circassian slave population. Stopping short of explicitly imposing a *mükatebe* on the master, the council implied a regularity of procedure which had to have general applicability. Nevertheless, nothing was said about the status of the families of slaves who would be drafted. Unfortunately, the paucity of available information on the matter makes it impossible at this stage to examine how the council's decision was actually implemented or what effects it had on the gradual process of manumitting the Circassian slaves. As regards the rest of the slave population (i.e., those not intended for military service, such as women, men over forty years old, disabled men, etc.), the cornerstone of government policy was still manumission through *mükatebe*. On this, the ministers were clear and adamant: no device other than the conclusion of a *mükatebe* was acceptable for resolving disputes between owner and slave.

Thus, the Council of Ministers was acting—by reaffirming the preeminence of the *mükatebe*—to stifle the tendency, expressed by the declaration of the Council of State and its adoption by some local authorities and government officials, to grant automatic manumission to all refugee slaves. One can, of course, ascribe this inconsistency of policy within the various branches of the administration and the seeming confusion merely to bureaucratic incompetence on the part of the Ottoman government. This, however, would be simplistic and unsatisfactory. After Abdülhamit II firmly established control over the government, no later than 1878, the Ottoman bureaucracy was fairly effective in carrying out the policies of the highly centralized administration. This is borne out by the available archival material, which can hardly support charges of laxity or ineptitude on the part of the central government even for much of the Tanzimat period; the situation in the provinces, of course, was quite different. We need, then, to look for explanations elsewhere.

Assessment of Ottoman Policy on Circassian Slavery

As ALREADY MENTIONED, it is feasible to assume that the ambiguity in the government's policy on Circassian slavery and slave trade actually served the interests of the Porte. It can be argued that the government deliberately refrained from clarifying matters in this area to enable itself to maneuver with greater ease between the rival factions in order to defuse tensions. On one side were the slaves, a sizable group, who demanded to be freed; on the other stood the slaveholders, influential men whom the government needed in order to communicate effectively with and control the whole of the Circassian population. Both parties had access to arms and were certainly capable of violence. Religious and conservative elements who opposed what could have amounted to the abolition of slavery in the empire, or at least what they thought might be a significant step toward it, lent their support to the slaveholders. The irony of this is, of course, that when they were in the Caucasus, the Circassians were only nominally Muslim. They maintained their own customary law and traditions, which often contradicted Islamic law. After their expulsion, however, it was the Şeriat which offered the slaveholders the best protection against government interference with their rights over their slaves. At the time, the Porte had neither the desire nor perhaps the power to side openly with one party, thereby bringing about a serious, probably armed and violent, clash with the other. So it chose the middle way.

All that notwithstanding, it is possible to say that the general mood of the Ottoman government was sympathetic to the slaves' demands. This becomes clear from the minutes of the Council of Ministers. In both 1867 and 1882, when Circassian slavery was discussed, the council stated that all Ottoman subjects were free persons.[48] In 1867 the ministers even rejected the use of the term "slave" in reference to any Ottoman subject, no doubt reflecting the debate over citizenship rights at the time. In 1882 the existence of a prohibition on the slave trade in Africans was mentioned, and the continuation of Circassian slavery was decried as being contrary to the proper

48. The grand vezir to the sultan, 24 Zilkâde 1283/30.3.67, BA/İrade/Meclis-i Mahsus/1407; BA/Meclis-i Vükelâ Mazbata ve İrade Dosyaları/vol. 225.

and just order. In both cases, the old and deeply rooted Circassian traditions, and the government's lack of desire to meddle in them, were cited as the reasons for allowing the refugees to maintain slavery. Here, derogatory remarks on the "wild, savage, vile, and uncivilized nature" of the Circassians abound.[49] But some of the government's actions spoke louder than words.

In a number of cases (e.g., the sale of the four freeborn boys and the separation of the slave family, both mentioned above), the Porte challenged existing Şerî court orders regarding the status of the plaintiffs. An unorthodox *mükatebe* between the Russian government and some Abaza slaves was recognized, and the claims of the former owners were rejected. In a similar case, the freedom of the slaves was upheld, though it was alleged that only a partial manumission fee *(bedel-i cüzi)* had been paid to the Russians.[50] In other instances, manumission was granted to groups of slaves who could not reach a settlement with their masters. Even when accepting the principle of *mükatebe* as the only legitimate way for slaves to realize their freedom, the government offered to use state land to cover manumission fees; it thereby facilitated the conclusion of *mükatebe* contracts that would otherwise not have been concluded.

In the two incidents of slave-master riots mentioned earlier, the Porte's mediation was aimed at and resulted in the liberation of the slaves and their resettlement. Central and local authorities were instructed to prevent the kidnapping of freeborn children and their sale into slavery. In one case the Ottoman consuls in Potide and Tiflis successfully negotiated with the Russians the release of more than forty persons who had been enslaved by Circassians living on Russian territory.[51] These actions—probably just a sample of a more ramified whole, the records of which are either lost or at present

49. See, e.g., the Porte to the president of the Immigration Commission, 29 Ramazan 1283/4.2.67, BA/Âyniyat/vol. 1136; enclosure 3, Osman Paşa to the High Council for Judicial Ordinances, 21 Rebiülâhir 1283/3.9.66, BA/İrade Meclis-i Mahsus/1407; the Porte to the Ministry of Justice, 12 Nisan 1295/25.4.79, BA/Âyniyat/vol. 1011. Cevdet, who described the Circassians very favorably, nevertheless stated that no manners, as known to the civilized world, existed among them (*"beynlerinde âdab ve rüsüm-i medeniye yoktur"*; Cevdet, *Tarih*, vol. 1, p. 295).

50. The Russian *mükatebe* is in the *vâli* of Konya to the *baş kâtip*, decoded telegram, 22 Mayıs 1307/3.6.91, BA/Yıldız/K35/2027/44/109.

51. The grand vezir to the sultan, 28 Zilhicce 1281/24.5.65 (and enclosures), BA/İrade/Hâriciye/12344. Some of these people were sold, presumably against their will, and the others were captured and enslaved after their boat had been wrecked near

unavailable—reflect the government's sympathetic attitude toward the slaves' complaints. Given this attitude, we may now ask what motivated the Porte to adopt it and, furthermore, what prevented a rigorous and uncompromising pursuit of a policy commensurate with such an attitude.

It has been suggested that the Ottoman government wanted to put an end to the slave trade in adult men among the Circassian refugees in order to channel as many of them as possible into the army.[52] This, however, ignores the important class distinctions within Circassian society between free persons and slaves. Four points should be made clear in this respect:

1. Men and women belonging to the slave class—and that included all Circassian agricultural slaves—were ineligible for military service.
2. For the most part, the Circassian slave trade targeted members of the slave class (*köle* or *cariye cinsi,* male or female slaves, as the case might be).
3. Even when freeborn persons were sold into slavery—which occurred more frequently during and after the Circassian influx—they were mostly young girls, who would never be drafted into the army, or boys who would not have been eligible for service before another ten or fifteen years would pass.
4. The only group regarding which military considerations could have played a part would have been freeborn adult males or teenage boys who were sold into slavery and thus became ineligible for military service. This group was very small and it would therefore be incorrect to suggest that the Porte's attempt to suppress the Circassian slave trade emanated from military considerations.

Rather, it is more likely that in this area of child trafficking, the main concern of the Ottoman government was to prevent the sale of freeborn Muslims into slavery. As noted, such sales were strictly forbidden by Islamic law. In sales of this kind, the government intervened, especially when deception was involved or the consent of the child's family had not been obtained.

---

the Russian coast. Russian cooperation in obtaining the release of the slaves is cited. The Ottoman vice-consul at Potide was recommended for a medal for his part in the negotiations.

52. Pinson, "Ottoman Colonization," pp. 81–82.

What did have bearing on recruitment to the army was the existence of a large class of agricultural slaves among the Circassians. Since only free men could be drafted, the manpower potential was, of course, reduced. Thus, the government's efforts to help these slaves to secure their freedom might have been motivated by the desire to make them eligible for the draft. There is no mention in Ottoman sources of any such considerations before 1882. While this is no proof that they did not play a role in shaping the Porte's policy, there seems to be no reason that mention of them should have been avoided in memoranda or minutes of the various councils—the argument itself being legitimate and even honorable. No attempt was made to conceal the military consideration when the imposition of the draft on refugee slaves was discussed by the Council of Ministers in February 1882. In any event, the military factor alone cannot account for government policy regarding Circassian slavery and slave trade.

The possibility that the Porte acted favorably toward the Circassian slaves in order to impress upon the European powers its enlightened and progressive disposition should be discounted. Nor can we say that any of the Porte's actions were taken under European pressure. The Ottoman government never reported to the foreign powers, not even to Britain—naturally interested in the matter—any of its actions concerning Circassian slavery and slave trade. In 1865 the Porte told the British ambassador, in response to his inquiry, about some of the plans that were being prepared by the Immigration Commission to cope with the problem. The British remonstrances regarding the clashes between Circassian slaveholders and their slaves were left unanswered. This was a domestic matter and the Ottoman government wanted to make sure that, unlike the traffic in Africans, it remained so.

We may, then, consider two other possible explanations, one pragmatic, the other cultural. Being practically minded, consecutive Ottoman governments realized full well that one of their most important tasks was to maintain public order (*hıfz-ı asayiş*). They had to contain sources of discontent which might disrupt law and order; failing to do so, they had to pacify the parties involved and restore order. The tension arising from the disaffection of the Circassian slaves with their masters and from outrage over deceitful slave dealing clearly endangered the public order in the empire. Frequent kidnapping and small-scale violence, occasional outbreaks of serious hostilities, and brigandage by bands of manumitted slaves who—through *mükatebe* agreements—lost the land plots they had been cultivating,[53] were some of the most conspicuous manifestations of the problem. The desire to defuse this growing tension has to be seen as the main driving force behind the government's actions regarding Circassian slavery and slave trade.

In forming the unfavorable attitude toward Circassian slavery which the Ottoman government came to hold during and after the Circassian influx into the empire, cultural differences certainly played an important role. Though ostensibly Muslim, the Circassians in fact retained many of their customs and practices, especially in the area of personal law, which also governed slavery. They were welcomed as refugees to the empire for reasons at once pragmatic and humanitarian, yet they were regarded by the Ottomans—and ample evidence of this is available[54]—as uncivilized and barbarian. The spirit of pluralism, though on the wane as a result of growing nationalism in the Balkans and of the increasing alignment between minorities and foreign powers, still held together this multinational empire. In that spirit, the Circassians were allowed to maintain their customs and social institutions, including their agricultural slavery.

Although slavery was practiced in the Ottoman Empire and the slave trade was still being pursued, agricultural slavery existed only among the Circassian refugees. Albeit subject to some restrictions of their freedom, mainly that of movement, peasants in the Ottoman Empire were free persons, not slaves. Hence, the Ottomans looked upon holding farmhands and their families in slavery with contempt and considered it socially backward. Ottoman slavery was mostly domestic and, in its nature, milder than the agricultural slavery prevalent among the refugees. The sale of children by their parents was also regarded as a "strange custom" *(adet-i garibe)*, which—being un-Islamic—was sure to bring upon the sellers damnation both in this world and the next.[55] These views must have had an impact on Ottoman policy and most likely led to the government's favorable disposition toward Circassian slaves and their demands.

53. On brigandage by manumitted slaves, see BA/Meclis-i Vükelâ Mazbata ve İrade Dosyaları/vol. 225.

54. For some examples, see Pinson, "Ottoman Colonization," pp. 81–82.

55. To cite only one of many examples: enclosure 3, Osman Paşa to the High Council for Judicial Ordinances, 21 Rebiülâhir 1283/3.9.66, BA/İrade/Meclis-i Mahsus/1407.

Why then, we must ask, did the Porte fail to enact a strong and clear policy on the issue, which would then be rigorously enforced? The answer lies in the nature and events of the time. The problems caused by the mass influx of the Circassian tribes into the empire in the years 1864–66 were indeed enormous. The government's lack of preparedness, and later its inability to cope with these problems, resulted in a chaotic process of settlement, which disrupted the life of the peasantry and increased discontent and lawlessness in the countryside. This period of transition also affected class relations among the Circassians themselves. The slaves felt less bound by the old social structure and, aware of changing realities and the breakdown of authority, challenged their masters' right of ownership.[56] Given the bellicose nature of the parties and the availability of arms, the situation was potentially explosive; and, whereas a one-sided policy might have produced a more rapid and drastic solution, it was also sure to result in a violent confrontation.

During the period under discussion, the Ottoman government could not afford even to risk such a confrontation, which would have added to its already numerous and pressing problems. We should remember that these were indeed troubled years in Ottoman history, a time of almost incessant external and internal difficulties that nearly destroyed the empire. Rebellions and attempts, ultimately successful, to achieve independence in virtually all of its European provinces, war with Russia on both the western and the eastern fronts, trouble in Lebanon, and the loss of Tunis and Egypt to France and Britain, respectively, kept the government fully occupied. Internal dissent, the Palace-Porte power struggle, financial bankruptcy, the turmoil preceding and following the promulgation of the 1876 Constitution, and the constant meddling by the European powers in the empire's domestic affairs, all left little desire in the councils of state for avoidable confrontations.

Thus, the government chose the middle road. It neither abolished Circassian slavery altogether nor fully supported the slaveholders' rejection of any changes in the status quo. Rather, it advocated manumission through *mükatebe* and facilitated the conclusion of

56. For assessment of the Ottoman efforts to absorb and settle the Circassian refugees, see Pinson, "Ottoman Colonization," pp. 80–81, 83–85; on the challenge to masters' authority, see also Blunt, *People of Turkey*, pp. 146–47.

such contracts by offering state land as manumission fee. Contested slave dealings were prohibited, but the government often turned a blind eye on trade involving "consenting adults" (excluding the slaves themselves, of course), and occasionally, according to circumstances, the Porte suspended even that traffic.

When we analyze the actions of the Ottoman government in comparative terms, we find that the series of steps taken during the second half of the nineteenth century eroded the foundations on which the institution of slavery was predicated. It is true that by giving the slaves recourse to the justice system, the Şeriat violated the total exclusivity of the owner-slave relationship. However, by allowing slaves access to the Immigration Commission and other government organs, the Ottomans restricted that exclusivity further, sometimes in a significant way. In that sense, the Ottomans moved on a course similar to that taken by various colonial states in Africa. What comes to mind in this context is the policy promulgated by the British high commissioner of northern Nigeria (1900–1906) Frederick D. Lugard, who preferred *mükatebe*-type solutions ("self-ransom" in the English terminology used then) arranged through the Islamic courts to government-imposed emancipation.[57]

In the same manner, the Ottoman government limited the market for slaves by restricting their transferability and by encouraging legal manumission through the *mükatebe*. By liberalizing the criteria for establishing free status, the Porte made it easier to avoid the heritability of slave status, thereby also restricting the size of the slave population and moving closer to the elimination of the practice altogether. Although no policy of abolishing slavery was ever adopted by the Ottoman government, the administrative measures it in fact resorted to ensured that the result would ultimately be to severely curtail slavery in the empire. Such an attitude is fully ingrained in Ottoman political culture, which was patient, mindful of the long term, gradual, indirect, always pragmatic, and in many cases ultimately quite effective.

57. See Paul E. Lovejoy and Jan S. Hogendorn, eds., *Slow Death for Slavery: The Course of Abolition in Northern Nigeria, 1897–1936* (Cambridge, 1993), pp. 98–126. In this case, Lugard might be said to have acted in the Ottoman way; when serving in East Africa, his previous posting, he strongly advocated self-ransom, but his plan was thwarted by the more radical abolitionists, who preferred to have slaves ransomed by the missions and the Imperial British East Africa Company (ibid., pp. 99–101).

FOUR

Slavery and Abolition

The Battle of Images

Thus far, we have treated the two most problematic and complex types of Ottoman slavery: *kul/harem* and agricultural. *Kul/harem* slavery was mainly an urban phenomenon, and by the nineteenth century the numbers involved were relatively small. Agricultural bondage among the Circassians was a rural institution, and although the slave population concerned was fairly large, it existed on the margins of Ottoman society, not at the core. Both categories consisted of non-African slaves, with the Caucasus supplying the lion's share. In the main urban centers of the empire, however, the overwhelming majority of the slaves—and of those imported into the empire—were domestic, female, and African, a social group that differed in many ways from the other two groups of Ottoman slaves.

Albeit important in itself and well deserving of a separate study, domestic slavery in the Ottoman Empire does not constitute, in my view, a major analytical stumbling block to the understanding of Ottoman slavery. Hence, greater attention has been devoted in chapters 1–3 to the less familiar and more ambiguous types of slavery practiced in the sultan's domains; I have treated the slave trade from Africa into the empire at great length elsewhere.[1] However,

1. Toledano, *Ottoman Slave Trade*, deals mostly with that traffic.

this chapter and the next will deal with two different aspects of Ottoman slavery as a whole—including urban domestic bondage of Africans. In this chapter I shall analyze the way in which the Ottoman officeholding and intellectual elites viewed slavery, and in chapter 5 I shall discuss the ways in which Ottoman slavery has been studied and written about.

In the following pages, the attitude of Ottoman statesmen and writers (many of whom were themselves slave owners) to slavery and their reaction to the European pressure to abolish it will be examined. This focus will reveal the bifurcated elite perception of *kul/harem* slavery versus domestic slavery. I shall also argue that it was the defense of *kul/harem* slavery that delayed full adoption of a clear abolitionist stance by the Ottoman governing elite. As already argued above, the slave-turned-general/minister and the *harem* lady were a small minority among Ottoman slaves and in some fundamental aspects were not "real" slaves nor seen as such. The Ottoman elite's refusal to repudiate *kul/harem* slavery clashed with the European insistence on lumping it together with the other—and far more painful—types of slavery. This inseparability ensured that the one could not be abolished without the other and only prolonged the suffering of domestic and agricultural slaves in the empire. But before we enter the thick of the matter, we ought to situate the story in its historical context.

One of the main themes of nineteenth-century Ottoman history is the process of change through reform from above. The period during which many reforms were carried out is known as the period of the Tanzimat, meaning "reforms," "reordering," "reorganization."[2] The Tanzimat is commonly considered to have been inaugurated by the Gülhane Rescript of 1839 and to have lasted through the first Ottoman constitution (1876) until the dissolution of Parliament and the renewal of sultanic autocracy in 1878, two years after the accession of Abdülhamit II (ruled 1876–1909). Since reforms had begun already in the 1830s and continued well into the reign of Abdülhamit II, I shall treat here what I call the "long-Tanzimat"

2. The standard accounts in English of the Tanzimat period are Bernard Lewis, *The Emergence of Modern Turkey* (Oxford, 1969); Roderic H. Davison, *Reform in the Ottoman Empire, 1856–1876* (Princeton, 1963); and Findley, *Bureaucratic Reform in the Ottoman Empire*.

period, spanning approximately the half century from the 1830s to the 1880s.

The Tanzimat period is generally regarded as a period of change in many areas of Ottoman life, although it is not certain how deeply the reforms affected non-elite groups—the overwhelming majority of Ottoman subjects—or even peripheral groups within the Ottoman elite. Visible changes in the army, the bureaucracy, the economy, law and justice, education, communication, transportation, and public health went along with the reinvigoration of central authority. While the government came to possess more efficient tools of repression, its reforms also sowed the seeds of political change, giving rise to a strong constitutional movement.

Too often, the Tanzimat was seen as a European-initiated and backed drive to import Western models and "modernize" the Ottoman Empire. However, modern scholarship has shown that the reforms were carried on the shoulders of a strongly motivated, Ottoman-centered group of able reformers, who were not merely the tools of Western influence but acted to implement their own agenda and further their own political program. On the other hand, the extent to which Western ideas—not just technology and fashion—were assimilated into Ottoman culture (integrated or "converted," in semiotic terms) is still under debate. Ideas about the security of life, honor, and property of the sultan's subjects figure already in the Gülhane Rescript of 1839. The concept of equality among all subjects, including non-Muslims, and notions of nationalism, liberty, political rights, and constitutionalism gained hold from the 1850s onward. Much more work is still needed on how these products of Western culture were understood, converted to Ottoman categories, and then consumed and disseminated.

A discussion of Ottoman slavery and slave trade during the Tanzimat offers a convenient opportunity to examine how the reformers contended with political and cultural "interference."[3] Except for the issue of equality for non-Muslims, the call for the abolition of Ottoman slavery was perhaps the most culturally loaded and sensi-

3. This concept is borrowed from literary and cultural historians and applied to the processes by which abolitionism was transferred (= converted) from Western (= source) culture into Ottoman (= target) culture. For an elaboration of the theory, see Even-Zohar's papers cited in n. 36, below.

tive topic processed in the Tanzimat period. Although it was rarely debated in public, it was a matter of daily and personal concern, since both the public and the private spheres of elite life were permeated by slaves on all levels. Encapsulating British diplomatic pressure for the suppression of the slave trade into the Ottoman Empire and the zeal of Western abolitionism,[4] abolitionism elicited a complex response from Ottoman reformers and thinkers on the political, as well as the ideological, plane. In that sense, slavery is an interesting—though not in all aspects typical—example of the critical choices confronting the Ottoman elite in the second half of the nineteenth century.

Thus, the history of Ottoman slavery went through one of its more eventful periods during the Tanzimat. It is, therefore, not surprising that scholars interested in the history of the institution have been attracted to the Tanzimat and the period that followed (see chapter 5). Whereas the political and socioeconomic aspects of the subject have received some attention in recent publications, the attitudes to slavery prevailing among Ottoman elite members and intellectuals have not been adequately treated. The publication in 1987 of İsmail Parlatır's study of slavery in the literature of the Tanzimat period goes a certain way toward filling that gap in modern scholarship.[5] I shall now take this work a few steps further and explore some of the more intriguing questions about Ottoman slavery and slave trade: How did Ottoman elite culture deal with the Western campaign against Ottoman slavery? How were Western notions of slavery received and processed? How did those notions affect attitudes to slavery in Ottoman society?

Ottoman Statesmen on Slavery

IT IS NOT WITHOUT FOUNDATION to argue that the politics of abolition and of suppression of the slave trade were nurtured

4. The term "abolitionism" is used throughout to denote the call for the abolition of slavery: in our case, in the Ottoman Empire from the 1840s onward. Abolitionism was the *idea* (= the cultural product) that Western, mostly British, culture tried to foist upon Ottoman elite culture.

5. İsmail Parlatır, *Tanzimat Edebiyatında Kölelik* (Ankara, 1987). Börte Sagaster is completing an extensive study about the ways in which slavery was viewed by Ottoman intellectuals during the last decades of the empire. Her thesis is tentatively entitled "Ottoman Attitudes to Slavery in Literary Sources as a Reflection of Ottoman Society at the Turn of the Twentieth Century" (see also the Conclusion, below, n. 26).

on strong moral sentiments, and that moral considerations motivated British pressure upon the Ottoman government on this issue, perhaps more overtly than on any other issue except that of equality for non-Muslim Ottoman subjects. The antislavery lobby in Britain was often seen by British politicians and diplomats as overzealous and lacking a sense of realpolitik. But they had to yield to its powerful evangelical appeal to the public and press the matter abroad even when they believed it to be useless or inexpedient. They too, however, seem to have welcomed the opportunity to trade, even if temporarily, the image of Perfidious Albion for that of the champion of a humanitarian cause. But when they met their Ottoman counterparts to discuss the issue, they soon found that no common ground could be reached if the moral basis of slavery was broached.

Perhaps no other issue during the Tanzimat so clearly pitted Ottoman against Western culture as slavery did. That moral flagship of Britain's civilizing mission sailed with all its zeal toward the Ottoman horizon, proudly flying its glorious colors. Curiously enough, however, the two "fleets" never really met. The few exchanges that will be treated below notwithstanding, Ottoman slavery and slave trade were never seriously debated, either on the political or on the intellectual plane. It was as if one party barged in fully armed with moral, economic, social, and political arguments, imbued with a strong sense of justice, while the other timidly turned its back, refusing to engage in a dialogue, claiming that there was basically no common ground, no common language, no frame of reference through which a true discussion could take place.

The nondialogue on slavery characterized British-Ottoman contacts on the subject from the outset. It was best expressed in the, by now famous, report of Lord Ponsonby, Britain's ambassador in Istanbul, to Lord Palmerston, the foreign secretary. Strongly urged by the Anti-Slavery Society, Palmerston instructed Ponsonby in November 1840 to clarify to the Ottoman government that, because of public opinion, continued British support depended on some action against slavery and the slave trade. In response, Ponsonby wrote (the emphases are mine):

> I have mentioned the subject and I have been heard with *extreme astonishment accompanied with a smile* at the proposition for destroying an institution closely interwoven with the frame of

> society in this country, and intimately connected with the law and with the habits and even the religion of all classes, from the sultan himself down to the lowest peasant. . . . I think that all attempts to effect your Lordship's purpose will fail, and I fear they might give *offence* if urged forward with importunity. The Turks may believe us to be their superiors in the Sciences, in Arts, and in Arms, but they are *far from thinking our wisdom or our morality greater than their own.*[6]

For much of the Tanzimat period, European abolitionist arguments were either taken as an offense or met with smiling dismissiveness, and thus, no real discussion of the issues could ensue. Since the question was immediately conceived in moral terms and translated into a competition between two value systems, no true exchange was possible. Subsequently, as already noted, Britain revised its goal from the abolition of Ottoman *slavery* to the suppression of the *slave trade* into the Ottoman Empire. However, it is noteworthy that for about a quarter of a century—from the 1840s to the 1860s—the Ottoman government, acting to accommodate its British ally, operated without an ideological support that would justify such a policy or endow it with meaning. For those who carried it out, this was change without genuine motivation, reform without conviction, a putting things "right" without accepting that they were indeed "wrong."

Throughout their dealings with the Tanzimat reformers, British diplomats noted that some of them were more inclined than others to assist in the suppression of the slave trade, for example, the leading reformer Mustafa Reşit Paşa, who served as grand vezir several times during the 1840s and 1850s. Some showed no interest whatsoever in promoting the cause, like another major reformer, Âli Paşa, who was grand vezir and foreign minister for a number of terms from the 1840s until his death in 1871. British records attribute the most forceful condemnation of slavery to Sultan Abdülmecit (ruled 1839–61), who reportedly told the first dragoman of the British embassy in Istanbul in 1851 that he hoped to abolish it in his dominions. "It is shameful and barbarous practice for rational beings to buy and sell their fellow creatures. Though slaves in Turkey are treated better than elsewhere, yet are they sometimes very ill-used. Are not

6. Ponsonby to Palmerston, 27.12.1840, PRO, FO 195/108.

these poor creatures our equals before God? Why then should they be assimilated to animals?"[7] Such evidence may indicate no more than that some Ottoman personages desired to impress their British interlocutors with their sincerity on this issue.

Nonetheless, Ottoman sources contain information suggesting that a few high- and middle-level officeholders supported anti–slave trade measures and even justified them in terms not entirely different from the language used in British discourse. In 1854, during the Crimean War, Grand Vezir Kıbrıslı Mehmet Emin Paşa forcefully argued in cabinet for a restriction of the slave trade in Circassians and Georgians. His view was praised by Mustafa Paşa, commander of the Batum Army during the war, in a letter to the British and French vice-admirals in the Black Sea. In 1860, Pertev Efendi, then governor of the Red Sea port of Massawa, strongly criticized slave raids in the Horn of Africa and proposed tough measures to stop them.[8]

Another example comes from the Ottoman regency of Tunis, which at the time enjoyed a very large measure of political autonomy, though it continued to belong to the same Islamic-Mediterranean-Ottoman culture. Under its reforming governor Ahmet Bey, Tunis tried to restrict the slave trade as early as 1841. On 31 October 1863 Husayn Paşa, the mayor of Tunis, literally turned the tables and assumed the role of an abolitionist preacher vis-à-vis the United States, then deeply embroiled in the bloody struggle of the Civil War. This was ten months after the Emancipation Proclamation and before the Thirteenth Amendment was passed by Congress on 1 February 1865 and ratified by two-thirds of the states at the end of the same year. The mayor addressed a letter to Amos Perry, the American consul general in Tunis, as a response to Perry's query regarding the Tunisian law on slavery.[9] In it, the obviously very Westernized official explains the Islamic concept of slavery and Ahmet Bey's policy to

7. Canning to Palmerston, 24.1.1851, PRO, FO 84/857/27–28.

8. Toledano, *Ottoman Slave Trade*, pp. 117–21, 206.

9. For details of attempts to restrict the slave trade in Tunisia, see Brown, *The Tunisia of Ahmad Bey*, pp. 321–25. Husayn Paşa's letter is cited in Salīm Fāris al-Shidyāq, ed., *Kanz al-Raghā᾽ib fī Muntakhab al-Jawā᾽ib* (Istanbul, 1295/1878), vol. 6, pp. 46–51. This text is also quoted in Ra᾽īf Khūrī, *Al-Fikr al-ʿArabī al-Hadīth* (Beirut, 1973), pp. 278–84. I could not locate the original text in the American archives, which may raise a question about the authenticity of the Arabic text. If the response is a forgery, we can ask who might have written it and for what purpose. Nonetheless, its very appearance in the *Kanz* in the late 1870s is in itself indicative of the changing views among certain literary

phase out the practice in Tunis. He then provides economic justification for abolition and argues that a free person is more productive than a slave, which accounts for the greater prosperity of countries where slavery no longer exists. The mayor concludes by urging the Americans—in the name of "human mercy and compassion"—to reconsider their attitude toward slavery.

Later in the century, we encounter additional cases of officials expressing criticism of the slave trade in the Ottoman Empire. In 1876, Midhat Paşa (a leading reformer and twice grand vezir in the 1870s) attempted, unsuccessfully, to include an anti–slave trade clause in the accession speech of Sultan Abdülhamit II.[10] As governor of Syria, Midhat Paşa suggested in 1879 the drastic measure of abolishing the pilgrimage caravan from Damascus to the Hijaz in order to prevent the importation of slaves into Syria. While this was never applied, other measures taken by the governor sharply reduced the traffic via that province during his tenure of office. On the less senior level of provincial administrators, we have in the 1880s the explicit condemnations of the slave trade by Ârifi Bey, governor of the major slaving port of Jidda, who described the trade as "repugnant."[11]

In almost all these cases, one can observe a fascinating cultural translation of Western-phrased opposition to slavery into Ottoman, indeed Islamic, terms. Not unexpectedly, the common ground here was humanitarian concern for the suffering of the slaves. This necessarily shifted the emphasis from slavery to the slave trade, thereby circumventing the futile head-on collision of values and mores, which was practically inevitable when slavery itself was touched.

Young Ottoman Writers on Slavery

OTTOMAN WRITERS AND INTELLECTUALS employed additional means of defusing the tension that any discussion of slavery seems to have produced, even when conducted within Ottoman society. But conclusive evidence of that internal debate comes only from

circles in Istanbul. See also Amos Perry to General Hussein (Husayn Paşa), 12.11.63, National Archives/Record Group 84, Tunis Consulate, pp. 178–80.

10. For a new interpretation of this peculiar episode, see Erdem, "Slavery in the Ottoman Empire," pp. 240–43. In his treatment the author also uses the published memoirs of Midhat Paşa's son.

11. See Toledano, *Ottoman Slave Trade*, pp. 229–31, 240.

very late in the Tanzimat period, that is, from the mid-1870s onward, though the debate certainly is still part and parcel of the phenomena generated by and associated with the Tanzimat.

The Young Ottomans were a leading group of writers, publicists, intellectuals, and activists who, from the 1860s to the late 1870s, opposed the Ottoman government for being too slow to introduce political and social reforms. One would intuitively expect such a group of socially aware people to adopt a clear position on slavery. However, it is indeed amazing how little interested in the institution and the traffic those men actually were. In his recent study of the treatment of slavery in Tanzimat literature, İsmail Parlatır rightly senses that opposition to slavery should follow naturally from support of political rights, liberty, equality, civil and human rights, for all of which the Young Ottomans firmly stood.[12] However, the evidence he adduces to back the claim that the Young Ottomans opposed slavery is insufficient. In fact, the very few statements that the subject elicited from leading Young Ottomans like Şinasi, Ali Suâvi, Ziya, and even Namık Kemal point out only too clearly how unenthusiastic they were to deal with it or how marginal they considered it to be to the larger issues they were fighting for.

Three factors underscore the Young Ottomans' virtual silence on slavery and suggest that it did not stem from mere indifference or insensitivity. First, as already alluded to, the subject matter undoubtedly belonged well in the realm of their concern. Second, these men spent much time in European capitals, where they also published their journals. Hence they could not be unaware of the currency of antislavery sentiments in Europe, nor were they constrained by censorship from printing their views on the matter, as perhaps they might have been within the Ottoman Empire. Third, they not infrequently used the *idiom* of slavery as a metaphor in their writings about political and social freedom. Even the name of Kemal and Ziya's journal, *Hürriyet* (freedom), is the Islamic legal opposite of the condition of slavery *(rıkkiyet* and *esaret)*.[13]

12. The best account of Young Ottoman thought is still Şerif Mardin, *The Genesis of Young Ottoman Thought* (Princeton, 1962). For Parlatır's comments, see Parlatır, *Tanzimat Edebiyatında Kölelik,* pp. 23–27.

13. The Şerî principle that governs issues relating to slave status asserts that "freedom is the overriding consideration" (*al-asl huwwa al-hurriyya* [= *hürriyet*]).

Note, for example, these lines from a poem written in 1856 by the prominent Young Ottoman writer Şinasi for the great reformer and grand vezir Mustafa Reşit Paşa (the emphases are mine):

> You have made us *free,* who were *slaves* to tyranny,
> *Bound as if in chains* by our own ignorance.
> Your law is an *act of manumission* for men.[14]

The slavery metaphor appears in other verses, such as by Sadullah Paşa ("Amr is not Zeyd's slave, nor is Zeyd Amr's master"), and in Namık Kemal's "Dream" (Rüyâ), where he plays on the words "slave" *(esir),* "slavery" *(esaret),* and "freedom" *(hürriyet).*[15] One may also quote Kemal's attack on Sultan Abdülaziz's speech in 1868 (the emphases are mine): "If the purpose is to imply that up to this day the people in the Ottoman Empire were the *slaves* of the sultan, who, out of the goodness of his heart, confirmed their *liberty,* this is something to which we can never agree, because, according to our beliefs, the rights of the people, just like divine justice, are immutable."[16]

However, when it came to Ottoman slavery, even Namık Kemal himself was not nearly as forceful. It was not until 1875 that he wrote the first of two plays in which slavery figures as a theme, although not as the main one. That play was not published until 1910. The second play was written in 1876 and treated the question of slavery in a secondary, though still noticeable, role. However, this surely fell short even of what another Young Ottoman, Ali Suâvi, might have had in mind when he suggested, in an article in *Hürriyet,* that the Young Ottomans "counsel" the nation to prevent the harm caused by slave trading in Istanbul.[17]

14. Cited in Lewis, *Emergence,* p. 137.

15. A translation of Sadullah's verse is in ibid., pp. 133–34 (Turkish text is cited in Parlatır, *Tanzimat Edebiyatında Kölelik,* p. 25). Kemal's verse is cited in Parlatır, *Tanzimat Edebiyatında Kölelik,* p. 26:

> Ne efsunkar imişsin ah ey didâr-i hürriyet
> Esiri aşkın olduk gerçi kurtulduk esaretten

16. Cited in Mardin, *Young Ottoman Thought,* p. 119.

17. Namık Kemal's *Kara Bela* (1875) is discussed in Parlatır, *Tanzimat Edebiyatında Kölelik,* pp. 130–32, and his *İntibah veyahut Âli Bey'in Següzeşti* (1876) is discussed in ibid., pp. 123–29. Ali Suâvi's appeal is cited in ibid., pp. 28–29.

Playwrights, Novelists, and Poets on Slavery

PARLATIR CITES SOME CLEAR-CUT condemnations of slavery and the slave trade by a number of celebrated Tanzimat writers. Dating from the mid-1870s onward, they were written mainly by Ahmet Midhat (who had fallen out with the Young Ottomans in the mid-1870s), Abdülhak Hamit, and Sâmi Paşazade Sezâi. Perhaps not surprisingly, all three had Circassian mothers brought to the empire as slaves, a phenomenon not uncommon among members of the Ottoman elite even during and after the Tanzimat period. The linkage between political freedom and the abolition of slavery—absent in the writing of leading Young Ottoman activists—is explicitly and naturally made by these novelists and playwrights. Yet, for them, too, Ottoman slavery was not a simple topic. As we shall see, they approached it carefully, as if treading on very thin ice.

Although the Tanzimat writers who deal in some measure with slavery are all critical of the practice, one feels that they are somehow reluctant to fully own up to it. In itself, that is an indication of the change that was taking place in the value system. This process manifests itself most strikingly in their total refusal to grant any resemblance between Western and Ottoman slavery. In an article published in 1869, Ahmet Midhat, one of the most prolific of nineteenth- and early-twentieth-century Ottoman writers, states categorically that "Europeans who do not know the manners and customs of the East think that slaves in Istanbul are like American slaves." In his plays, a clear dichotomy is drawn between Ottoman slavery and slavery elsewhere.[18]

Accordingly, American slaves are described as beasts *(behaim)* tied together to a wooden board, slaves in antiquity are said to have been regarded as animals *(hayvanat)* and not counted as human beings, and the killing of a Russian slave is alleged to have been considered no more than the killing of a dog. On the most vulnerable point, sexual relations, Midhat deflects Western insinuations embodied in the "*harem* fantasy" of male European literary fame.[19] Here, he

18. My interpretation in this and the following paragraph is based on a selection of Midhat's texts cited in Parlatır, *Tanzimat Edebiyatında Kölelik*, pp. 42–43. On Ahmet Midhat, see Lewis, *Emergence*, pp. 189–90.

19. Melman, *Women's Orients*, especially pp. 59 ff.

inverts the charge by stating that female slaves, in Russia for example, were sexually available *(istifraş edebilir)* to their masters even if married, a travesty of Islamic and Ottoman slavery.

Ottoman slavery, on the other hand, is described in humane, almost benign terms. The human sensitivity of Ottoman society is taken for granted and appealed to in order to mitigate the circumstances that surround slavery and the traffic that feeds it. Making a clear distinction between the nonhuman status of slaves in other societies and the status of slaves in Ottoman society, Tanzimat writers dwell mostly on *harem* slavery, which despite its sexual problematics was relatively the most comfortable type of servitude for women. The implication is that many of the slaves in Ottoman society were actual members of the elite. Thus, Ahmet Midhat—only an example here—states that many female slaves become queen mothers, that the overwhelming majority of the wives of Ottoman "noblemen" are of slave origin, that slavery is, in fact, a way of choosing one's wife, or lady of the house, and that slavery does not debase any female slave.[20]

This strong defense of Ottoman (actually Islamic) slavery vis-à-vis Western slavery comes from the same author who, in another play, strongly identifies with the pains of separation brought about by Ottoman slavery. The heroine, a young female slave, exclaims at one point: "May the eyes of those who sold us [into slavery] be blinded!" Ahmet Midhat, as narrator, concludes by saying: "I vowed never to buy a slave again. I began cursing the sellers and buyers [of slaves] for thus separating the poor children from their mothers and fathers and for causing this and thousands of similar painful tragedies."[21]

This striking contradiction reflects a very real and honest inner conflict. In the 1870s, patriotic, Westernized Ottomans were torn between a growing rejection of slavery and a deep attachment to their sociocultural heritage, of which they remained proud. They tried hard to reconcile the conflict between a system in which they were born and raised—often by mothers, wet nurses, nannies, and female relatives of slave origins—and the demands and principles of a foreign culture they grew to respect, wanted to acquire, and wished to be recognized by as equals.

20. Parlatır, *Tanzimat Edebiyatında Kölelik*, pp. 42–45.

21. Condemnation of slavery and quotations are from Ahmet Midhat's *Esaret* as printed in his collection *Letaif-i Rivayat* (Istanbul, 1290/1873–74), vol. 1, pp. 73–74.

To many of them, there was something perplexingly incomprehensible about the juxtaposition of Western and Ottoman slavery. What they came to know about American slavery, in particular, had almost nothing to do with their familiar home-bred type of slavery: the word was the same, but the experience, the meaning, the feelings it conjured up in their hearts and minds, were all so different, virtually irreconcilable. If the reactions of people like Ahmet Midhat to British admonitions seem cynically manipulative, they should not be taken as such. Rather, they reflect an honest—at least in most cases—misapprehension, confusion, and anger caused by the inability to offer a persuasive cultural translation of what these writers felt was the true nature of Ottoman slavery.

The defensive attitude that many of these writers came to espouse in consequence was by no means limited to the Istanbul-centered Ottoman elite of the time. Rather, everywhere across the Muslim world, intellectuals were grappling, inwardly and outwardly, with the inroads made by Western ideas and their effect on Islamic culture.[22] On 1 July 1888 Cardinal Lavigerie, one of France's most active abolitionists, gave a speech in the church of Saint Sulpice in Paris. The cardinal condemned Islam for the evils of slavery and the slave trade in Central Africa. In the audience sat a French-educated Egyptian, Ahmad Shafiq Bey, who took great offense at the cardinal's words. In a reaction to the speech, he wrote in French a short book entitled *L'esclavage au point de vue musulman.*[23]

Shafīq's book is a defense of Islam and its humane view of slavery. The author claims that Islam wished to abolish slavery, but since it could not do so without causing much damage to the social fabric, it chose at least to mitigate the institution. He goes on to state that the slaves found in Egypt at the time were not in fact slaves in the legal ("Sharʿī"; Turkish "Şerî") sense but abducted persons who should be set free immediately. In Shafiq's book we have a

22. Compare the extensive debates among U.S. Southern intellectuals over progress and slavery, discussed in Eugene D. Genovese, *The Slaveholders' Dilemma: Freedom and Progress in Southern Conservative Thought, 1820–1860* (Columbia, S.C., 1992); Genovese, *The World the Slaveholders Made*, pp. 118–244; and David Brion Davis, *Slavery and Human Progress* (New York, 1984)

23. Ahmed Chefik, *L'esclavage au point de vue musulman* (Cairo, 1891), translated into Arabic by Ahmad Zakī under the title *Al-Riqq fī ʾl-Islām* (Cairo, 1892); references are to the Arabic translation. This work is discussed by Gabriel Baer in Baer, "Slavery," pp. 187–88.

clear reference to African slavery and to the slave trade in a direct response to Western criticism.[24] Appropriately enough, it comes from Egypt, where ownership of African slaves was widespread, and where members of the Ottoman-Egyptian elite were as much in contact with Europeans as were their counterparts in Istanbul, if not more so.

The book was debated in the foreign and Egyptian press and was translated into Arabic and Ottoman Turkish. It also elicited an interesting response from a former Ottoman foreign minister, Karatodori Paşa, then the Ottoman ambassador to Belgium and the Porte's representative at the Brussels Conference of 1889–90.[25] In his letter to Shafiq, this high-ranking non-Muslim official reveals his frustrations in trying to convey to the Europeans the humane, Muslim position on slavery and the traffic. Karatodori Paşa goes on to charge the Europeans with ignorance and thanks Shafiq for providing him with useful ammunition to counter their arguments.

However, setting Ottoman slavery apart from Western slavery was not the only device employed by Ottoman writers sensitized to the subject. In addition, when condemning Ottoman slavery and slave trade, they also tried to distance the object of their criticism from their immediate "high Islamic," elite milieu. Thus, they preferred to direct their comments against slavery to "uncivilized" Muslim peoples, most readily and pertinently to the Circassians. Sezâi unequivocally denounced the old Asian savageness *(Asya vahşet-i kadimesi)* that enslaved young children. But quite astonishingly—and contrary to any historical account—Sezâi stated that "African traders" were to blame for the enslavement of the "noble people" of the Caucasus. As for Ahmet Midhat, he opposed Circassian slavery, no matter how benign it might be, while at the same time questioning and bemoaning

24. Similar sentiments are expressed in what is probably one of the strongest critiques of slavery and the slave trade produced in a nineteenth-century Islamic country. It was written in 1881 by the Moroccan historian Ahmad al-Nāsirī in his history of the Maghrib: *Kitāb al-Istiqsā'*. Al-Nāsirī condemns the slave raids in Africa as being contrary to humanity and to Islam. The importance of his argument lies in his attempt to show that the law of Islam prohibits enslavement and slave trading. Like Shafīq seven years later, al-Nāsirī too asserts that the Islamic permission to enslave the heathen who are defeated in Holy War no longer applies. The majority of Africans in the regions bordering on the Abode of Islam, he adds, have already accepted the Prophet's message, and it is, therefore, illegal to enslave them (Ahmad al-Nāsirī, *Kitāb al-Istiqsā' li-Akhbār Duwal al-Maghrib al-Aqsā'* [Casablanca, 1955], vol. 5, pp. 131 ff.).

25. Shafīq, *Al-Riqq fi'l-Islām*, pp. 130–33.

the very use of the term "slavery" with regard to the kind of servitude existing in the Caucasus.[26]

Sezâi's antislavery play *Sergüzeşt* was published in 1889,[27] not long before the Ottoman government became a signatory to the Brussels Act against the slave trade. Although the mood had already changed by then, a zealous abolitionist movement did not emerge in the empire, nor did an active, mobilizing antislavery lobby appear. The voices calling for the end of the practice came from literary, rather than political, figures, and more from second-stratum writers than from major authors. Even these voices were cautious and not too forceful. Nonetheless, there was no real difference in the sentiments prevailing in literary, intellectual, and political circles on this issue.

Attitudes of the Ottoman Elite toward Abolition

IN SCHOLARLY LITERATURE, two explanations have usually been given for this lack of enthusiasm, if not outright reluctance, to consider the abolition of slavery. Before mentioning them, I should note that no economic reason has been proposed for the Ottomans' reluctance to abolish slavery. Given the fact that slavery in the empire was, by and large, domestic and of the *kul/harem* type, this is hardly surprising, though economic historians, quite naturally, are unlikely to be fully satisfied with current explanations. As one of the most prominent economic historians of slavery has suggested with regard to the economic aspect of abolition, "it is perhaps indicative of the perceptions (as well as the power) of political elites that when both slavery and serfdom were ended it was most frequently with some compensation paid—in cash, securities, land, or labor time—to slaveowners and serfowners, presumably as partial payment for their expected economic losses."[28] This was indeed so in the case of agricultural slavery among the Circassian refugees who settled in the Ottoman Empire from the mid-1850s onward (see chapter 3).

26. Texts of Sezâi and Midhat are cited in Parlatır, *Tanzimat Edebiyatında Kölelik*, pp. 37–40. Writing about Recaizade Mahmut Ekrem's *Vuslat*, Mizancı Murat accuses female slave dealers of bringing upon society damages worse than those caused by murderers (text cited in Parlatır, *Tanzimat Edebiyatında Kölelik*, p. 41).

27. For an analysis of Sezâi's play *Sergüzeşt*, see Parlatır, *Tanzimat Edebiyatında Kölelik*, pp. 135–47. For an analysis of two of Sezâi's other plays that treat slavery, see ibid., pp. 148–55.

28. Engerman, "Slavery and Emancipation in Comparative Perspective," p. 330.

The first explanation for the absence of Ottoman abolitionism is the relatively mild nature of slavery in the empire and the obvious gap between the prototype of American slavery and Ottoman realities. Members of the Ottoman elite could not but feel that what British and other European critics of the institution were talking about and what they themselves were familiar with in Ottoman society were two completely different phenomena. The fact that the horrors of the slave trade were quite similar in both cases was conveniently brushed aside—if not repressed—by the "collective mind" of the Ottoman elite, which only reinforced their view of the benign, if not benevolent, nature of Ottoman slavery. Most wealthy, urban, and urbane Ottomans encountered slaves in their own houses and in those of their friends and relatives. They could pretend that this was where the story actually began and that what had happened before belonged to another world—uncivilized, unruly, beyond their control.

The second explanation is that slavery enjoyed a high degree of legitimacy in Ottoman society. That legitimacy derived from Islamic sanction and the unshakable conviction that Islamic law (the Şeriat) was predicated on deep human concern *(insaniyet)* and could not possibly condone any practice that was not humane, caring, and cognizant of the suffering of the weak and poor members of society. Slavery was "part and parcel of the Ottoman family," an institution scrupulously guarded against any outside interference. Since slavery was thus doubly shielded by social and religious practice, any attempt to impugn it as morally reprehensible was perceived as an indictment of the culture as a whole.[29]

29. It is interesting to note here that in modern scholarship, the question of comparing attitudes to slavery in Western and non-Western societies has been pushed aside for reasons of political correctness: the desire to avoid pronouncing judgment on an "entire culture" is often cited as the reason (for more on that, see chap. 5, below). An exception is a short work by a Sudanese scholar who compares American and Egyptian-Sudanese views of Nile Valley slavery before and during the American Civil War (Ahmed E. Elbashir, *The United States, Slavery, and the Slave Trade in the Nile Valley* [Lanham, Md., 1983]). In conclusion, the author writes: "Evidently more research is needed to explore the question of why the United States produced an indigenous abolition movement, which culminated in a protracted civil war and the final abolition of slavery, while the Nile Valley failed to produce such a movement, and required foreign intervention and domination in order to bring slavery and the slave trade to an end. Cultural, religious, and economic factors were involved in the way these two slave societies responded to abolition and its aftermath" (p. 141).

That no antislavery sentiments prevailed even among members of the elite who were sensitized to ideas of political freedom, equality, and civil rights should not perhaps be so surprising after all. The recent debate in American history over the views and actions of Thomas Jefferson can tell us a great deal about the contradictions that often inhere in situations and within personalities where we have come not to expect them.[30] In any event, the question is clearly asked from a Western, non-Ottoman perspective, and we should not assume that abolitionism is a universally "natural" reaction to slavery rather than a specific response by Western elites, in given historical circumstances, to the kind of slavery practiced in the Americas during the nineteenth century. Also, we should not fall into the fallacy of imagining the Other—here the Ottoman elite—as an "imperfect Self," that is, as lacking the human sentiment of abolitionism so integral to nineteenth-century Western elite identity, and hence as being fundamentally deficient.

The attitude of the Ottoman elite is reminiscent of the Brazilian case, where no internal pressures for emancipation existed before the 1870s, and an abolitionist lobby, the Brazilian Anti-Slavery Society, was founded only in 1880. The Rio Branco Law, which was enacted in 1871, was the first measure that supposedly limited slavery. It was passed under French pressure and with the hope of placating foreign abolitionists and alleviating external pressures. In effect, however, the law was what Philip Curtin calls "a statistical trick," since it "freed" children of slave mothers but placed them in bonded custody as *ingenuos* until the age of twenty-one, thereby significantly postponing the actual impact of manumission. Another similar feature is that the Brazilian national narrative argued that Brazilians were less racist than other Westerners, that slave owners voluntarily manumitted

30. See, e.g., Paul Finkelman, "Jefferson and Slavery: 'Treason against the Hopes of the World,' " in *Jeffersonian Legacies*, ed. Peter S. Onuf (Charlottesville, 1993), pp. 181–221; and Stanton, " 'Those Who Labor for My Happiness,' " pp. 147–80. In his harsh criticism of Jefferson, Finkelman writes that "this 'apostle of liberty' [Jefferson] could never reconcile the ideals of freedom, expressed in the Declaration of Independence and his other writings, with the reality of his ownership of men and women and his leadership of a slaveholding society" (p. 181). Stanton argues that "the constant tension between self-interest and humanity seems to have induced in him [Jefferson] a gradual closing of the imagination that distanced and dehumanized the black families of Monticello [where Jefferson's plantation was located]" (pp. 162–63).

many slaves, and that their model of emancipation was gradual, hence more peaceful and sensible.[31]

Be that as it may, we should try to work from inside Ottoman culture itself and seek to understand it on its own terms. The sociocultural approach to the intricate history of slavery and abolition during the Tanzimat, which will be offered in the following pages, emphasizes the *nexus* between the *kul/harem* and the domestic types of slavery.[32] When the evidence presented in this chapter is analyzed, it becomes clear that the Ottoman elites acted as if *kul/harem* slavery differed in *quality of kind* from domestic slavery or Circassian agricultural slavery. They viewed the practice much in the same way as they did the servile components in officeholding—namely, as a *privileged position with certain inherent disabilities*. Painful though they were at times, such disabilities were greatly outweighed by the advantages that accrued with office and elite status.

Because of European condemnation of *all* types of slavery in the Ottoman Empire, a bifurcated view of *kul/harem* slaves evolved. Within Ottoman society, these were considered to be persons "of slave origins" who had been socialized in a *mamlūk* or *kul*-type pattern, which by definition assumed a patron-client relationship of the master-slave kind. To have been raised under the shadow of slavery attached no stigma to *kul/harem* slaves, nor did it assimilate them into the group of domestic slaves familiar to members of the elite from their own households. In all senses, Ottoman society treated *kul/harem* slavery as one of the paths to patronage, like kin, marriage, adoption, suckling, etc. Therefore, the dichotomy which Patterson draws between patronage and slavery, because one is voluntary and the other is not, is alien to Ottoman realities.[33]

At the same time, however, and as a defense mechanism of sorts, when faced with Western criticism of Ottoman slavery, the same

31. See Curtin, *Plantation Complex*, pp. 190–95.

32. As already mentioned in chapter 3, agricultural slavery was dealt with in different terms from other types by both the Ottoman government and the British, and its tacit exclusion from the cross-cultural debate on slavery and abolition leaves it outside our discussion here. The African slave army that operated in the Sudan under the Ottoman-Egyptian administration from the 1820s to the 1850s (see the Introduction, nn. 26 and 27) was clearly a fringe phenomenon, existing in a frontier situation that was totally peripheral to the Ottoman core.

33. Patterson, *Slavery and Social Death*, p. 309.

elite mind collapsed the category of domestic slavery into that of *kul/harem* slavery. Consequently, defense of Ottoman slavery was predicated on drawing a sharp distinction—which obviously existed—between the lot of slaves in Western society and the lot of Ottoman grand vezirs and elite ladies. Another version of the argument claimed that the track of "rags-to-riches" was open to *all* Ottoman slaves. This unrealistic claim was most often put forth with regard to female slaves.

A striking example of that can be found in Ahmet Midhat's work *Âcaib-i Âlem* (Wonders of the World) in a dialogue between one of the main characters, Suphi, and a Russian princess. Suphi is trying to disabuse the princess of the notion that female slaves in the empire were objects of sexual pleasure for Ottoman men. He says to her:

> They [female slaves] are not [intended] for pleasure but for general household chores. All our female slaves perform duties that women do, from what are called in Europe maids of honor, or [just] maids, to cooks. . . . If the master's wife dies or falls into illness or old age, [he] takes a female slave for a concubine, and there is no difference [then] between her and a legal wife. The children of that woman are [considered] legitimate.[34]

There can be little doubt that the author himself knew that this was not the normal course. The various categories within *harem* slavery were quite familiar to all members of the Ottoman elite. As is vividly related in Fatma Âliye's four-part novel *Muhadarat*, the practice had its unhappy, as well as happy, aspects. There were three major types of female slaves: the menial domestic *(cihaz halayiği)*, the concubine *(odalık)*, and the girl brought up in the household and later married off and set up in life *(çirak/çirağ* and *besleme)*. Fatma Âliye claims that custom limited concubinage to cases of infertility—which is inaccurate—and required the consent of both the wife and the intended concubine. If the concubine did not bear children, she was then treated as *çirak* and married off comfortably. Other writers

34. The text is reproduced in Parlatır, *Tanzimat Edebiyatında Kölelik*, p. 43.

point out that concubinage was often the stepping stone to marriage (as the first wife) and was not necessarily related to infertility.[35]

It is perhaps not surprising that, as a woman, Fatma Âliye displays greater empathy with the plight of even the most privileged of *harem* slaves, the *odalıks*. Thus, we learn of the pain of the wife whose husband takes two concubines, one after the other, but still cannot beget children because the infertility—naturally attributed to her—is probably his. We read about the anger and humiliation of the wife who attempts to prevent her husband from flirting with the slaves of the family. We also get a more realistic picture of the hard work of the menial slaves in wealthy elite households. But even Fatma Âliye deals mostly with the better-off slaves, those populating the mansions of the great, who were usually Circassian or Georgian. The majority of Ottoman domestic slaves during the Tanzimat were, however, African and Ethiopian women who served in less congenial circumstances. As for male slaves, the *kul*-type track was open only to a select group of, almost exclusively white, candidates.

Thus, although to both Ahmet Midhat and Fatma Âliye, Ottoman slavery is actually *harem* slavery, the works cited above exhibit different approaches. Ahmet Midhat in *Âcaib-i Âlem* and other works, though certainly not in all, constantly addresses Western criticism of Ottoman slavery. He, therefore, *assimilates* all types of slavery in the empire into the *kul/harem* type, which is the most easily defendable practice and does not resemble slavery as known in the West. Fatma Âliye, on the other hand, is not animated by the same polemical concern but instead writes about Ottoman gentlewomen and the world they inhabited. Slavery to her is just one of the experiences of womanhood. Nonetheless, even in her work, a clear status distinction is maintained between the ladies of the house—bond or free—and the domestic slaves, whether belonging to the household or working outside in less enviable dwellings.

The split representation of *kul/harem* bondage, indeed the dualism in the attitude to slavery in general, may have prolonged the existence of the institution in Ottoman society beyond the Tanzimat period. So long as Western perceptions of Ottoman slavery were deemed by

35. For texts and some observations, see ibid., pp. 156–63, 183. On Fatma Âliye, see Carter Vaughn Findley, "La soumise, la subversive: Fatma Aliye, romancière et féministe," *Turcica* 27 (1995): 153–76.

the Ottoman elite as fundamentally wrong, demands to abolish it on moral grounds could be easily deflected. If, according to leading statesmen and intellectuals, slavery in the inhuman form did not exist in Ottoman society, but only in ancient and modern European or American societies, then it was not an Ottoman problem. The strong attachment of elite members to this pillar of their sociocultural heritage—slavery of the *kul/harem* type—blinded them to the unpleasant fact that Ottoman slavery was not all that different from slavery elsewhere in two major respects: the plight of black domestic slaves and the slave trade.

As suggested at various points above, the dynamic processes that took place during the Tanzimat in Ottoman elite thinking can also be interpreted within the framework of semiotic theories of culture. The formulation and reformulation of Ottoman attitudes to slavery can be seen as a result of "cultural interference."[36] The concept of slavery took about half a century to gradually infiltrate, or be "converted,"[37] from Western (source) culture into Ottoman (target) culture. By comparison to the appropriation of other, related components of Western culture, the conversion of Western ideas about slavery was slow and late. Ideas about the security of life and property became current in the empire during the 1830s, and by the 1850s a campaign for political and civil rights, liberty, and equality was under way. But in spite of measures to suppress the slave trade from the mid-1850s onward, ideas about slavery began to change only in the mid-1870s.

In this chapter, we have been dealing only with the center of "canonized culture"[38]—that of the Istanbul-oriented Ottoman elite, who were located in all the major cities of the empire. With regard to slavery, the process of conversion involved three broadly and loosely

36. The theoretical framework used here is an elaboration of Russian Formalist and Czech Structuralist theories by Itamar Even-Zohar. The works of Jurij Tynjanov and Roman Jakobson form the basis for Even-Zohar's theory. For the most recent formulation of Polysystem Theory, see Itamar Even-Zohar, *Polysystem Studies: Papers in Historical Poetics and Semiotics of Culture,* Special Issue of *Poetics Today* 11/1 (1990); especially relevant to our discussion are "Polysystem Theory" and "Laws of Literary Interference."

37. Conversions are the moves, or transfer processes, of cultural products (here Western abolitionism) from one cultural system to another or from one stratum to another within a cultural system.

38. Much of what constituted that culture is convincingly described in great detail in Carter V. Findley, *Ottoman Officialdom: A Social History* (Princeton, 1989).

defined groups of cultural producers/disseminators. In descending order of strata, from the center to the semiperiphery of the Ottoman elite, these groups were (1) Ottoman statesmen, (2) Young Ottoman publicists and activists, and (3) playwrights, novelists, and poets.[39] This is also the order in which the groups became exposed to European abolitionist demands over a period of more than half a century. It is, however, the reverse group order as far as ideological reception, cultural conversion, and formulation of a critical attitude toward Ottoman slavery were concerned. Thus, it may be said that Western abolitionism first interfered with a lower stratum of Ottoman elite culture. It then spread to other, higher and lower, strata, partially as an internal Ottoman process of conversion from semiperiphery to center.

The first to be faced with the need to formulate an attitude to slavery were the statesmen, who from the 1840s onward had to deal with British pressure to suppress the slave trade. On the ideological level, they responded in the defensive manner described above, although they accepted the need to prevent the human suffering caused by the slave trade and issued edicts to effect such a change without touching slavery itself. The Young Ottomans were next to address slavery, but they were too absorbed in their struggle for political rights to deal with it more than marginally. The last to confront the unpleasant subject were the writers. They came to slavery late in the day, during the mid-1870s, but made the most impressive effort to grapple with it. In spite of these differences, all three groups coped with the Western image of Ottoman slavery and the denunciation thereof by adopting a strategy of bifurcation.

The result was that they projected back and out *kul/harem* slavery as being the *only* type of Ottoman slavery while simultaneously, at home, they treated domestic and agricultural slavery as being the *only* type of Ottoman slavery. To be able to do so, they intuitively applied to the variegated reality of Ottoman slavery procedures of selection, deletion, and amplification. Since the economic value of slavery was not the issue, British abolitionism must have touched

39. Owing to the predominance of the Young Ottomans in intellectual circles from the 1860s to the late 1870s, there was some overlapping between the second and third groups. The case of Ahmet Midhat comes to mind, as he was close to the Young Ottomans until the second half of the 1870s, when he began to operate under the aegis of Abdülhamit II's government. For his career, see Lewis, *Emergence,* pp. 189–90.

the very core of Ottoman elite culture, where the belief and value systems were most vulnerable to criticism. Otherwise it would be quite difficult to explain why cognate products of Western culture (e.g., ideas about political freedom) faced much less resistance and were converted relatively early, whereas abolitionism was rejected on the ideological, not merely the political, level.

Because of the unmitigated and uncompromising nature of Western abolitionism, no other Ottoman counterstrategies were developed. A campaign to abolish only domestic and agricultural slavery—indeed the predominant and most painful types—was never contemplated by Western proponents of abolition. That similar or other pragmatic alternatives were not suggested may be safely laid at the door of nineteenth-century European zeal, moralism, and inability to differentiate and empathize across cultural boundaries.

FIVE

Discourses on Ottoman and Ottoman-Arab Slavery

THE SCHOLARLY STUDY of the history of slavery in Ottoman society—and in Muslim societies as a whole—is characterized by a deafening silence, which is only seldom broken by lone voices. Although scattered works by individual scholars have been published in recent years,[1] a sustained program of research with a concomitant

1. Thanks to the efforts of Joseph C. Miller, we possess an excellent bibliography of such works in his "Muslim Slavery and Slaving: A Bibliography," in Savage, *The Human Commodity*, pp. 249–71. For the most pertinent to our topic see, in order of publication, Baer, "Slavery and Its Abolition"; Muhammad Ali, *The British, the Slave Trade, and Slavery in the Sudan;* Borge Fredriksen, "Slavery and Its Abolition in Nineteenth-Century Egypt" (Ph.D. diss., University of Bergen, 1977); Alan Fisher, "The Sale of Slaves in the Ottoman Empire: Markets and State Taxes on Slave Sales," *Boğaziçi Üniversitesi Dergisi* 6 (1978): 149–74; Halil İnalcık, "Servile Labor in the Ottoman Empire," in *The Mutual Effects of the Islamic and Judeo-Christian Worlds: The East European Pattern*, ed. A. Ascher, T. Halasi-Kun, and Bela Kiraly (New York, 1979); Halil Sahillioğlu, "Onbeşinci Yüzyılın Sonu ile Onaltıncı Yüzyılın Başında Bursa'da Kölelerin Sosyal ve Ekonomik Hayattaki Yeri," *ODTÜ Gelişme Dergisi*, 1979–80 Özel Sayısı, pp. 67–138 (an English version of this paper was presented at a conference on the economic and social history of the Islamic Middle East, 700–1900, held at Princeton in 1974; the papers were published by Abraham L. Udovich in 1981, but this one was not included); Joseph Gaston, *L'esclavage en Tunisie* (Tunis, 1980); Hans Müller, *Die Kunst des Sklavenkaufs nach arabischen, persischen, und türkischen Ratgeben vom 10. bis zum 18. Jahrhundert* (Freiburg, 1980); Alan Fisher, "Chattel Slavery in the Ottoman Empire," *Slavery and Abolition* 1 (1980): 25–45; Patricia Crone, *Slaves on Horses: The*

discourse has yet to emerge in the field. This is in stark contrast to the well-developed discourse on slavery and the slave trade in North and South America, Africa, European and Mediterranean antiquity, the Far East, and Russia. The rich and complex literature on slavery as practiced in these diverse societies is the result of over a century of individual efforts by members of both Western and non-Western—though Western-influenced—scholarly communities.[2] The methods and issues discussed in that by now fairly coherent and well-integrated discourse have been further articulated in the scholarly debates waged during the 1970s in the United States. These debates were mainly stimulated by Fogel and Engerman's *Time on the Cross* and the renewed controversy over the volume of the Atlantic traffic. The discussion of the economic and social aspects of slavery was soon extended to include the cultural and intellectual ones.[3]

Evolution of the Islamic Polity (Cambridge, 1980); Pipes, *Slave Soldiers and Islam;* Reda Mowafi, *Slavery, Slave Trade, and Abolition in Egypt and the Sudan, 1820–1882* (Malmö, Sweden, 1981); Elbashir, *United States, Slavery, and the Slave Trade in the Nile Valley;* Lewis, *Race and Slavery in the Middle East;* Toledano, *Ottoman Slave Trade;* Toledano, "Slave Dealers, Women, Pregnancy, and Abortion"; Toledano, "The Imperial Eunuchs of Istanbul: From Africa to the Heart of Islam," *Middle Eastern Studies* 20/3 (1984): 379–90; Toledano, "Ottoman Concepts of Slavery in the Period of Reform, 1830s–1880s," in *Breaking the Chains: Slavery, Bondage, and Emancipation in Modern Africa and Asia,* ed. Martin A. Klein (Madison, 1993), pp. 37–63 (substantially revised versions of the last three items are woven into various parts of the present book); Judith E. Tucker, *Women in Nineteenth-Century Egypt* (Cambridge, 1985), chap. 5; Le Gall, "End of the Trans-Saharan Slave Trade," pp. 25–56. For studies on slavery in African Muslim societies, see further below.

2. It might be instructive to note that a quick search of the term "slavery" in the computerized version of University Microfilms International's *Dissertation Abstracts* yields an amazing quantity of research on the topic: between January 1961 and December 1981, slavery is mentioned in 338 author-provided abstracts, which means either that the whole dissertation is devoted to the subject or that at least some aspect thereof is discussed in the thesis; for the period between January 1982 and December 1987, slavery is mentioned in 308 abstracts; between January 1988 and December 1992, it appears in 339 abstracts; and between January 1993 and March 1994, 117 abstracts refer to slavery.

3. See R. W. Fogel and S. L. Engerman, *Time on the Cross: The Economics of American Negro Slavery* (Boston, 1974) (for a critique of this work, see Herbert G. Gutman, *Slavery and the Numbers Game: A Critique of "Time on the Cross"* [Urbana, Ill., 1975]); Philip D. Curtin, Roger Anstey, and J. E. Inikori, "Discussion: Measuring the Atlantic Slave Trade," *Journal of African History* 17/4 (1976): 595–627, following the debate around Curtin's *The Atlantic Slave Trade: A Census* (Madison, 1969) and Inikori's "Measuring the Atlantic Slave Trade: An Assessment of Curtin and Anstey," *Journal of African History* 17/2 (1976): 197–225. Among the most widely used studies, one might cite also the following works (a fuller list can be found in Klein, *Breaking the*

In the late 1970s and throughout the 1980s, Africanists have taken up the challenge and developed an impressive corpus of scholarly literature on slavery in African societies.[4] Considerably more restricted in their written source materials than writers on slavery in the United States South, Africanists used colonial archives but also had to develop new methodologies to deal with oral sources and evidence from material culture. Slavery in African Muslim societies, too, has been investigated in this wave of studies, and in 1977, John Ralph Willis organized at Princeton University a conference on slavery and related institutions in Islamic Africa. The revised papers were published in two volumes eight years later.[5] In the early 1980s, Patricia Crone and Daniel Pipes published books on military slavery under Islam, supplementing the earlier works of David Ayalon on the Mamluk Sultanate; these were later used by comparative historians of slavery, such as Orlando Patterson, to incorporate Islamic slavery into their global models. However, the importance of military-administrative

---

Chains, pp. 28–36): Curtin, *Plantation Complex;* Davis, *Problem of Slavery in the Age of Revolution;* Davis, *Slavery and Human Progress;* Seymour Drescher, *Capitalism and Antislavery: British Mobilization in Comparative Perspective* (London, 1986); Elkins, *Slavery;* David Eltis, *Economic Growth and the Ending of the Transatlantic Slave Trade* (New York, 1987); Moses Finley, *Ancient Slavery and Modern Ideology* (London, 1980); Genovese, *The World the Slaveholders Made;* Genovese, *Roll, Jordan, Roll;* Richard Hellie, *Slavery in Russia, 1450–1725* (Chicago, 1982); Herbert Klein, *African Slavery in Latin America and the Caribbean* (New York, 1986); Patterson, *Slavery and Social Death;* Anthony Reid, *Slavery, Bondage, and Dependency in Southeast Asia* (St. Lucia, 1983); James L. Watson, ed., *Asian and African Systems of Slavery* (Oxford, 1980).

4. Some of the main works in this area are (a fuller list can be found in Klein, *Breaking the Chains*, pp. 28–36) Ralph A. Austen, "From the Atlantic to the Indian Ocean: European Abolition, the African Slave Trade, and Asian Economic Structures," in *The Abolition of the Atlantic Slave Trade*, ed. David Eltis and James Walvin (Madison, 1981); Austen, "The 19th Century Islamic Slave Trade from East Africa"; Austen, "The Mediterranean Islamic Slave Trade out of Africa"; Cooper, *Plantation Slavery;* Klein, *Breaking the Chains;* Paul Lovejoy, ed., *The Ideology of Slavery in Africa* (Beverly Hills, 1981); Lovejoy, *Transformations in Slavery: A History of Slavery in Africa* (Cambridge, 1983); Claude Meillassoux, *Anthropologie de l'esclavage: Le ventre de fer et d'argent* (Paris, 1986) (English trans., *The Anthropology of Slavery: The Womb of Iron and Gold* [Chicago, 1991]); Miers and Kopytoff, *Slavery in Africa;* Suzanne Miers and Richard Roberts, eds., *The End of Slavery in Africa* (Madison, 1988); Joseph Miller, *Slavery: A World-wide Bibliography, 1900–1982* (New York, 1985); Joseph Miller, *Way of Death: Merchant Capitalism and the Angolan Slave Trade, 1730–1830* (Madison, 1988); Richard Roberts, *Warriors, Merchants, and Slaves: The State and the Economy in the Middle Niger Valley, 1700–1914* (Stanford, 1987); Robertson and Klein, *Women and Slavery in Africa;* Abdul Sheriff, *Slaves, Spices, and Ivory in Zanzibar* (London, 1987).

5. J. R. Willis, *Slaves and Slavery in Muslim Africa*, 2 vols. (London, 1985).

slavery in Muslim societies has lured scholarly attention away from the less glamorous and intriguing, though more widely prevailing, forms of servitude.[6]

In light of the new wave of works on slavery in many societies across the globe, the study of Ottoman slavery appeared even more neglected and external to the highly articulated discourse on slavery. My own ventures into the suppression of the Ottoman slave trade in the nineteenth century and, later, into some aspects of Ottoman slavery have attempted to rescue the topic from the oblivion it does not merit and to launch it into the orbit of slavery studies. The current volume is yet another effort in this direction. Owing to recent work by Turkish scholars and others (see further below), the discourse on Ottoman slavery and the slave trade now coheres with the discourse on slavery in other societies and forms a part of it. In the following pages I will argue that a separate and ancillary discourse on slavery in other Muslim societies still exists, especially in the Arab world. As will be shown, this partly stems from attitudes prevailing in political and academic communities in Arab societies, but it is also partly the result of political and scholarly constraints in Muslim societies on Western-trained scholars working on slavery. Only very recently can one detect the beginnings of a dialogue between that discourse and the other two.

It is by now a cliché that the subject of slavery in Islamic societies is a highly sensitive issue. Bernard Lewis, one of the few writers on Islamic slavery, notes that this "extreme sensitivity . . . makes it difficult, and sometimes professionally hazardous, for a young scholar to turn his [or her] attention in this direction." Lewis adds that "the mere mention of [the subject] . . . is often seen as a sign of hostile intentions. Sometimes indeed it is, but it need not and should not be so, and the imposition of taboos on topics of historical research can only impede and delay a better and more accurate understanding."

6. Crone, *Slaves on Horses;* Pipes, *Slave Soldiers and Islam;* David Ayalon, *L'esclavage du Mamelouks* (Jerusalem, 1951); David Ayalon, *Gunpowder and Firearms in the Mamluk Kingdom: A Challenge to a Medieval Society* (London, 1956); David Ayalon, *Studies on the Mamluks of Egypt (1250–1517)* (London, 1977); David Ayalon, *The Mamluk Military Society* (London, 1979); Patterson, *Slavery and Social Death.* Nonmilitary slavery in Muslim societies has been discussed mostly by legal historians interested in various aspects of Islamic law (the Sharīʿa), but one should also note here again Brunschvig's excellent article "ʿAbd" in the *Encyclopædia of Islam.*

As for his own efforts in his book, Lewis asserts that he has "tried to deal fairly and objectively with a subject of great historical and comparative importance and to do so without recourse to either polemics or apologetics."[7]

But perhaps in the hope of avoiding an added controversy, Lewis refrains from naming the political atmosphere in the field of Middle Eastern studies in the United States as a major deterrent against the study of "sensitive topics." Unlike the situation in the European discourse on the Middle East, the self-imposed censorship dictated by the rules of *political correctness* in the United States—under the lingering impact of Edward Said's works on "Orientalism"—has severely restricted the scholarly discussion of topics that are somehow viewed as potentially unflattering to the image of Muslims, especially those living in the Middle East. This resembles the milder predicament of some Africanists who, in the words of Claire Robertson and Martin Klein, "find it uncomfortable to study stratification and exploitation within African societies" because of "a romantic view of an egalitarian Africa."[8]

At the same time, the intense political interest in the history of African American slavery has spawned a sustained scholarly activity in the field. While African Americans have now come to see in it their own "holocaust," for which social, economic, and political reparations are due,[9] Africanists have, beginning in the late 1970s, devoted greater attention to slavery in Africa itself and to the impact of the slave trade on African societies, including Muslim ones. Consequently, a great deal of excellent work has appeared on slavery in Africa, with some of the more interesting methodological contributions that one can find in the field of slavery studies. Nonetheless, several Africanists have displayed the same "geocentric" bias that Americanists have, studying African slavery in complete isolation from slavery elsewhere. In a way, this is an even greater fallacy than

7. Lewis, *Race and Slavery,* p. vi.

8. Robertson and Klein, "Introduction," p. 13.

9. Steven T. Katz, "Quantity and Interpretation—Issues in the Comparative Historical Analysis of the Holocaust," *Holocaust and Genocide Studies* 4/2 (1989): 127–48, compares five historical cases of persecution and extermination—including African American slavery (pp. 137–41)—with the Jewish Holocaust in Nazi Germany. This is an obvious response to the political arguments advanced by African Americans. Patrick Manning considers the whole moral issue of reparations under the rubric of "the response to past injustice," in his *Slavery and African Life,* pp. 174–76.

that committed by Americanists, since Africa is far closer to, in fact borders on, regions in which slavery was rife, such as the Ottoman dominions. African societies have had continuous—at times intense—commercial, political, and religious links to the Ottoman Middle East and North Africa, with the pilgrimage to Arabia and the trans-Saharan connection as the main channels of exchange. Moreover, slavery in Africa, especially among its Muslim societies, had a great deal more in common with slavery in the adjacent Ottoman world than did slavery in the Americas.

Thus, for example, in a long review article published in 1987, Humphrey J. Fisher makes no reference to one of the major elements that linked the main Muslim power of the time—the Ottoman Empire—to the continent of Africa, namely the slave trade.[10] In that piece, Africa seems to exist in isolation, a closed system which can be studied most legitimately by itself, ignoring the web of networks that extended across the continent between its Muslim peoples and the world of Islam outside, mostly via North and East Africa or the Red Sea and Persian Gulf networks. Incidentally, in December 1988 a special issue of *Slavery and Abolition*, edited by Gervase Clarence-Smith, was devoted to the Indian Ocean slave trade, which included, of course, the East African, Red Sea, and Persian Gulf traffic. Luckily, though quite artificially, this volume is included in what purports to be a comprehensive review of works on African slavery and on the slave trade from Africa published by Janet J. Ewald as recently as 1992.[11] However, Ewald's article is an even more blatant example of "Africanist isolationism" in the discussion of slavery and the slave trade. This approach stems from a parochial insistence that the source societies, from which the slaves came, are the most—if not the only—relevant frame of reference, ignoring the societies which imported and absorbed African slaves.

But if some Africanists choose not to deal with the slave trade to the Ottoman-Arab world, the sheer politics of it has driven the issue right to the fore. African-Arab relations have been tainted, some might say

10. "Of Slaves and Souls of Men: Review Article," *Journal of African History* 28 (1987): 141–49. The work under review is Willis's *Slaves and Slavery in Muslim Africa*.

11. "Review Article: Slavery in Africa and the Slave Trade from Africa," *American Historical Review* 97/2 (1992): 465–85. The article treats seven books on slavery in Africa, including Clarence-Smith's volume on the Indian Ocean slave trade, that were written by Africanists and published between 1983 and 1990.

poisoned, by the historical role attributed to Arab slave dealers and slave owners in Africa, particularly in East and North Africa. The renewal of interest in African slavery since the late 1970s, which followed the larger wave of works on African American slavery in the 1970s, seems to have rekindled the debate between Arabs and Africans over the meaning of that painful heritage. The issue has since been aired in various forums within what might loosely be called the intellectual-academic-political discourse. Thus, for example, in an article published in 1982 in *Arab Studies Quarterly,* Ghada Talhami complains that "modern Western scholarship on Africa . . . has marred the memory of this long and historic association [between Islam and Africa] with detailed emphasis on the nineteenth-century Arab involvement in the slave trade." The author tries to minimize the magnitude of the traffic by mentioning only the Zanzibari and Sudanese trade in slaves, then admits it constituted "stark exploitation," but curiously asserts that it lasted only a "limited period," and pleads that it not be "allowed to obscure the memory of the previous centuries of peaceful Arab migrations and intermarriage."[12]

In 1984, the debate was openly and poignantly carried to the pages of a more canonic platform, *Issue: A Journal of Africanist Opinion,* published by the African Studies Association.[13] The Focus section in that issue was devoted to "Afro-Arab Relations" and guest-edited by Ali A. Mazrui and Omari H. Kokole. Mazrui entitled his opening paper "The Semitic Impact on Black Africa: Arab and Jewish Cultural Influences" but somehow managed to ignore the issue of the slave trade while spending much time on the influence of Arabic and Islam on African societies. However, in a strongly worded piece entitled "African-Arab Relations from Slavery to Petro-Jihad," Dunstan M. Wai addressed the historical residue in that loaded and complex relationship:

> The African collective memory of Arab participation in the slave trade and proselytization of Islam, more often by the sword and

12. "The Muslim African Experience," *Arab Studies Quarterly* 4 (1982): 17–33. Quotations are from p. 32. It need only be mentioned that other important branches of the slave trade to Muslim lands included the trans-Saharan, Ethiopian, and Persian Gulf routes, and that the traffic was active—in varying degrees—well before the nineteenth century, hardly a limited period.

13. *Issue: A Journal of Africanist Opinion* 13 (1984), edited by Edmond J. Keller. Mazrui's article, discussed below, is on pp. 3–8, and Wai's is on pp. 9–13.

> through trade, produces a negative attitude towards Arabs. Africans perceive Arabs as cunning, crafty, dishonest, untrustworthy, and racially as well as culturally arrogant. Many Africans do not feel at ease in dealing with Arabs: for educated and Westernized Africans, Arab culture is unattractive, and for the masses of Africans, they are mystified in general by most foreigners. . . .
>
> . . . Many Africans tend to view Arab relations with Africa in a historical continuum: Arabs as accomplices in Africa's enslavement, Arabs competing with other foreigners for political influence in Africa, Arabs increasing the price of their oil thereby contributing to [the] strangling of Africa's economies.[14]

How authentic these sentiments are, and how much the dialogue between Africans and Arabs is still affected by the slavery issue can amply be seen in the 1989 publication of a special volume on the question of slavery in Africa.[15] Sponsored by an organ of the Arab League—the Arab Organization for Education, Culture, and Sciences—it contains papers presented at a seminar held in Tunis on 27–29 June 1985. Some twenty scholars from Egypt, Jordan, Morocco, Iraq, Lebanon, Kuwait, Tanzania, Uganda, Nigeria, and Senegal took part in what might be described as an official Arab attempt to academically revise the image of Arabs as slave dealers and slaveholders. In their opening speeches, the administrative organizers complained that the image of the Arabs was deliberately distorted and—skirting the actual point under debate—resorted at times to absurdities such as the claim that Western scholarship on slavery and the slave trade accuses the Arabs of controlling and masterminding

14. Quotations are from pp. 9 and 13. Wai further argues that such perceptions still persist and are continually reinforced by ongoing contacts and experiences. He adds that despite the sense of Islamic solidarity with the Arabs, many African Muslims "don't feel at ease with non-African Muslims. Islam doesn't seem to provide the religious bond that would cement relations between African Muslims and Arabs" (p. 9). His argument is borne out by some of the views expressed at the first Arab-African writers' meeting, held in Algiers in May 1983. In the proceedings, published in *Al-Kātib al-ʿArabī* 6 (1983): 7–46, the residue of past experiences of the Arab presence in Africa surfaced despite attempts to gloss over it. Thus, the Senegalese writer Mamadou Traor Diop surveys Arab-African relations in the past and clearly mentions "the enslavement of large black societies" (p. 36).

15. Al-Munazzama al-ʿArabiyya li-l-Tarbiyya wa-l-Thaqāfa wa-l-ʿUlūm, *Masʾalat al-Riqq fī Ifrīqyā* (Tunis, 1989) (papers by Arabs are in Arabic; those by Africans are in French and English).

the *Atlantic* traffic.[16] While more serious and less flagrant than the introductions, the papers presented by the Arab scholars still exude an uncomfortably apologetic air.

By contrast, the African contributions to this volume are considerably more critical. They all clearly implicate the Arabs in the slave trade and in using Africans as slaves, sometimes directly accusing them of ill-treatment. Thus, for example, having mentioned Tippu Tip and the slaving port of Zanzibar, T. Shaaban Y. Sengo writes:

> The Arabs were quite happy to enslave the Africans who worked in their clove and coconut plantations, in their houses and who served them indoors and fought for them different wars both in East Africa and abroad. They went too far in the maltreatment of their slaves. . . . Whatever the previous attempts to make East Africa forget and forgive, the Arab slave trade in the zone left a serious mark against the Arabs and everything else associated with them.[17]

Yet, Sengo sees the very convening of the conference as "a sign of maturity and sincerity on the part of the Arabs." Whereas the proceedings can hardly convince one that the parties managed to engage in a serious exchange leading to a rapprochement of sorts, it seems to me that the first signs of a future dialogue are, nevertheless, beginning to emerge. This is mostly because some debate on the issue of slavery in Muslim societies and the slave trade to territories controlled by Muslim powers already was initiated in the 1980s by a few Arab scholars,[18] who are still faced with stiff opposition from establishment scholars. In both the eastern and western parts of the Arab world, nationalist historians were—and no few still are—engaged in writing a defensive narrative, which is often a belated polemic against "foreign" *(ajānib)* writers on the Middle East and

16. Ibid., pp. 12–13 (Arabic). Arguing against this bogus accusation, the organizers completely ignore the actual charge by Africans that a vast slave trade was carried on from Africa to Muslim territories and that African slaves were widely used in Muslim and Arab societies.

17. Ibid., p. 8 (English).

18. An early precursor is perhaps Samir M. Zoghby, "Blacks and Arabs: Past and Present," *Current Bibliography on African Affairs* 3/5 (May 1970): 5–22. My only reservation is that this article appeared in English and in a Western publication rather than in Arabic and in the Arab world.

North Africa (many of whom, in fact, wrote several decades back and were not professional historians). There is still precious little scholarly dialogue in writing that takes into account recent historical works on the region composed by Western-trained scholars. A value-laden subject such as slavery, alongside a mélange of issues on the nationalist agenda, has too frequently attracted the kind of rhetoric that is not conducive to any meaningful exchange of views or the accumulation of new knowledge.

A typical example of the historian qua "defender of the flag" is Tamām Humām Tamām of Cairo University, who published an article entitled "Slaves and the Army in Muhammad ʿAlī's View" in 1981.[19] The author openly admits that he was motivated to study the question because he views foreign (i.e., Western) writings on it as blemishing not only the history of Muhammad ʿAlī but also that of Egypt itself. It is claimed by such writers that the governor of Egypt conquered the Sudan in 1820–21 mainly in order to capture slaves for his army, that he mistreated his slave recruits, and that his slaving activities brought devastation upon the Sudan. Tamām's painstaking efforts in the archives have led him to some rather bizarre conclusions, including the assertion that the Sudan actually benefited from the enslavement of its people by Muhammad ʿAlī, since this enabled the slaves to gain awareness *(waʿy)* of the modern world and created nuclei of military units that laid the foundations of the modern Sudanese army.[20]

19. "Al-Raqīq wa-l-Jundiyya fī Nazar Muhammad ʿAlī," *Al-Majalla al-Tārīkhiyya al-Misriyya* 27 (1981): 120–57. Mehmet Ali Paşa (in Arabic, Muhammad ʿAlī), Ottoman governor of Egypt from 1805 to 1848, is still considered "the Founder of Modern Egypt" by nationalist historians. On the man and his reign, see my article "Muhammad ʿAlī," in the *Encyclopædia of Islam*, 2d ed. (Leiden, 1991), vol. 7, pp. 423–31.

20. One way of "retaliating" against the alleged misrepresentation of the historical record on slavery in Muslim (here mainly Ottoman-Arab) societies is to attack the Western record on slavery, which is admittedly no better than that of Muslim societies, and sometimes certainly worse. A classic example of this genre is an article by ʿAbdallāh ʿAbd al-Rāziq Ibrāhīm entitled "The International Efforts toward the Abolition of Slavery in Africa" ("Al-Juhūd al-Dawliyya li-Ilghāʾ al-Riqq fī Ifrīqyā," *Al-Majalla al-Tārīkhiyya al-Misriyya* 32 [1985]: 181–219). The author uses strong language to condemn the European powers for enslaving West Africa, ignores completely the existence of an East and North African market, and accuses Britain for having ulterior motives in its abolitionist policies. Using inflated numbers for the Atlantic traffic, he charges that it depopulated Africa and left behind only the elderly, who were incapable of productive

Although milder in tone, the following three examples are still within the same nationalist defensive tradition. In 1985, a Tunisian establishment figure, ʿAbd al-Jalīl al-Tamīmī (often spelled Abdeljelil Temimi), published in the main Tunisian historical journal an article entitled "Liberation of Slaves and Their Number in the [Ottoman] Province of Tunis in the Middle of the Nineteenth Century."[21] This largely apologetic and often inaccurate piece begins with another familiar theme, namely the complaint that "we" (presumably Muslim historians) will no longer accept that the civilizing role of Islam (with regard to slavery?) continue to be ignored—supposedly by Western historians of Muslim societies. The author later repeats yet another common claim about the mild nature of Islamic slavery and the good treatment of slaves (see the Introduction, above) in Ottoman Tunis. He also quibbles with Lucette Valensi's estimate of the number of slaves in Tunis at the time, not surprisingly suggesting a much smaller slave population.

Another disturbing paper on slavery in Africa, by ʿAbd al-Rahmān ʿAbdallāh al-Shaykh, appeared in the same journal two years later.[22] Its author blames the Portuguese missionaries and the Jews for the Atlantic slave trade and accuses the British of unholy motives in their prosecution of abolitionism in Africa. By hijacking all the glory for abolition, Britain distorted the fact that it was indeed Islamic expansion in Africa that deserved the credit for the actual suppression

---

work. Hence, he claims that the success of the West and the endemic problems of Africa all stem from the slave trade, presumably only that part of it for which the Western powers were responsible (see especially pp. 181, 204–5, 214–16).

21. "ʿItq al-ʿAbīd wa-ʿAdaduhum fī Muntasaf al-Qarn al-Tāsiʿ ʿAshar bi-Iyālat Tūnis," *Revue d'Histoire Maghrebine* 12/39–40 (1985): 590–96 (Arabic section). At the outset, Temimi criticizes my *Ottoman Slave Trade* for offering an "unscientific" comparison between the volume of the slave trade to the Muslim world and that to the New World (p. 590). His point is, of course, that the Muslim traffic was immeasurably smaller than the Atlantic one. However, currently accepted estimates show that my statement was actually too conservative with regard to the Muslim traffic (for the Atlantic slave trade figures, see Eltis, *Ending of the Transatlantic Slave Trade,* table A.8, p. 249). In n. 41 (p. 595), Temimi also attributes to me the opposite of what I am saying about the Ottoman government's 1846 view of the bey's 1841 action (see Toledano, *Ottoman Slave Trade,* pp. 98–99).

22. "Sabʿ Mulāhazāt Jadīda ʿan al-Riqq fī Ifrīqyā hattā Nihāyat al-Qarn al-Tāsiʿ ʿAshar" [Seven New Observations on Slavery in Africa until the End of the Nineteenth Century], *Revue d'Histoire Maghrebine* 14/45–46 (1987): 49–61 (Arabic section).

of the slave trade. Al-Shaykh then asserts that slaves in African (Muslim?) societies were not worse off than other family members, their position in fact resembling that of adopted children.

In 1986, Muhammad al-Razūq, chairman of the history department of the Faculty of Humanities in Casablanca, Morocco, published in a Libyan journal an article under the promising title "The Problem of Slavery in the History of the Maghrib."[23] Maghribi and Arab historians, he asserts, have neglected the study of North African slavery, leaving the field to "the Europeans," who treat Maghribi—and by extension Arab and Muslim—slavery as if it were similar to European (and American) slavery. However, "it is well known," al-Razūq continues, that this was not so and that there were two major differences between the two: the Moroccan expansion into Africa—unlike the European penetration—was not motivated by the desire to recruit slaves; and slaves in the Maghrib were treated in a humane way, joined their owners' families, enjoyed the owners' social status, were often educated, and could rise to positions of high responsibility.[24] Perhaps because much of the evidence adduced by the author hardly supports these assertions, his tone is both moralizing and defensive.

Although one might be tempted to dismiss as mere propaganda these three articles, and others written in the same vein, they do serve a purpose in our discussion of the state of research on slavery and the slave trade in the Middle East and North Africa. Whereas it is certainly naive to believe that scholarship and politics can be totally separated, it is quite distressing to note the extent to which the political and the academic are still so confiningly intertwined. One should also notice that for both Temimi and al-Shaykh, the defensive posture centers on abolition, which then conveniently enables them to "improve" the view of the last phase of slavery. It seems to make the issue somehow more palatable to them and their audience and to place the debate on a more comfortable plane. This tradition goes back to the late-nineteenth-century reaction of certain intellectuals to the attack by Western abolitionism on slavery in the Ottoman Empire

23. Muhammad al-Razūq, "Qadiyyat al-Riqq fī Tārīkh al-Maghrib," *Majallat al-Buhūth al-Tārīkhiyya* 8/2 (1986): 269–89.

24. Ibid., pp. 269–70. On the situation in Morocco, see Daniel Schroeter, "Slave Markets and Slavery in Moroccan Urban Society," in Savage, *The Human Commodity*, pp. 185–213.

and other Muslim countries (see chapter 4). Yet we should not lose sight of another, though not dominant, tradition among Arab and Muslim scholars dealing with slavery in their societies.

This different corpus consists mainly of Western-influenced works, written in Western languages and often the product of graduate work done at Western universities. Perhaps because of the political constraints mentioned above, the study of slavery benefited from a rather small number of such endeavors. Thus, ʿAlī ʿAbd al-Wāhid's French doctoral thesis in sociology, published in 1931, was a pioneering effort.[25] In his *Contribution à une théorie sociologique de l'esclavage: Etudes des situations génératrices de l'esclavage,* the author describes the sources and causes of slavery in three different periods: slavery in antiquity (Hebrews, Greeks, and Romans); Islamic slavery in the medieval period; and slavery in the French Antilles in modern times. The Islamic part is the most original, using primary sources and analyzing legal and religious institutions, literary works, and historical texts. The author later taught in Egypt and published various works, including a critical edition of Ibn Khaldūn's *Al-Muqaddima,* though his book on slavery never appeared in Arabic. Another little-known work in this small group is M. F. Shukry's doctoral dissertation, entitled "The Khedive Ismail and Slavery in the Sudan."[26]

The following three decades did not see any meaningful additions to this limited corpus of works, which is hardly surprising given the fact that during that time Western and Western-trained scholars, too, did very little work on slavery in Muslim societies. In 1972, however, Abbas Ibrahim Muhammad Ali published in Khartoum his intriguing and problematic work *The British, the Slave Trade, and Slavery in the Sudan, 1820–1881.* Drawing on British archival sources—mainly consular correspondence—the author, nonetheless, idealizes the plight of slaves in the Sudan to the point of arguing that "by the standards of western slavery, most slaves, if not all, in

25. For a short evaluation of this and other sociological work done in France by Arab scholars, see Mustapha al-Ahnaf, "Sur quelques Durkheimiens Arabes," *Peuples Méditerranéens* 54–55 (Jan.–June 1995): 41–51 (references to the work on slavery are on pp. 44–45 and 49–50). The dissertation of ʿAlī ʿAbd al-Wāhid (spelled Ali Abd el Wahid) was published in Paris by Éditions Albert Mechelinck and contains 438 pages.

26. M. F. Shukry, "The Khedive Ismail and Slavery in the Sudan" (D.Phil. diss., University of Liverpool, 1935). For comment on the author's views, see Spaulding, "Slavery, Land Tenure, and Social Class," especially pp. 8–13 (and as cited in the Introduction, above).

the Sudan who were categorized by British writers as slaves were not slaves." This work sets out to demolish British views regarding Sudanese slavery and the slave trade, which the author describes as "distortions, exaggerations and misconceptions." He further argues against linking the persistence of slavery with the influence of Islam, as against the notion that Samuel Baker and Charles Gordon had contributed to the suppression of the slave trade in the Sudan. All that notwithstanding, this work clearly belongs—in terms of method, issues, sources, and vocabulary—to the Western discourse on slavery in Muslim societies.

Additional contributions to that discourse by Western-trained Arab scholars writing in English followed the 1970s revival of interest in American slavery and the Atlantic traffic. Thus, in 1981 an Egyptian scholar, Reda Mowafi, published his *Slavery, Slave Trade, and Abolition in Egypt and the Sudan, 1820–1882.*[27] Based mainly on British documents and European travelogues and memoirs, and using works on slavery by Western-trained scholars, this is a straightforward account, free from apologies and other related encumberments. Mowafi cogently argues that "in the northern and western Sudan, slavery permeated society to a much more fundamental degree" than in Egypt. This, among other factors, accounted for the longevity of Sudanese slavery, while in Egypt, antislavery measures taken by the government, "coinciding with the socio-economic transformation of the Egyptian society, had effectively undermined the demand for slaves" and brought about the demise of slavery at the end of the nineteenth century.

Works comparing attitudes to slavery in Western and non-Western societies have been relatively rare in modern scholarship, partly due to the trendy desire to avoid pronouncing judgment on an "entire culture." An exception is a short book by Ahmed E. Elbashir, a Western-trained Sudanese scholar, comparing American and Egyptian-Sudanese views of Nile Valley slavery before and during the Civil War in the United States.[28] The author traces American reaction to and involvement in the suppression of the slave trade in that region

27. Specific references here are to pp. 97–98 of Mowafi's *Slavery, Slave Trade, and Abolition.*

28. Elbashir, *United States, Slavery, and the Slave Trade in the Nile Valley*. For further comment on and quotation from the book, see chap. 4, above, n. 29.

and boldly addresses the absence of an abolitionist movement in Egypt and the Sudan. Elbashir's long association with Howard University, the leading African American school, has probably sensitized him to the issue and might have induced him to undertake such a comparative project.

With all their importance for cross-discourse fertilization, the works mentioned above did not break the language barrier, thereby allowing the treatment of slavery among Arab scholars to remain a fairly isolated discourse. In the 1980s, however, the Western discourse on slavery began to make some inroads into the Middle Eastern and North African discourse in Arabic. Thus, for example, in 1983, the Moroccan historian Muhammad al-Nājī published in Rabat an article entitled "Concerning the [Question of] Slaves in the Maghrib before Imperialism."[29] The author argues that before the French occupation, slaves in the Maghrib were badly treated and that trivial transgressions were severely punished, at times resulting in the death of the slave. He also asserts that slaves ran away frequently, which attests to their ill-treatment, and that the negative attitude toward slaves, presumably African, is not surprising in a society that considered Africans to be markedly inferior. Al-Nājī explains that by pointing out these phenomena, he hopes to open up a debate concerning the whole question of slavery in the Maghrib. Indeed, this challenge was met by his compatriot Muhammad al-Razūq in the article mentioned above. In a footnote, al-Razūq rebukes his colleague, arguing that one opens up a debate by offering questions for discussion, not by pointing out negative phenomena—a curious approach, to say the least, that underlines the resistance that criticism of this sort has been facing.

In 1990, ʿAbd al-Mālik Khalaf al-Tamīmī, of the history department at the University of Kuwait, published an interesting article in Arabic on the slave trade in the Gulf region between 1820 and 1928.[30] The author used the India Office Records in Britain and some local sources to describe the political, social, and economic

29. "Hawla al-Raqīq fī al-Maghrib mā qabla al-Istiʿmār," *Abhāth* (Rabat) 1 (Jan.–Feb. 1983): 45–57.

30. "Barītānyā wa-Tijārat al-Raqīq fī Mintaqat al-Khalīj al-ʿArabī, 1820–1928," *Al-Majalla al-Tārīkhiyya al-ʿArabiyya li-l-Dirāsāt al-ʿUthmāniyya* [Arab Historical Review for Ottoman Studies] 1+2 (1990): 73–91 (Arabic section) (a brief abstract in English is provided on p. 147 of the English and French section).

mechanisms that operated in the Gulf slave trade. He clearly asserts that no sociologist or social historian can avoid dealing with the important and sensitive issue of slavery and the slave trade. This piece is undoubtedly well within the Western discourse on slavery and is almost free of the defensive-apologetic tone. The only exception is in the opening paragraph, where al-Tamīmī admits that "European" writings on slavery provide (reliable) information but claims that they share a bias in depicting slavery and the slave trade as an Eastern phenomenon rather than stress the fact that these prevailed in both East and West. While patently wrong, this is a small price to pay for what is otherwise an important contribution, presented by the author as "an attempt to pave the way for more comprehensive research on the slave trade in the future."[31]

An even bolder contribution to the Arab discourse on slavery in Arabic is ʿAbd al-ʿAlīm ʿAlī ʿAbd al-Wahhāb Abū Haykal's article on African slaves in the Hijaz during the first half of the twentieth century.[32] Based on a wide array of American, British, and Saudi archival material, as well as Western and Arab studies and newspapers, this is a rare and even-handed discussion of the last phase of slavery in the Arabian Peninsula. The author describes the modes of enslavement, the number of slaves, their prices, and the various types of work they did. He reserves judgment on the issue of how domestic slaves were treated and cites opposing views by Arab and European writers. Abī Haykal then concludes that slavery was affected by the political, economic, and social changes that were taking place in the Hijaz at midcentury. Slavery, he asserts, belonged to the domestic issues that had been shelved by the Saudi leadership due to the pressing need to formulate a coherent foreign policy. When it was addressed,

31. Ibid., p. 147 (the English abstract). The "European" writers mentioned are J. J. Lorimer, Arnold T. Wilson, John B. Kelly, and Ehud R. Toledano (p. 73). The position attributed by the author to these writers is nowhere to be found in their books (e.g., a quick look at the opening pages of the introduction to my *Ottoman Slave Trade,* pp. 3–5, would easily show that the very opposite is true). The author makes no attempt to engage in any debate with the traditional Arab discourse on slavery, though he does mention two of the articles referred to above (by Abdeljelil Temimi—who happens to be the editor of the journal in which ʿAbd al-Mālik Khalaf al-Tamīmī's article appeared—and by Muhammad al-Razūq). The article contains some legitimate criticism of British policies, which is, needless to say, part and parcel of the Western discourse on slavery.

32. "Al-Raqīq al-Afrīqī bi-l-Hijāz khilāl al-Nisf al-Awwal min al-Qarn al-ʿIshrīn," *Al-Majalla al-Tārīkhiyya al-Misriyya* 36 (1989): 317–51.

the issue became entangled in the struggle between promodern and conservative forces in the developing world and in the campaign for human rights, until its resolution through the official abolition of slavery in Saudi Arabia in 1962.

While Arab scholars and political academics have often been critical and defensive about the work of Western and Western-trained scholars on slavery in Muslim societies,[33] the reaction in modern Turkey to the study of Ottoman slavery has been markedly different. This is partially because of the impact of forced secularization; a more open atmosphere in Turkish academic circles with regard to Western scholarship on the Ottoman Empire; an only limited commitment during the early years of the Republic to defend the Ottoman past, which yielded a sober, balanced treatment of that Ottoman heritage in later years; and the large presence in Turkish universities of liberal-minded, Western-trained scholars. Although old-guard scholars have often treated archival materials about slavery and the slave trade in the familiar *explication de texte* genre, their work is relatively free of the defensive sentiments described above for the conservative Arab discourse on slavery.[34] Needless to say, the work of Turkish scholars such Halil İnalcık, Ömer Lutfi Barkan, Halil Sahillioğlu, Metin Kunt, and others is well within the Western discourse on Ottoman slavery.

For the late 1980s and early 1990s, one can note an even greater willingness among Turkish academics to deal with Ottoman slavery. İsmail Parlatır's 1987 study in Turkish on the motif of slavery in the literature of the long-Tanzimat period (1830s–1880s) is an honest, if somewhat mechanistic, scholarly endeavor that reflects a readiness to deal with "unpleasant" components in one's own heritage.[35] Gülnihal Bozkurt studied the legal history of Islamic and Ottoman slavery

33. We should not forget that these deficiencies are mostly evident in the study of domestic slavery in its last phase and the abolition of slavery. Serious work has been done by Arab scholars on medieval military slavery in Muslim societies, most notably in the Mamluk Sultanate but also in earlier and later Islamic states.

34. Various items on slavery in Pakalın's historical dictionary, published in Istanbul during the 1940s and 1950s, still contain what I would call a mildly defensive attitude about the Islamic view of slavery. See Mehmet Zeki Pakalın, *Osmanlı Tarih Deyimleri ve Terimleri Sözlüğü*, 5 vols. (Istanbul, 1946–56), s.v., e.g., *Köle, Kölelik, Kul, Kulluk*, and related terms.

35. Parlatır, *Tanzimat Edebiyatında Kölelik*. A German dissertation by Börte Sagaster is expected to appear shortly. Sagaster covers both fiction and nonfiction writings by Ottoman intellectuals and explores also the changing image of the slave in Ottoman society. I am indebted to her for kindly providing this information.

as early as 1981.[36] And in 1993 an Oxford-trained Turkish scholar, Y. Hakan Erdem, completed a dissertation entitled "Slavery in the Ottoman Empire and Its Demise, 1800–1909," which is both critical and empathetic, examining Ottoman archival material in light of Western-developed methodologies. In 1994, my own book on the Ottoman slave trade in the nineteenth century appeared in Turkish translation under the auspices of the Economic and Social History Foundation.[37] However, the Islamic revival in Turkey in recent years has rekindled some of the old-fashioned sentiments on the issue and has already yielded a number of polemical pieces by Islamic intellectuals.[38]

All these comments lead to the conclusion that we might be at the beginning of a slow, gradual process of integrating two different discourses on the history of slavery in Muslim societies, particularly with regard to slavery in the Ottoman Empire. This process resembles in many ways what has been occurring between the various discourses on the history of Muslim societies in general. Until recently, the Western discourse on Islamic slavery has formulated and treated questions that had not concerned the Arab discourse on the subject. The methods used by Western and Western-trained scholars have also been quite different from those employed by Arab scholars. Even the languages used in the discourse, and concomitantly the vocabulary and the constructs, have not been the same: one uses Arabic; the other, European languages. This has been most strikingly demonstrated in the volume produced by the Arab League's Tunis conference mentioned above: Western-trained African scholars used English and French, and Arab scholars used Arabic, all in the same book. The authors were clearly writing within two separate and only marginally related discourses on slavery.

36. Bozkurt's unpublished dissertation dealt with slavery in Islamic and Ottoman law ("İslâm ve Osmanlı Hukukunda Kölelik," Ankara, 1981). The paper she presented at the Bellagio conference on the Mediterranean and trans-Saharan slave trade (Dec. 1988) treated the legal suppression of the Ottoman slave trade. The paper was not included in Savage's collection but was published in Turkish under the title "Köle Ticaretinin Sona Erdirilmesi Konusunda Osmanlı Devletinin Taraf Olduğu ki Devletlerarası Anlaşma," in *Osmanli Tarihi Araştirmalari Mecmuâsi* (Ankara, 1990), pp. 45–77.

37. Erdem's thesis was published in the St. Antony's series in 1996; the title and publisher of my translated book are *Osmanlı Köle Ticareti, 1840–1890*, Tarih Vakfı Yurt Yayınları (Istanbul, 1994).

38. See, e.g., an article by Ali Bulaç in *Türk Edebiyatı*, Apr. 1994.

Most notably perhaps, the Arab discourse has suffered from the stultifying effects of a defensive and apologetic streak, which has hampered true cross-discourse exchanges. The Turkish discourse on Ottoman slavery has already integrated to a very large extent with its Western-influenced counterpart, and the flow of ideas in both directions is now taken for granted. The Arab discourse on slavery in the Ottoman period is gradually entering into a fruitful dialogue with the other two, though it seems to me that a more serious debate within Arab discourse must still take place in earnest, in which Arab establishment scholars will face their own heritage and come to grips with it. Such internal dynamics might be stimulated by contributions from Arab scholars such as the three articles already noted and by critical input from African scholars, especially African Muslim ones, who are already demanding that the Arabs own up to their past role as slave dealers and slave owners (see above on the Tunis conference).

In conclusion, it might be illuminating to add that a great deal of this debate is a reflection of the larger dispute concerning relativism and universalism in human rights.[39] Although slavery as we knew it is fairly dead in the former domains of the Ottoman Empire, the battle over the heritage of slavery is not. Whereas in the West historians of Muslim societies are often inclined to embrace a relativist view, they must not allow the emergence of "forbidden agendas" in scholarly research, no matter how "sensitive" the issues might seem. One should not mix the empathy that is due to the slaves and their plight with sympathy for those who write about them and who seek to defend the past record of slave dealers and slave-owning societies. That very defense and the ensuing apologia stem from a profound change in the value system that would never have come about if nineteenth-century abolitionists had accepted the tenets of relativism.

One should not, however, automatically treat Western standards and ideas as being somehow "universal" and view non-Western belief and value systems as "local cultures" that are in various ways deficient or not fully developed versions of the desired norm. A

39. On this, see, e.g., Douglas Lee Donoho, "Relativism versus Universalism in Human Rights: The Search for Meaningful Standards," *Stanford Journal of International Law* 27 (1991); Jack Donnely, *Universal Human Rights in Theory and Practice* (Ithaca, 1989); Alison Dundes Renteln, *International Human Rights: Universalism versus Relativism* (Newbury Park, 1990); and Abdullahi Ahmed An-Naʿim, ed., *Human Rights in Cross-Cultural Perspectives: A Quest for Consensus* (Philadelphia, 1992).

growing awareness of this pitfall has clearly emerged over the past decade within the Western discourse on slavery. Whereas such an awareness has enriched our understanding of non-Western slavery, the moral—as distinct from what might be termed methodological—relativism that has at times accompanied it is obfuscating the main analytic issues and creating new "attitude" problems.

CONCLUSION

Ottoman Slavery in World Slavery

Despite some exceptions, slavery in Muslim societies has figured only marginally in comparative studies on slavery. Such projects have most frequently been undertaken by specialists in slavery in North and South America, Africa, and the Far East. This is indeed a striking phenomenon, given the undisputed social and political importance of slavery in Muslim societies, the rising interest in the social and cultural history of these societies, and the ongoing publication of studies on slavery in other societies. The reasons are, however, relatively easy to explain, though they need to be spelled out and grappled with if the problem is to be overcome, which it should be and is fairly likely to be in coming years.

"The study of slavery and the slave trade," writes W. G. Clarence-Smith in a collection of articles on the slave trade in the Indian Ocean, "has become one of the fastest growing areas of academic research into the economic and social history of the 'Third World,' but the 'Eastern' slave trade has not received its due share of attention."[1] As he points out, the international congresses on slavery and the slave trade (Nantes in 1985 and São Paulo in 1988) focused almost exclusively on the Atlantic trade. His is one of the very few attempts

1. Clarence-Smith, *Indian Ocean Slave Trade*, p. 1.

"to begin to right the balance," as he puts it, between the great attention devoted to the Atlantic slave trade and the paucity of studies on what he calls the "Eastern" traffic. As far as Ottoman slavery is concerned, however, Clarence-Smith's collection is but a modest contribution, since only two out of its twelve articles deal with territories directly under Ottoman rule (Egypt and the Sudan, and Arabia), and three more touch on the periphery of Ottoman territory. Yet, a quick look at the map provided by the editor himself (p. 2) reveals that most of the arrows indicating the direction of the slave trade from East Africa lead to the Ottoman Empire.

In 1982, Michael Craton assessed the progress of studies in comparative slavery, which he saw as the third of three waves in the post–Stanley Elkins historiography of slavery, following the Marxian-influenced works on slavery and the interdisciplinary studies under the impact of the Annales school and the Cambridge Group.[2] Craton admits though that only in recent years have American scholars begun to examine non–United States slavery, and that their efforts have only been extended to the Caribbean and Latin America. This is clearly demonstrated in the Presidential Address delivered at the American Economic History Association meeting in 1986 by the eminent historian of slavery Stanley L. Engerman.[3] Surveying the major debates in the field, Engerman treats mainly the United States and mentions, for example, the debate over the economic value of slave versus free labor and the argument about why and how slavery exhausts its usefulness and how long it takes it then to actually end. He then extends his discussion to include only "the Americas," referring at times also to slavery in Greek and Roman antiquity, India, and Mauritius and scattered Pacific cases. Engerman even ventures some comparative comments regarding Russian serfdom, but he completely ignores slavery in Muslim societies.

A staunch believer in the need for comparative studies, Craton still argues that "indeed, it is only by knowing more about slavery in Africa and Asia as well as North America and plantation slavery in America at large, and about slavery in post-imperial and ancient times

2. "A Cresting Wave? Recent Trends in the Historiography of Slavery, with Special Reference to the British Caribbean," *Historical Reflections/Réflexions Historiques* 9/3 (1982): 403–19.

3. "Slavery and Emancipation in Comparative Perspective: A Look at Some Recent Debates," *Journal of Economic History* 46/2 (1986): 317–39.

as well as in the age of European expansion and dominance . . . , that we can fully understand, or even justify, the study of . . . localised slavery."[4] But only a few years later, Peter Kolchin still concludes that works on non–United States slavery have actually shown the uniqueness of the American case in its self-reproductive, racial, mainly agricultural, and non-elite character. He also claims, unjustly, that students of non–United States slavery have not followed the dominant trend among scholars of United States slavery, that is, to look at the slaves themselves, as subjects rather than objects, using evidence emanating from slave sources.[5] Furthermore, George M. Fredrickson asserts that although the character and consequences of African American slavery were "the most highly developed subject of comparative historical study in the United States," scholars have recently preferred to undertake microlevel research on various aspects of slavery in specific places.[6]

This is certainly one of the reasons for the paucity of comparative studies on slavery, and the trend toward microhistorical research has indeed often come at the expense of larger, comparative efforts. However, perhaps a more salient factor, in my view at least, has been that historians of American slavery believe, by and large, that non-American slavery, especially that practiced by Muslim societies, is not suitable for comparison with slavery in the United States. Islamic societies, certainly the Ottoman one, were not "slave societies/economies" in the classical sense of the term, since agricultural slavery was not widespread in them, but rather the milder forms of domestic and elite slavery were dominant. Hence, rather than attract the interest of American and non-American comparativists, as Kolchin hoped for, the lack of similarity has inhibited interest by Americanists in non-American slavery, because the latter's relevance to their subject matter has been harder to establish.

An additional reason for the limited number of comparative works in general, not only in the history of slavery, is what Fredrickson

4. "A Cresting Wave?" p. 404.

5. "Slavery outside the United States," pp. 767–77. Kolchin's point on different methods is on p. 774, but this is certainly not the case in the study of slavery in Africa (see, e.g., Robertson and Klein, *Women and Slavery in Africa*); I hope that the present volume has shown that, with regard to Ottoman slavery too, this is not so, and indeed has not been so for more than a decade.

6. Fredrickson, "Comparative History," p. 465.

identifies as the organization of historical studies in the United States, which favors intense specialization in one country or culture.[7] This might have contributed to the lack of enthusiasm among historians of the American South for studying slavery in the Ottoman Empire or, for that matter, in any other Muslim society. But it can hardly account for the reluctance among Islamicists to undertake the study of slavery or the slave trade in the societies whose social, political, economic, and cultural history is the focus of their scholarly endeavors.

There are, I believe, three possible explanations for that reluctance. The first is political and is often disguised under the convenient label of "the sensitivity of the topic," that is, the disinclination to investigate potentially conflictual and divisive topics across a cultural divide. The second is that—unlike in the United States and to a lesser extent in Latin America—there is no large, self-aware, and sociopolitically important community of slave descendants in the formerly Ottoman Middle East; nor is there a community that sees itself as descended from, or heir to, the slaveholders. Hence, there are no active "constituencies" that create a demand to have their slave or slaveholding past investigated so that they can come to terms with it.[8] And third, there is a scholarly-analytic reason: the inherent difficulty in comprehending a rather complex social, economic, and cultural phenomenon, such as Ottoman slavery, that contains apparent internal contradictions. In the following pages I sum up and contextualize some of the main conceptual difficulties involved in that multifaceted institution.

Martin A. Klein's systematic introduction to his recent edited collection *Breaking the Chains: Slavery, Bondage, and Emancipation in Modern Africa and Asia* provides a typology of the existing definitions of slavery, which he breaks down into three main categories: (1) definitions that stress the slave's *kinlessness* in the slave-owning society and use that as a major interpretive tool (notably Patterson, Meillassoux, Miers and Kopytoff, and Watson); (2) definitions based

7. Ibid., pp. 472–73.

8. Such a demand could, of course, come from an "external" constituency: the African societies whose men, women, and children were carried off to the Ottoman Empire (but see chap. 5, above, for the problematics involved). The interesting question of why the fairly large slave trade into the eastern Mediterranean has left such minimal traces in the populations of the present-day Middle East and North Africa is treated in Manning, *Slavery and African Life,* pp. 38–48, and Hunwick, "Black Africans," pp. 5–38.

on the *proprietary relations* between owners and slaves; and (3) definitions that stress the *power relations* between master/mistress and slave, beginning with the violence of enslavement and continuing with the constant need for coercion to retain the enslaved person in slavery.[9] This is a rather useful departure point to locate and analyze Ottoman slavery, but we must first consider some additional definitions that are relevant to the Ottoman situation.

Some of the general analytic frameworks developed for understanding slavery worldwide suffer from what might be called theoretical "totalism" and risk losing the historian's sympathy. An appropriate example of that can be found in Claude Meillassoux's *The Anthropology of Slavery: The Womb of Iron and Gold,* where he opts for an ideal-type definition of slavery that rarely fits any given historical reality.[10] The notion of the slave's kinlessness—admittedly based on the African model—is carried to an unrealistic extreme, thereby losing its explanatory power for the historian, certainly for the historian of Ottoman society. It was the slave's master, writes Meillassoux, "who gave birth to him each day, by letting him live another day. Only the master could grant him the attributes of a person, albeit fictitious and precarious." Thus, his account of the "revenge of the anti-kin" may apply to some African societies, but it hardly fits the Ottoman Empire. Nonetheless, his description of slaves in high positions would seem familiar, to some extent, to students of Ottoman military-administrative slavery.[11]

Still, ideas such as those developed by Patterson and Meillassoux, among others, at least attempt to bring cultural analysis and social psychology into the historical interpretation of slavery. One would naturally expect psychological interpretations to contribute useful

9. "Introduction: Modern European Expansion and Traditional Servitude in Africa and Asia," in Klein, *Breaking the Chains,* pp. 3–36. The typology of definitions for "slave" referred to in this paragraph is on pp. 4–5.

10. Comments in this paragraph draw on Meillassoux's discussion on pp. 138–40 of his *Anthropology of Slavery.*

11. On this Meillassoux writes: "In societies ruled by kinship, the anti-kin could be an effective agent of social and political manipulation. By replacing free men with slaves, the masters could protect themselves from ambitious relatives or rebellious subjects; and at the same time they could protect themselves from these henchmen, by granting them differentiated privileges which divided them among themselves and further attached them to their master" (*Anthropology of Slavery,* pp. 139–40).

insights to the discussion of slave *mentalité*, the peculiar predicament of the military slave as both bondsman and commander, the effects of castration on the personality of eunuchs, the impact of *harem* life on women, or the role of sexuality in the social and political life of slave-owning societies. However, there has generally been very little input of this kind infused into the slavery debate. Hence, although based on surprisingly limited and unrepresentative data regarding Islamic slavery, Dean A. Miller's article "Some Psycho-social Perceptions of Slavery" is a welcome venture. The status of slaves, as that of other dominated groups, Miller believes, was strongly tied to the "psychologically-motivated diminution or reduction of the[ir] image . . . by the dominant [slave-owning] group."[12]

Slave owners used expressions, Miller asserts, that imputed to the slaves "sets of natural (in the sense of innate, immutable) characteristics that firmly identify the slave within a derogated continuum which extends from the less than adult (less than fully socialized or socializable) to the less-than-human, or truly inhuman, characteristic zone." In Miller's universal model, the slave-owning, dominant group "affects to see, or believes that it *must* see, various proofs of both natural *and* unnatural anomaly and thus inferiority in the dominated group: its slaves." While slave owners were driven by contempt and fear, slaves possessed a negative power that emanated from the ambiguity and anomaly of their status. Thus, slaves were variously regarded as children, animals, or monsters, and their sexuality and " 'unnatural' morphism" were feared. In turn, slaves had "compensatory, if negative power—real or suspected"—that ranged from the supernatural to the military and political. In these capacities slaves were believed to be endowed with "death-dealing" powers, which only increased the ambiguity of their position in society.

This book has attempted to show that Ottoman slavery is better explained by models, such as Miller's, that stress the mutually conditioning effect of the owner-slave relationship, with all its human complexity and reciprocity. In the same vein, Richard Harvey Brown argues that the representation of slaves is a form of domination that—across cultures and societies—facilitates and legitimates slavery itself. He asks why the image of African slaves in medieval Muslim societies

12. *Journal of Social History* 18/4 (1985): 587–605. Quotations in this and the following paragraphs are from pp. 522 and 588–89.

resembles the "Sambo personality" in American slavery and asserts in response that, in addition to other factors, "the discourse and practice of slavery itself creates the 'Sambo personality,' both as a stereotype held by slaveholders to legitimate their domination, as well as a tactic of adaptation used by the oppressed to survive psychically and to limit exploitation."[13] To this line of argument, too, belongs Patterson's concept of "human parasitism," which deals in a satisfying way with the complexities of owner-slave relations by addressing the "cooperation and mutualism between holder/parasite and slave/host."[14]

Hence, whether we accept Patterson's metaphor or some other device, Ottoman slavery must be understood as a *social relationship,* as a dynamic give-and-take between owner and slave in a variety of changing situations.[15] This applies to all types of Ottoman slaves. One must not assume, however, that owner-slave relations in the empire were necessarily harmonious; rather, the material presented in this book provides ample evidence of the slaves' resistance to the total control imposed by their owners. To begin with, the exclusivity of the owner-slave relationship that typifies slavery systems was never part

13. "Cultural Representation and Ideological Domination," *Social Forces* 71/3 (1993): 666.

14. On human parasitism, see Patterson, *Slavery and Social Death,* pp. 334–42; the quotation is from p. 337.

15. A legitimate question in this respect is whether the evidence exists to support the suggested shift of emphasis to the slaves themselves and the *relationships* they formed. For this agenda, official sources—both Ottoman and non-Ottoman—are likely to become less useful. We may not have slave diaries, archeological evidence from former plantation sites, or similar materials, which exist for the study of slavery in the United States, for example, but we are fortunate to possess a mine of relevant information in the Ottoman court records. Such detailed accounts of legal cases adjudicated by Ottoman *kadıs* (Şerî court judges) are available for most, if not all, the provinces. Information about slaves can be teased out not only from cases in which slaves were directly involved but also from cases in which testimony rendered by witnesses mentions slaves and slave owners. Records exist also of cases adjudicated before the new administrative councils/courts established during the Tanzimat as part of a wide array of reforms. While it is possible, on the basis of such records, to transcend the "community of litigants" and reconstruct a full picture of social realities, one must still be aware of the fact that both the law and the courts applying it reflect the worldview and value system of the dominant groups in Ottoman society, not those of the slaves. In any event, it seems that the stage is now set for an expansion of the study of slavery in various parts of the Ottoman Empire. New questions can and should be asked of old and new sources in order to gain fresh insights into Ottoman society and culture and bring the study of Ottoman slavery into the mainstream of studies on slavery in other societies around the globe.

of Ottoman realities. The Şeriat-based court system breached that exclusivity by allowing slaves to complain of ill-treatment, which could lead to forced manumission. Although, as we have seen, the courts were reluctant to intervene in owner-slave relations, and the state was careful not to force owners to manumit slaves involuntarily, an arbitration mechanism was at all times available in the background, able if necessary to step into that relationship.

In the nineteenth century, the Ottoman state marched right into the conflicts that erupted between Circassian agricultural slaves and their masters. It empowered the Immigration Commission to manage these conflicts and also to resolve problems that emerged from the traffic in Circassian refugee girls and boys. Its consultative councils and administrative courts deliberated matters relating to slavery, enacted codes with clauses concerning slavery, and adjudicated disputes between owners and slaves. The Ottoman government also restricted the market for slaves in various ways and eventually suppressed the African slave trade into the empire.

The slaves' resistance to exploitation was overt and violent, and ultimately they achieved their goal and were gradually liberated. As the nineteenth century wore on, Britain's abolitionist interventionism drove yet another wedge between owner and slave, as not a few of the slaves flocked to consulates across the empire—in Jidda, Izmir, and Istanbul, as in Tripoli, Cairo, Damascus, and Baghdad—in search of refuge and manumission. Owners resisted their slaves' attempt to break away and sought to protect their privileged way of life. But as the story of Şemsigül shows, even before such external options were open to slaves, it was possible to make a stand against exploitation and oppression from within. It was precisely inside the household *(kapı)* that even humble slaves had to negotiate their position vis-à-vis the powerful figures at the family compound since, for slavery to work efficiently, labor could not be extracted solely by the constant threat of force.

As much as the worlds of owners and slaves were demarcated by status and wealth, these worlds were not in fact physically separate. Rather, most domestic slaves and their owners inhabited the same space; the *kapı* was the home they shared and the place where their reciprocal relationships were formed and developed. Elite households were of course stratified internally—as all families indeed are—and the distribution of power within them was never in doubt. However, to view slaves as always standing on the "receiving end," never having any agency, seems to me to somehow miss the "real-life" situation in such households. With free and bond sharing the same space, a multiplicity of relationships developed that often transcended the owner-slave one. In these relationships roles were switched, transposed, and recast.[16]

Kul/harem slavery was conceived of as an *origin,* rather than a *status,* whereas domestic and agricultural slavery definitely constituted a *status.* Accordingly, there was no opposition to the participation of *kul/harem* slaves in husband-wife or patron-client relations, and they were allowed to own property, including slaves of all types, hold state offices, and fully engage in the political, economic, and cultural life of Ottoman society. In fact, an inversion of sorts occurred when *kul/harem* origin (i.e., slave origin) became a mark of high status and privilege. As already mentioned, female social roles were clearly differentiated within nineteenth-century elite *harem*s, with the menial domestics *(cihaz halayiği)* ranking at the bottom together with the free servants, and the concubines *(odalık*s) reigning at the top with the free ladies of the household. Although domestic and agricultural slaves were legally restricted persons, needed formal manumission to become free subjects, and had a low social status, even they could often find themselves in role relations that in effect mitigated and even overrode their bondage.

A suckling relationship, which was an extremely important institution, could elevate an African female slave, for example, to a "mothering" relationship with the freeborn children of the master and mistress of the house, thereby also enabling her own children to be considered "brothers" and "sisters" of the children of the family. These were often lifetime relationships that entailed protection, patronage, loyalty, and mutual affection. In Ottoman elite *kapı*s, such bondage-extenuating mechanisms were more apt to develop because of the intimate "home situations" that prevailed in them.

16. A similar point is also made by Kolchin in his *Unfree Labor.* Kolchin calls for shifting the focus to the slaves themselves and asserts that "although the former [owners] supposedly were in charge, the latter [slaves] were far from passive and never conformed entirely to the masters' wishes or expectations. Their relationship therefore represented an uneasy equilibrium, a compromise with which no one was entirely happy. If the masters had the upper hand, the slaves and serfs played major roles in shaping—and setting limits to—their own bondage" (p. xi).

This resembled the case in the United States South, where bonded house servants were considered by themselves and by slave society as the most privileged of slaves. In Russia, on the other hand, domestic slaves were seen as the least fortunate, because they were subject to greater owner supervision and lost the freedom and relative economic leeway that life within the bonded village community afforded.[17] With the limited evidence and research available at the moment on Circassian agricultural slavery, we can only assume that it shared properties with both systems of bondage but that it was perhaps closer to the situation in Russia, which, after all, was the next-door neighbor in the Caucasus.

Throughout the nineteenth century—but probably also before and increasingly more so with the shrinking of the market for slaves—households would take in girls, and sometimes also boys, from poor families within their patronage orbit, bring them up within the household, use their labor in return for food and shelter, train them according to need and talent, and later marry them off and set them up in life *(çirak/çirağ* and *besleme),* thereby further expanding patronage networks. The role relations that developed in such a context do not lend themselves to a simple, mechanistic analysis. The complexity and richness of these life situations are the stuff of which the weblike environment of the *kapı* was made, a subject matter that has been justifiably attracting a growing number of scholars in recent years.

Looking at all this, it is quite obvious that the complexity of the phenomenon of slavery is not amenable to simple, clear-cut definitions

17. For the view that on American plantations the relationship between the master's family and the house slaves was closer than that with the farm and workshop laborers, see, e.g., Stanton, " 'Those Who Labor for My Happiness,' " pp. 150–53. The intimate mingling of white slaveholders and their African slaves within the owners' houses was very much on the mind of a slaveholder such as Thomas Jefferson, who was terrified by the impact it would have on white society in the long run (see Rhys Isaac, "The First Monticello," in Onuf, *Jeffersonian Legacies,* p. 99). For a comparison with the situation of house slaves on Russian estates, see Kolchin, *Unfree Labor,* pp. 352–57. Kolchin's explanation is predicated on the essential difference between community life in the Russian serf village and in the African American slave quarters on the plantation. To that we might add that in both the United States and the Ottoman Empire, the slaves were imported from the outside and became "alien," or "kinless," whereas in Russia, slaves were drawn from Russian society itself, not infrequently remaining within their own village community. Still, in all these societies, female house slaves were exposed to sexual abuse, though the legitimacy and relative security of concubinage in the Ottoman Empire might have improved the lot of women in elite households.

despite their enormous appeal, especially to scholars who study a large number of slave societies and attempt to produce global comparative works.[18] For Ottoman slavery, however, one must provide a framework for analysis that accommodates such diverse phenomena as military-administrative slavery, *harem* slavery, domestic slavery, and agricultural slavery. In such realities, any single-factor definition is likely to prove unsatisfactory, unless of course one chooses to exclude a certain category from the class of slaves (e.g., *kul/harem* slaves), which in my view is unnecessary and would create inconsistencies in the historical analysis of this phenomenon.[19]

Thus, considering the Ottoman case, the sweeping concept of *social alienation* (or kinlessness) has a limited explanatory power for slavery in the empire, since the proximity and intimacy of daily interaction between owner and slave produced what is sometimes called "fictive-kin" relations that incorporated the slave—via the elite household—into the social networks *(intisap)* of Ottoman society, often effectively compensating for the lack of natural kin relations, though certainly at a psychological cost.[20] *Proprietary relations,* too, are only one component of the condition of slavery, and when the legal, Şerî aspect is overemphasized, the often mitigating impact of social realities is lost, thereby privileging a formalistic discussion of legalistic-normative nuances. Even the basic notion of *power relations* is not very effective if carried beyond the banal and self-evident

18. Peter Kolchin's view, in "Slavery outside the United States," pp. 767–77, reflects a seemingly pervasive frustration with the poor results of most attempts at some grand universal definition of slavery. He suggests that the diversity of the phenomenon and the usage of the term are similar to those of many other terms, such as "liberty," "democracy," or "terrorist," and cogently argues that the meaning of such terms "cannot . . . be deduced by examining many cases and noting shared characteristics" (p. 772). However, his suggestion that "slavery" should mean what we mean by it assumes the usefulness of a universal term, which I feel is somewhat doubtful. Rather, we should strive to understand what "slavery"—and other terms—meant in given, historical social environments, regardless of whether it meant something different in other societies and at other times.

19. A striking resemblance that still remains to be explored exists between slavery in the Ottoman Empire and the *kholopy* of Russia regarding, among other features, the varieties of slave types involved (see Kolchin, *Unfree Labor,* pp. 2–3).

20. As mentioned in n. 17, above, one can also point to cases such as Russian slavery, where most slaves were in fact indigenous (see, e.g., Hellie, *Slavery in Russia,* pp. 390 ff.). A concept related to that of fictive kin can be found in the rehumanization of the "nonperson" (the slave) in his or her new social setting, as described by Miers and Kopytoff, *Slavery in Africa,* pp. 17, 23.

level. It is certainly true that Circassian agricultural slavery required continued coercion (see chapter 3), but *kul/harem* slavery certainly required no force, nor in many cases did domestic slavery in elite households throughout the Ottoman Empire.

In an earlier attempt at a definition of the position of African female slaves, Claire Robertson and Martin Klein offered the following characterization: "the slave is involuntarily servile, has a marginal position within her social unit, and is subject to the control of another."[21] In other words, this is a combination of several of Klein's later types, transcending earlier definitions that stressed property relationship or kinlessness. Because in the Ottoman Empire during the nineteenth century most slaves were female, as in African societies, one might expect this definition to also be applicable here. However, it is largely (though not always) not, mainly because in the Ottoman case, servility was voluntary for many domestic slaves, many free servants were under the control of another person (at times himself or herself a slave), and *kul/harem* slaves were certainly not marginal and often controlled other persons, free and slave.

Hence, we must try a more differentiated approach to the complex realities of Ottoman slavery, which might perhaps also be relevant to other, non-Ottoman situations. It is quite obvious to me that what we are dealing with here is a *continuum* of various degrees of bondage rather than a *dichotomy* between slave and free. At one end of the spectrum stand the domestic, agricultural, and Sudanese military slaves, the most restricted of Ottoman slaves. Officeholders stand at the other end, with much less to tie them to the phenomenon of slavery. Not very far from officeholders we find our *kul*-type slaves, or state functionaries of slave origins. A little further down the steep road leading to the depths of bondage, we come upon *harem* ladies of slave origins. These last three groups, however, are located quite apart from those who populate the rest of our continuum. By walking this path rather than that of contrasting dichotomies, we avoid forcing rigid categories upon a complex social phenomenon that rebels against them. In so doing, we can also accommodate culture-bound, historical nuances that would otherwise elude us.

This is certainly not the first time the concept of a continuum has been suggested for overcoming the problems inherent in any

21. Robertson and Klein, "Introduction," pp. 3–4.

definition of slavery, whether in the Ottoman Empire or elsewhere. Frederick Cooper also offers a continuum approach to the evaluation of slave usage and social status on the Muslim east coast of Africa. Cooper talks about a "balance between the divergent roles of slaves in a given society at a given time" that can situate a slave anywhere on a continuum from a person absorbed into the owner's social group to a mere worker.[22] He offers a very sensible interpretation of slavery, which is predicated on his brilliant comparison of plantation slavery in two remote locations—the Muslim east coast of Africa and the United States South.

Cooper's analysis integrates various types of seeming dichotomies: the social versus the economic aspects of slavery; the slave as an extension of the owner's will versus the slave as possessing a will of his or her own; the varying degrees of trust that slave owners harbored toward their slaves, from high to low; and the prestige that accrued as a result of owning slaves versus the fact that slaves did have economic value. Perhaps because he deals with a Muslim society, Cooper's *inclusivist* approach seems to me more suitable to the realities of Ottoman slavery than *exclusivist* approaches that view one component in a slave's identity as—analytically—overriding all others.[23]

Although the Islamic legal concept of slavery, *grosso modo,* admits only the basic distinction between free and slave, pre-Ottoman and Ottoman practice accepted the usage of additional terms to accommodate phenomena such as military-administrative slavery (*kul, gulam,* etc.). However, after the changes that occurred in the *kul* system from the sixteenth century onward and the ensuing distinction that emerged between the notion of officeholders' servility and actual slavery, the once convenient terminological distinction ceased to reflect reality. Consequently, the terms *köle* and *câriye* gradually gained ascendance, coming to denote all types of male and female slaves, re-

22. *Plantation Slavery,* p. 253.

23. The categories in my own continuum are nevertheless less fluid, or flexible, than Cooper's seem to be. In the East African society studied by Cooper, slaves were sometimes workers and sometimes soldiers in the service of their household head, since they were his "dependent followers," whereas in Ottoman society (or societies, if we wish to grant local culture greater weight), slaves tended to remain within their category, although some mobility did occur. Cooper's analysis, however, is quite close to my view of agricultural slavery among the Circassians in the Caucasus and later in the Ottoman Empire (see chap. 3, above).

spectively. Other terms, most notably *esir* for a male slave (pl. *üsera*), were also in use, though clearly accorded a lower preference.[24] The survival of *kul*-type slavery—in the revised form of the slave-turned-general/minister—was only partially represented in central Ottoman Turkish terminology, although in the Arab provinces men recruited and socialized in that fashion were called *mamlūks*.[25]

Thus, the Islamic legal unity of the notion of slavery, the lack of ready-made terminology in Western languages to accommodate the phenomenon of *kul/harem* slavery, the gradual changes in the *kul* system, and the emergence of the term *köle* to denote all types of Ottoman slaves, all yielded the uniform, undifferentiated view in the West of that rather complex Ottoman institution. Concomitantly, the slave prototype in Western eyes was, more or less, that of the African slave in the Americas, whereas the slave prototype which the Ottomans sought to project to the outside world, for polemical reasons, was that of the *kul/harem*. Within Ottoman society, however, the slave prototype was that of the domestic and, to a lesser extent, the agricultural slave, while *kul/harem* slaves were practically indistinguishable from their free social peers.[26] Such perceived internal contradictions, or inconsistencies, are only to be expected in a culture that was coping with internal and external challenges, responding to change, and adjusting to the transformation of the world around it. That world was increasingly interfering with internal Ottoman affairs, and slavery was just one of the vehicles employed in the power play of the nineteenth century.

24. On terminology, see Toledano, *Ottoman Slave Trade,* pp. xiv–xv (Ottoman), and Pipes, *Slave Soldiers and Islam,* pp. 195–98 (Arabic).

25. For this Ottoman phenomenon, not to be confused with realities in the Mamluk Sultanate (1250–1517), see Toledano, "Emergence of Ottoman-Local Elites."

26. Börte Sagaster has found that during the first decades of the twentieth century, the image of slaves in Ottoman society worsened (I believe that this reflected growing criticism of the institution, as opposed to its earlier defense). This will be reported in her forthcoming German dissertation, tentatively entitled "Ottoman Attitudes to Slavery in Literary Sources as a Reflection of Ottoman Society at the Turn of the Twentieth Century." I am grateful to her for sharing this information with me via personal communication.

BIBLIOGRAPHY

ARCHIVES

Archives of the British and Foreign Anti-Slavery Society, Rhodes House, Oxford

Archives of the Prime Minister's Office, Istanbul (Başbakanlık Arşivi = BA):
- İrade Collection:
  - Bab-ı Asafi/Ayniyat
  - Bab-ı Âli Evrak Odası (BAEO)
  - Meclis-i Vükelâ Mazbata ve İrade Dosyaları
- Kepeci Collection
- Yıldız Collection

British Museum, Western Manuscripts (BM):
- BM/Add. MS 42565, Brant Papers
- BM/Add. MS 39028, Layard Papers
- BM/Add. MS 43138, Aberdeen Papers
- BM/Add. MS 46094, Gladstone Papers

Egyptian National Archives (Dār al-Wathā᾿iq al-Qawmiyya), Cairo:
- Police Records (Dabtiyyat Misr)

Ministère des Affaires Étrangères, Paris:
- Correspondance Politique, Turquie
- Correspondance Consulaire, Turquie

Public Record Office (PRO), London:
- Foreign Office 84—Slave Trade (FO 84)
- Foreign Office 78—Turkey (FO 78)
- Foreign Office 195—Turkey, Consular (FO 195)

United States National Archives, Department of State, Washington, D.C.:
Despatches from U.S. Ministers to Turkey, 1818–1906 (M46)
Despatches from U.S. Consuls to Tripoli, Libya, 1796–1885 (T40)

BOOKS AND ARTICLES

Abd el Wahid, Ali. *Contribution à une théorie sociologique de l'esclavage: Études des situations génératrices de l'esclavage*. Paris, 1931.

Abū Haykal, ʿAbd al-ʿAlīm ʿAlī ʿAbd al-Wahhāb. "Al-Raqīq al-Afrīqī bi-l-Hijāz khilāl al-Nisf al-Awwal min al-Qarn al-ʿIshrīn." *Al-Majalla al-Tārīkhiyya al-Misriyya* 36 (1989): 317–51.

al-Ahnaf, Mustapha. "Sur quelques Durkheimiens Arabes." *Peuples Méditerranéens* 54–55 (Jan.–June 1995): 41–51.

Aristarchi, Grégoire. *Legislation ottomane*. 7 vols. Istanbul, 1873–88.

Ata, Tayyarzade Ahmet. *Tarih-i Ata*. Vol. 1. Istanbul, 1874.

Austen, Ralph A. "From the Atlantic to the Indian Ocean: European Abolition, the African Slave Trade, and Asian Economic Structures." In *The Abolition of the Atlantic Slave Trade*, ed. David Eltis and James Walvin. Madison, 1981.

———. "The 19th Century Islamic Slave Trade from East Africa (Swahili and Red Sea Coasts): A Tentative Census." In *The Economics of the Indian Ocean Slave Trade in the Nineteenth Century*, ed. William Gervase Clarence-Smith, *Slavery and Abolition* 9/3 (1988).

———. "The Mediterranean Islamic Slave Trade out of Africa: A Tentative Census." *Slavery and Abolition* 13/1 (1992): 214–48.

Ayalon, David. *L'esclavage du Mamelouks*. Jerusalem, 1951.

———. *Gunpowder and Firearms in the Mamluk Kingdom: A Challenge to a Medieval Society*. London, 1956.

———. "The Eunuchs in the Mamluk Sultanate." In *Studies in Memory of Gaston Wiet*. Jerusalem, 1977.

———. *Studies on the Mamluks of Egypt (1250–1517)*. London, 1977.

———. *The Mamluk Military Society*. London, 1979.

———. "On the Eunuchs in Islam." *Jerusalem Studies in Arabic and Islam* 1 (1979): 67–124.

Baer, Gabriel. *Egyptian Guilds in Modern Times*. Jerusalem, 1964.

———. *Studies in the Social History of Modern Egypt*. Chicago, 1969.

Barkan, Ömer Lûtfi. "Le sérvage éxistait-il en Turquie?" *Annales ESC* 11 (1956): 54–60.

Blunt, Lady F. J. *The People of Turkey*. 2 vols. London, 1878.

Bozkurt, Gülnihal. "İslâm ve Osmanlı Hukukunda Kölelik." Ph.D. diss., University of Ankara, 1981.

———. "Köle ticaretinin sona erdirilmesi konusunda Osmanlı Devletinin taraf olduğu ki devletlerarası anlaşma." In *Osmanlı Tarihi Araştırmaları Mecmuâsı*. Ankara, 1990.

Brown, Demetra. *Haremlik*. Boston and New York, 1909.

Brown, L. Carl. *The Tunisia of Ahmad Bey, 1837–1855*. Princeton, 1974.

Brown, Richard Harvey. "Cultural Representation and Ideological Domination." *Social Forces* 71/3 (1993): 657–76.

Brunschvig, R. "ʿAbd." In *Encyclopædia of Islam*, 2d ed., vol. 1. Leiden, 1960.

Cevdet, Ahmet. *Tezakir.* Ed. Cavid Baysun. 4 vols. Ankara, 1953–67.

Chefik, Ahmed. *L'esclavage au point de vue musulman.* Cairo, 1891. Translated into Arabic by Ahmad Zakī under the title *Al-Riqq fī ʾl-Islām* (Cairo, 1892).

Cole, Juan R. I. *Colonialism and Revolution in the Middle East: Social and Cultural Origins of Egypt's ʿUrabi Movement.* Princeton, 1993.

Cooper, Frederick. *Plantation Slavery on the East Coast of Africa.* New Haven and London, 1977.

Craton, Michael. "A Cresting Wave? Recent Trends in the Historiography of Slavery, with Special Reference to the British Caribbean." *Historical Reflections/Réflexions Historiques* 9/3 (1982): 403–19.

Crone, Patricia. *Slaves on Horses: The Evolution of the Islamic Polity.* Cambridge, 1980.

Curtin, Philip. *The Atlantic Slave Trade: A Census.* Madison, 1969.

———. *The Rise and Fall of the Plantation Complex: Essays in Atlantic History.* Cambridge, 1990.

Curtin, Philip D., Roger Anstey, and J. E. Inikori. "Discussion: Measuring the Atlantic Slave Trade." *Journal of African History* 17/4 (1976): 595–627.

Davis, David Brion. *The Problem of Slavery in the Age of Revolution, 1770–1823.* Ithaca, 1975.

———. *Slavery and Human Progress.* New York, 1984.

Davison, Roderic H. *Reform in the Ottoman Empire, 1856–1876.* Princeton, 1963.

Drescher, Seymour. *Capitalism and Antislavery: British Mobilization in Comparative Perspective.* London, 1986.

Düstur. 1st ed. 5 vols. Istanbul, 1872–92.

Elbashir, Ahmed E. *The United States, Slavery, and the Slave Trade in the Nile Valley.* Lanham, Md., 1983.

Elkins, Stanley. *Slavery.* Chicago, 1959.

Eltis, David. *Economic Growth and the Ending of the Transatlantic Slave Trade.* New York, 1987.

Engerman, Stanley L. "Slavery and Emancipation in Comparative Perspective: A Look at Some Recent Debates." *Journal of Economic History* 46/2 (1986): 317–39.

Erdem, Y. Hakan. *Slavery in the Ottoman Empire and Its Demise, 1800–1909.* London and New York, 1996.

Eren, Ahmet Cevat. *Türkiye'de göc ve göcmen meseleleri.* Istanbul, 1966.

Even-Zohar, Itamar. *Polysystem Studies: Papers in Historical Poetics and Semiotics of Culture. Poetics Today* 11/1 (1990).

Ewald, Janet J. "Review Article: Slavery in Africa and the Slave Trade from Africa." *American Historical Review* 97/2 (1992): 465–85.

Fahmy, Khaled M. "All the Paşa's Men: The Performance of the Egyptian Army during the Reign of Mehmed Ali Paşa." D.Phil. diss., University of Oxford, 1993.

Findley, Carter V. *Bureaucratic Reform in the Ottoman Empire.* Princeton, 1980.

———. *Ottoman Civil Officialdom: A Social History.* Princeton, 1989.

Finkelman, Paul. "Jefferson and Slavery: 'Treason against the Hopes of the World.' " In *Jeffersonian Legacies,* ed. Peter S. Onuf. Charlottesville, 1993.

Finley, Moses. *Ancient Slavery and Modern Ideology.* London, 1980.

Fisher, Alan. "The Sale of Slaves in the Ottoman Empire: Markets and State Taxes on Slave Sales." *Boğaziçi Üniversitesi Dergisi* 6 (1978): 149–74.

———. "Chattel Slavery in the Ottoman Empire." *Slavery and Abolition* 1 (1980): 25–45.

Fisher, Humphrey J. "Of Slaves and Souls of Men: Review Article." *Journal of African History* 28 (1987): 141–49.

Fogel, R. W., and S. L. Engerman. *Time on the Cross: The Economics of American Negro Slavery.* Boston, 1974.

Fredriksen, Borge. "Slavery and Its Abolition in Nineteenth-Century Egypt." Ph.D. diss., University of Bergen, 1977.

Fredrickson, George M. "Comparative History." In *The Past before Us: Contemporary Historical Writing in the United States,* ed. Michael Kammen. Ithaca and London, 1980.

Gammer, Moshe. *Muslim Resistance to the Tsar: Shamil and the Conquest of Chechnia and Daghestan.* London, 1994.

Garnett, Lucy. *The Women of Turkey and Their Folk-Lore.* London, 1891.

———. *Home Life in Turkey.* New York, 1909.

Gaston, Joseph. *L'esclavage en Tunisie.* Tunis, 1980.

Geertz, Clifford, et al. *Meaning and Order in Moroccan Society.* Cambridge, 1979.

Genovese, Eugene D. *The World the Slaveholders Made.* New York, 1969.

———. *Roll, Jordan, Roll.* New York, 1972.

———. *The Slaveholders' Dilemma: Freedom and Progress in Southern Conservative Thought, 1820–1860.* Columbia, S.C., 1992.

Gibb, H. A. R., and H. Bowen. *The Islamic Society and the West.* Vol. 1, pt. 1. Oxford, 1950.

Gutman, Herbert G. *Slavery and the Numbers Game: A Critique of "Time on the Cross."* Urbana, Ill., 1975.

Hathaway, Jane. *The Politics of Households in Ottoman Egypt: The Rise of the Qazdağlı Bayt.* Cambridge, 1997.

Hellie, Richard. *Slavery in Russia, 1450–1725.* Chicago, 1982.

Hodgson, Marshall G. S. *The Venture of Islam.* Vol. 2. Chicago, 1974.

Hunwick, John O. "Black Africans in the Mediterranean World: Introduction to a Neglected Aspect of the African Diaspora." In *The Human Commodity: Perspectives on the Trans-Saharan Slave Trade,* ed. Elizabeth Savage. London, 1992.

Ibrāhīm, ʿAbdallāh ʿAbd al-Rāziq. "Al-Juhūd al-Dawliyya li-Ilghāʾ al-Riqq fī Ifrīqyā." *Al-Majalla al-Tārīkhiyya al-Misriyya* 32 (1985): 181–219.

İnalcık, Halil. "Hüsrev Paşa." In *Islam Ansiklopedisi*, vol. 5. Istanbul, 1950.

———. "Čerkes—iii, Ottoman Period." In *Encyclopædia of Islam*, 2d ed., vol. 2. Leiden, 1960.

———. *The Ottoman Empire: The Classical Age, 1300–1600*. New York, 1973.

———. "Servile Labor in the Ottoman Empire." In *The Mutual Effects of the Islamic and Judeo-Christian Worlds: The East European Pattern*, ed. A. Ascher, T. Halasi-Kun, and Bela Kiraly. New York, 1979.

Inikori, J. E. "Measuring the Atlantic Slave Trade: An Assessment of Curtin and Anstey." *Journal of African History* 17/2 (1976): 197–225.

Isaac, Rhys. "The First Monticello." In *Jeffersonian Legacies*, ed. Peter S. Onuf. Charlottesville, 1993.

Jwaideh, Albertine, and J. W. Cox. "The Black Slaves of Turkish Arabia during the 19th Century." In *The Economics of the Indian Ocean Slave Trade in the Nineteenth Century*, ed. William Gervase Clarence-Smith, *Slavery and Abolition* 9/3 (1988).

Karasch, Mary. "Anastacia and the Slave Women of Rio de Janeiro." In *Africans in Bondage: Studies in Slavery and the Slave Trade*, ed. Paul E. Lovejoy. Madison, 1986.

Keller, Edmond J., ed. *Issue: A Journal of Africanist Opinion* 13 (1984).

Khunke, Lavern. *Lives at Risk*. Berkeley, 1990.

Klein, Herbert. *African Slavery in Latin America and the Caribbean*. New York, 1986.

———, ed. *Breaking the Chains: Slavery, Bondage, and Emancipation in Modern Africa and Asia*. Madison, 1993.

Kolchin, Peter. "Some Recent Works on Slavery outside the United States: An American Perspective." *Comparative Studies in Society and History* 28/4 (1986): 767–77.

———. *Unfree Labor: American Slavery and Russian Serfdom*. Cambridge, Mass., and London, 1987.

Kunt, Metin I. "Kulların Kulları." *Boğaziçi Üniversitesi Dergisi, Hümaniter Bilimler*, 3 (1975): 27–42.

———. *The Sultan's Servants: The Transformation of Ottoman Provincial Government, 1550–1650*. New York, 1983.

Lane, Edward W. *An Account of the Manners and Customs of the Modern Egyptians*. 1860; reprint, New York, 1973.

Le Gall, Michel. "The End of the Trans-Saharan Slave Trade: A View from Tripoli, 1857–1902." *Princeton Papers on the Near East* 2 (1993): 25–56.

Lewis, Bernard. *Race and Slavery in the Middle East: An Historical Inquiry*. New York and Oxford, 1990.

Lovejoy, Paul. *Transformations in Slavery: A History of Slavery in Africa*. Cambridge, 1983.

———, ed. *The Ideology of Slavery in Africa*. Beverly Hills, 1981.

Lovejoy, Paul E., and Jan S. Hogendorn, eds. *Slow Death for Slavery: The Course of Abolition in Northern Nigeria, 1897–1936*. Cambridge, 1993.

Manning, Patrick. *Slavery and African Life*. Cambridge, 1990.

Mardin, Şerif. *The Genesis of Young Ottoman Thought*. Princeton, 1962.

McCarthy, Justin. "Nineteenth-Century Egyptian Population." In *The Middle Eastern Economy*, ed. Elie Kedourie. London, 1976.

Meillassoux, Claude. *Anthropologie de l'esclavage: Le ventre de fer et d'argent*. Paris, 1986. Translated into English under the title *The Anthropology of Slavery: The Womb of Iron and Gold* (Chicago, 1991).

Melek-Hanum. *Thirty Years in the Harem*. 2 vols. Berlin, 1872.

Melman, Billie. *Women's Orients: English Women and the Middle East, 1718–1918*. Ann Arbor, 1992.

Miers, Suzanne, and Igor Kopytoff, eds. *Slavery in Africa*. Madison, 1977.

Miers, Suzanne, and Richard Roberts, eds. *The End of Slavery in Africa*. Madison, 1988.

Miller, Dean A. "Some Psycho-social Perceptions of Slavery." *Journal of Social History* 18/4 (1985): 587–605.

Miller, Joseph C. *Slavery: A World-wide Bibliography, 1900–1982*. New York, 1985.

———. *Way of Death: Merchant Capitalism and the Angolan Slave Trade, 1730–1830*. Madison, 1988.

———. "Muslim Slavery and Slaving: A Bibliography." In *The Human Commodity: Perspectives on the Trans-Saharan Slave Trade*, ed. Elizabeth Savage. London, 1992.

Mowafi, Reda. *Slavery, Slave Trade, and Abolition in Egypt and the Sudan, 1820–1882*. Malmö, Sweden, 1981.

Muhammad Ali, Abbas Ibrahim. *The British, the Slave Trade, and Slavery in the Sudan, 1820–1881*. Khartoum, 1972.

Müller, Hans. *Die Kunst des Sklavenkaufs nach arabischen, persischen, und türkischen Ratgeben vom 10. bis zum 18. Jahrhundert*. Freiburg, 1980.

al-Munazzama al-ʿArabiyya li-l-Tarbiyya wa-l-Thaqāfa wa-l-ʿUlūm. *Mas'alat al-Riqq fī Ifrīqyā*. Tunis, 1989.

al-Nājī, Muhammad. "Hawla al-Raqīq fī al-Maghrib mā qabla al-Istiʿmār." *Abhāth* (Rabat) 1 (Jan.–Feb. 1983): 45–57.

Necipoğlu, Gülru. "The Formation of an Ottoman Imperial Tradition: The Topkapı Palace in the Fifteenth and Sixteenth Centuries." Ph.D. diss., Harvard University, 1985.

Osmanoğlu, Ayşe. *Babam Abdülhamid*. Istanbul, 1960.

Owen, Roger. *Cotton and the Egyptian Economy, 1820–1914*. Oxford, 1969.

———. *The Middle East in the World Economy, 1800–1914*. London, 1981.

Pakalın, Mehmet Zeki. *Son Sadrazamlar ve Başvekiller*. 5 vols. Istanbul, 1940–48.

———. *Osmanlı tarih deyimleri ve terimleri sözlüğü*. 5 vols. Istanbul, 1946–56.

Parlatır, İsmail. *Tanzimat Edebiyatında Kölelik*. Ankara, 1987.

Patterson, Orlando. *Slavery and Social Death.* Cambridge, Mass., 1982.

Peirce, Leslie P. *The Imperial Harem: Women and Sovereignty in the Ottoman Empire.* New York and Oxford, 1993.

Penzer, Norman H. *The Harem.* Philadelphia, 1936.

Pinson, Marc. "Ottoman Colonization of the Circassians in Rumili after the Crimean War." *Études Balkaniques* (Sofia) 3 (1972): 71–85.

Pipes, Daniel. *Slave Soldiers and Islam.* New Haven and London, 1981.

Piterberg, Gabriel. "The Formation of an Ottoman Egyptian Elite in the 18th Century." *International Journal of Middle East Studies* 22/3 (1990): 275–89.

Prunier, Gerard. "Military Slavery in the Sudan during the Turkiyya (1820–1885)." In *The Human Commodity: Perspectives on the Trans-Saharan Slave Trade,* ed. Elizabeth Savage. London, 1992.

al-Razūq, Muhammad. "Qadiyyat al-Riqq fī Tārīkh al-Maghrib." *Majallat al-Buhūth al-Tārīkhiyya* 8/2 (1986): 269–89.

Reid, Anthony. *Slavery, Bondage, and Dependency in Southeast Asia.* St. Lucia, 1983.

Ricks, Thomas M. "Slaves and Slave Traders in the Persian Gulf, 18th and 19th Centuries: An Assessment." In *The Economics of the Indian Ocean Slave Trade in the Nineteenth Century,* ed. William Gervase Clarence-Smith, *Slavery and Abolition* 9/3 (1988).

Rivlin, Helen. *The Dār al-Wathā'iq in 'Abdīn Palace at Cairo as a Source for the Study of the Modernization of Egypt in the Nineteenth Century.* Leiden, 1970.

Roberts, Richard. *Warriors, Merchants, and Slaves: The State and the Economy in the Middle Niger Valley, 1700–1914.* Stanford, 1987.

Robertson, Claire C., and Martin A. Klein, eds. *Women and Slavery in Africa.* Madison, 1983.

Sagaster, Börte. "Ottoman Attitudes to Slavery in Literary Sources as a Reflection of Ottoman Society at the Turn of the Twentieth Century." Ph.D. diss., University of Hamburg, 1996.

Sahillioğlu, Halil. "Onbeşinci Yüzyılın Sonu ile Onaltıncı Yüzyılın Başında Bursa'da Kölelerin Sosyal ve Ekonomik Hayattaki Yeri." *ODTÜ Gelişme Dergisi,* 1979–80 Özel Sayısı, pp. 67–138.

Schroeter, Daniel. "Slave Markets and Slavery in Moroccan Urban Society." In *The Human Commodity: Perspectives on the Trans-Saharan Slave Trade,* ed. Elizabeth Savage. London, 1992.

Senior, Nassau W. *Conversations and Journals in Egypt and Malta.* 2 vols. London, 1882.

Shaw, Stanford J., and Ezel Kural. *History of the Ottoman Empire and Modern Turkey.* Cambridge, 1976–77.

al-Shaykh, 'Abd al-Rahmān 'Abdallāh. "Sab' Mulāhazāt Jadīda 'an 'l-Riqq fī Ifrīqyā hattā Nihāyat al-Qarn al-Tāsi' 'Ashar." *Revue d'Histoire Maghrebine* 14/45–46 (1987): 49–61 (Arabic section).

Sheriff, Abdul. *Slaves, Spices, and Ivory in Zanzibar.* London, 1987.

Shukry, M. F. "The Khedive Ismail and Slavery in the Sudan." D.Phil. diss., University of Liverpool, 1935.

Slade, Adolphus. *Record of Travels in Turkey, Greece, &c. . . . in the Years 1829, 1830, and 1831.* 2d ed. 2 vols. London, 1854.

Spaulding, Jay. "Slavery, Land Tenure, and Social Class in the Northern Turkish Sudan." *International Journal of African Historical Studies* 15/1 (1982): 1–20.

Stanton, Lucia. " 'Those Who Labor for My Happiness': Thomas Jefferson and His Slaves." In *Jeffersonian Legacies*, ed. Peter S. Onuf. Charlottesville, 1993.

Süreyya, Mehmet. *Sicill-i Osmani.* 4 vols. Istanbul, 1890–98.

Talhami, Ghada. "The Muslim African Experience." *Arab Studies Quarterly* 4 (1982): 17–33.

Tamām, Tamām Humām. "Al-Raqīq wa-l-Jundiyya fī Nazar Muhammad ʿAlī." *Al-Majalla al-Tārīkhiyya al-Misriyya* 27 (1981): 120–57.

al-Tamīmī, ʿAbd al-Jalīl. "ʿItq al-ʿAbīd wa-ʿAdaduhum fī Muntasaf al-Qarn al-Tāsiʿ ʿAshar bi-Iyālat Tūnis." *Revue d'Histoire Maghrebine* 12/39–40 (1985): 590–96 (Arabic section).

al-Tamīmī, ʿAbd al-Mālik Khalaf. "Barītānyā wa-Tijārat al-Raqīq fī Mintaqat al-Khalīj al-ʿArabī, 1820–1928." *Al-Majalla al-Tārīkhiyya al-ʿArabiyya li-l-Dirāsāt al-ʿUthmāniyya* 1+2 (1990): 73–91 (Arabic section). A brief abstract in English is provided on p. 147 of the English and French section.

Toledano, Ehud R. "Slave Dealers, Women, Pregnancy, and Abortion: The Story of a Circassian Slave-Girl in Mid–Nineteenth Century Cairo." *Slavery and Abolition* 2/1 (1981): 53–68.

———. *The Ottoman Slave Trade and Its Suppression, 1840–1890.* Princeton, 1982.

———. "The Imperial Eunuchs of Istanbul: From Africa to the Heart of Islam." *Middle Eastern Studies* 20/3 (1984): 379–90.

———. *State and Society in Mid-Nineteenth-Century Egypt.* Cambridge, 1990.

———. "Muhammad ʿAli." In *Encyclopædia of Islam*, 2d ed., vol. 7. Leiden, 1991.

———. *Osmanlı köle ticareti, 1840–1890.* Istanbul, 1994.

———. "The Emergence of Ottoman-Local Elites in the Middle East and North Africa, 17th–19th Centuries." In *Essays in Honour of Albert Hourani*, ed. I. Pappé and M. Ma'oz. Oxford and London, forthcoming.

Tucker, Judith E. *Women in Nineteenth-Century Egypt.* Cambridge, 1985.

Tugay, Emine Foat. *Three Centuries: Family Chronicles of Turkey and Egypt.* London, 1963.

Uluçay, Çağatay. *Harem ii.* Ankara, 1971.

Uzunçarşılı, İsmail Hakkı. *Osmanlı devletinin saray teşkilatı.* Ankara, 1945.

Walz, Terence. *Trade between Egypt and Bilād as-Sūdān, 1700–1820.* Cairo, 1978.

Watson, James L., ed. *Asian and African Systems of Slavery.* Oxford, 1980.

White, Charles. *Three Years in Constantinople.* 3 vols. London, 1846.
Willis, J. R. *Slaves and Slavery in Muslim Africa.* 2 vols. London, 1985.
Zoghby, Samir M. "Blacks and Arabs: Past and Present." *Current Bibliography on African Affairs* 3/5 (May 1970): 5–22.

INDEX

www.ingramcontent.com/pod-product-compliance
Ingram Content Group UK Ltd.
Pitfield, Milton Keynes, MK11 3LW, UK
UKHW040846120325
456138UK00002B/26

* 9 7 8 0 2 9 5 9 7 6 4 2 6 *